知库

教育与语言

—

英语词汇习得研究

李庆新　等 编著

吉林大学出版社

·长春·

图书在版编目（CIP）数据

英语词汇习得研究 / 李庆新等编著. --长春：吉林大学出版社，2023.4
ISBN 978－7－5768－1643－3

Ⅰ.①英… Ⅱ.①李… Ⅲ.①英语—词汇—教学研究 Ⅳ.①H319.34

中国国家版本馆 CIP 数据核字（2023）第 091504 号

书　　名	英语词汇习得研究 YINGYU CIHUI XIDE YANJIU	
作　　者	李庆新　李庆建　迟雯雯　张卫东　刘海英　闫凤霞　李明贤 李延波　房红芳	
策划编辑	李潇潇	
责任编辑	刘　丹	
责任校对	闫竞文	
装帧设计	中联华文	
出版发行	吉林大学出版社	
社　　址	长春市人民大街 4059 号	
邮政编码	130021	
发行电话	0431-89580028/29/21	
网　　址	http://www.jlup.com.cn	
电子邮箱	jdcbs@jlu.edu.cn	
印　　刷	三河市华东印刷有限公司	
开　　本	787mm×1092mm　1/16	
印　　张	13	
字　　数	208 千字	
版　　次	2023 年 4 月第 1 版	
印　　次	2023 年 4 月第 1 次	
书　　号	ISBN 978－7－5768－1643－3	
定　　价	85.00 元	

版权所有　翻印必究

前　言

词汇是语言的基础和核心，也是交际过程中至关重要的因素。词汇量的大小会影响着交流的顺畅和交际的效率。为了培养学生的英语语言综合应用能力，更好地帮助学生有效地习得英语词汇，极大地促进其听、说、读、写、译能力的提高，重视英语词汇的教学和学习显得尤为重要。

近年来，教育部陆续颁布了《大学英语课程教学要求》《大学英语教学指南》和《中国英语能力等级量表》等教学文件，对学生的英语词汇量等都有明确的规定和要求。词汇是语言中最基本、最活跃、最丰富、不可缺少的组成成分，英语词汇能力直接影响着学习者的学习效果和英语综合水平的提高。

然而，传统的词汇教学存在一些问题。由于缺乏系统理论指导，在如何促进词汇习得、提高词汇能力等方面，教师在词汇教学的认识上仍存在误区，一味地要求学生通过死记硬背来掌握词汇，忽视了学生对单词识记的深度。而学生对词汇能力的理解过于简单化，认为词汇能力就是词汇量的多少，将词汇习得和认识词汇被混为一谈。

词汇习得是第二语言习得的基础，但是在实际的教学中，并没有充分重视词汇习得的理论研究，常常忽视科学的单词记忆方法指导、语境因素以及文化内涵，把单词视为简单的音形义的结合体而进行孤立讲解，然后要求学习者背诵记忆，最后通过听写检查其记忆效果。由于没有文化背景的导入以及语言环境的依托，记忆的单词变得机械，没有灵魂和活力。

在英语词汇学习方面，由于学习方法不得当，词汇习得缺乏广度和深度，词汇运用和输出能力不强，从而造成学习者在英语语言综合应用能力方面事倍功半，即投入大、收效小，达不到预期的目标。因此，我们编著《英语词汇习得研究》一书，以期帮助学习者提高英语词汇习得效率，增强词汇能力，更有效地运用词汇，提高英语能力。

本书的编著者均为从事英语教学多年的一线教师，教学经验较为丰富，并具有较强的科研能力，接触过不同年龄层次、不同基础水平的英语学习者，了解其英语词汇学习中存在的问题；同时，在多年的英语教学实践中，积累了一定的经验，在词汇习得方面也进行了较深入的研究，并在实践中取得了较好的效果。为此，我们在本书中力求探索如何将词汇习得理论和策略科学且合理地运用到教学实践中，以便改善英语词汇教与学，帮助学习者最大限度地提高英语词汇学习效果，促进英语教学。

《英语词汇习得研究》是《英语词汇记忆研究》的姊妹篇。《英语词汇习得研究》一书分为英语词汇习得理论研究篇和英语词汇习得实践篇。英语词汇习得理论研究篇从教和学两个方面分析了在英语词汇的方面存在的问题和原因，并依据英语词汇习得相关理论，提出了有效的词汇习得方法和策略；英语词汇习得实践篇，依据《大学英语词汇表》和教学实践，选取大学英语四、六级范围内的词汇，通过例句、辨析、拓展等途径，详尽分析重点和难点词汇，有助于学习者记忆和掌握单词，并举一反三，融会贯通。

《英语词汇习得研究》和《英语词汇记忆研究》两本书具有较为相似的特点：

（1）理论研究通俗易懂，可操作性强。词汇习得理论与英语学习实践相结合，并应用于词汇记忆中，便于学习者理解领会，提高英语词汇能力。

（2）词汇精挑细选，解析深入浅出。本书所选词汇均属高频词汇，并以字母顺序分章节编排，与《英语词汇记忆研究》所选词汇不重复，并配有详细的中文解析、实用例句、中文翻译和词汇辨析等讲解和记忆手段。

（3）美籍专家录制音频文件，纠正发音方便学习。本书所有词汇统一标注美音音标，学习者可以模仿、跟读标准词汇发音，增强语感，加强记忆，自我检测，有助于英语学习者的词汇学习。

（4）适用范围广。本书可供英语词汇研究者及英语教师研究和教学使用，也适合大学生、研究生以及有一定基础的英语学习者作为英语词汇教材使用。

《英语词汇习得研究》是山东科技大学外国语学院"英语教育研究科研团

队"的研究成果，是团队成员多年潜心研究共同努力的结果。

《英语词汇习得研究》由李庆新、李庆建、迟雯雯、张卫东、刘海英、闫凤霞、李明贤、李延波、房红芳参加编著。全书由李庆新负责拟定编写提纲、统稿和定稿。

本书得到了美籍专家 Shavon Austin 的帮助，对本书所选词汇进行音频录制，并由山东科技大学网络与信息中心制作了音频文件，非常感谢他们为本书付出的劳动。

本书的编著过程中，参阅了大量相关文献资料、英语词汇方面的著作、教材、书籍、报纸杂志和网上资源等，在此不一一列出，对相关作者表示衷心的感谢。

在本书的编著过程中，我们虽已竭尽全力，但不足之处在所难免。真诚希望广大读者和学界同仁提出宝贵意见，将有助于我们在英语词汇领域的研究，同时欢迎更多的英语教师了解该项研究成果，并适时运用到自己的词汇教学中去。

编著者
2021 年 7 月于青岛

目 录
CONTENTS

第一部分　英语词汇习得理论研究篇

1　大学英语词汇教学现存的问题 …………………………… 3
  1.1　教师在词汇教授上的问题 …………………………… 3
  1.2　学生在词汇学习上的问题 …………………………… 6

2　英语词汇习得的理论基础 ………………………………… 11
  2.1　记忆理论 …………………………………………… 11
  2.2　加工层次理论 ……………………………………… 13
  2.3　语义场理论 ………………………………………… 14
  2.4　词汇的"板块性"理论 ……………………………… 17
  2.5　词汇附带习得 ……………………………………… 18

3　运用词汇习得理论和策略，改善词汇教与学 …………… 20
  3.1　教师积极干预，设计丰富多样的词汇课堂活动 …… 20
  3.2　结合信息加工理论，对词汇进行词形和语义的加工 … 22
  3.3　运用语义场理论，提高学生词汇习得的效果 ……… 24
  3.4　强化词汇的文化内涵，突出词汇的文化载体作用 … 25

3.5　提供丰富的语料库，利用网络资源促进学生词汇习得 ………… 26
　　3.6　提供灵活多元的词汇输入渠道，虚拟现实语言输出环境 ………… 28

4　遵循英语词汇习得规律，提高词汇习得效果 ………………………… 30

第二部分　英语词汇习得实践篇

1　A, B …………………………………………………………………… 35
　　1.1　A …………………………………………………………………… 35
　　1.2　B …………………………………………………………………… 53

2　C, D …………………………………………………………………… 62
　　2.1　C …………………………………………………………………… 62
　　2.2　D …………………………………………………………………… 73

3　E, F, G, H ……………………………………………………………… 80
　　3.1　E …………………………………………………………………… 80
　　3.2　F …………………………………………………………………… 86
　　3.3　G …………………………………………………………………… 88
　　3.4　H …………………………………………………………………… 92

4　I, J, K ………………………………………………………………… 95
　　4.1　I …………………………………………………………………… 95
　　4.2　J …………………………………………………………………… 113
　　4.3　K …………………………………………………………………… 116

5　L, M, N ……………………………………………………………… 119
　　5.1　L …………………………………………………………………… 119
　　5.2　M …………………………………………………………………… 127

5.3 N …………………………………………………………… 132

6 O, P ……………………………………………………………… 136
　6.1 O …………………………………………………………… 136
　6.2 P …………………………………………………………… 141

7 Q, R, S …………………………………………………………… 154
　7.1 Q …………………………………………………………… 154
　7.2 R …………………………………………………………… 155
　7.3 S …………………………………………………………… 172

8 T, U, V, W, X, Y, Z …………………………………………… 180
　8.1 T …………………………………………………………… 180
　8.2 U …………………………………………………………… 185
　8.3 V …………………………………………………………… 187
　8.4 W …………………………………………………………… 191
　8.5 X …………………………………………………………… 193
　8.6 Y …………………………………………………………… 193
　8.7 Z …………………………………………………………… 194

后　记 ……………………………………………………………… 195

第一部分 01
英语词汇习得理论研究篇

1 大学英语词汇教学现存的问题

每种语言都存在着大量的词汇，英语也不例外。词汇是语言的基础，也是语言的核心，是语言中最基本、最活跃、最丰富、不可缺少的组成成分。并且，词汇是交际过程中至关重要的因素；掌握词汇量大，交际极有可能会顺畅得多，交际效率也极有可能会提高；掌握词汇量小，交际极有可能受阻，交际效率也有可能变得较低。掌握一定量的词汇可以极大地促进沟通交流，不管是书面交流还是口头交流。就像英国著名语言学家 D. A. Wilkins 说的："没有语法，人们不能表达很多东西，而没有词汇，人们则无法表达任何东西。"英语学习者对词汇学习的需求几乎贯穿于整个英语学习的过程。英国学者迈克尔·万斯特（Michel West）早就论述过："学习语言的主要任务是习得词汇量，并在运用中逐步熟练掌握。"夏慧言等（2015）强调了外语词汇习得的重要性以及对外语学习者语言能力的影响。

1.1 教师在词汇教授上的问题

芬兰学者罗尔夫·帕尔姆伯格 1986 年在《英语教学论坛》杂志上撰文指出："真正认识一个外语词汇，要求学习者做到能识别其口头与笔头的形式；能随时回忆起其词义及形式；能把它与相应的实物或概念联系起来；能以适当的语法形式应用它；能以公认的方式读出它；能正确拼写出它；明白它的内在含义及其关联意义；能将它用于合宜的语体及适当的语境中。"也就是说，一个人只有对一个词的形式、语法模式、相关搭配、语义和语用特点、社会文化内涵等有所了解后，他才真正称得上掌握词汇（陈斌，2005）。

堵楠楠（2015）认为对我国大学生二语词汇习得现状的研究起步较晚，借鉴国外理论与实际情况相结合的研究和创新还有值得探讨的空间。对于如何教词汇，虽然是仁者见仁，智者见智，但是通常都未脱离"发音、拼法、词性、意义"的框架（王寅，2001）。在这样的"音、形、义"的传统词汇教学框架下，按照传统的套路进行词汇教学，学生往往不能透彻理解和掌握单词的确切意义与文化内涵，并由此滋生了"石化现象"，即一段时间出现的语言能力止步不前，极有可能导致学生在使用单词时错误频繁，学习效率低下。总体来说，教师在教词汇上的问题，主要如下：

1.1.1 缺乏系统的理论知识指导

虽然教师和学生对词汇能力的重要性达成了共识，但是对于什么是词汇能力，如何促进词汇习得、提高词汇能力这样根本性的问题却没有系统的理论知识用作指导，教师在词汇教学的认识上也存在误区。例如，词汇能力被简单地理解为是掌握词汇量的多少，词汇习得和认识词汇被混为一谈。对于词汇的教学，许多教师简单地认为"词汇没有什么好教的，反正让学生在课外自己去背、去记就行了"（戴聪腾，1997）。这势必使得学生们也误以为词汇学习毫无方法可言，只能靠自己死记硬背，并且把词汇能力差统统归咎为努力不够的结果。

事实上，词汇能力包含理解性词汇能力、使用性词汇能力、已有的多义水平和词义扩展的逻辑性想象能力；词汇习得涉及信息论、认知理论和语义理论等多种理论。提高词汇教学的效果必须要从理论出发，接受科学的指导思想，进而联系学生个体的实际情况，制定因人而异的词汇习得方案。

在第二语言的教学实践中，词汇教学似乎没有得到足够的重视。尽管教师深知词汇习得是第二语言习得的基础，没有一定的词汇量就无法进行有效的言语交际，但是，在有关词汇教学的问题上，他们在主观认识上却存在较大的误区，认为词汇不应是课堂教学所考虑的对象，因为借助于教材和理想的字典，学生完全可以在课后通过自己的努力来扩大词汇量。在这种思想的指导下，少有教师会在课堂上系统地教授词汇学方面的知识，更难得有教师能够潜心钻研词汇学方面的教学法。客观地讲，教师主观意识上的忽视是造成词汇教学及相应的教学法在大学英语教学中缺失的主要原因之一。

也有部分教师在教学的过程中一味地强调学生的词汇量，让学生识记大量的单词，却明显忽视了学生对单词识记的深度。有的教师在授课的过程中会给学生推荐一些词汇书，要求学生背书，并拥有6,000~10,000的英语词汇量。这样看似增加了学生的词汇量，导致学生看似记住了单词，但缺乏对单词的相应理解，缺乏对其不同用法的理解，最终无法正确使用这些词汇，跟没记住单词的同学并没有什么太大的差别，这种教学方法仍不可取。

1.1.2 缺少科学的单词记忆方法及策略引导

对教师来讲，词汇教学的理念、内容以及方法都有待改进。一些大学英语教师对词汇教学采取传统僵化的翻译法，孤立地讲解单词。在讲解的过程中，教师把单词视为简单的音、形、义的结合体而进行孤立讲解，然后要求学生背诵记忆，之后通过听写检查学生的记忆效果。这样的词汇教学方法容易导致学生对单词死记硬背，而且只是利用了自己的短期记忆通过眼前的测试，在考试过后便把单词遗忘在脑后，再也不去回顾这些单词，无法形成对单词的长期的、永久性的记忆。对于外语学习者，尤其是非英语专业的大学生来说，使用英语单词的机会相对较少，因此，这样"死记硬背"地记单词而之后却不复习的做法并不是学习单词的最佳方式，很容易导致混淆和遗忘。对于教师来讲，这种教授方法存在一定的问题，有需要改进之处。

教师未充分地教授学生科学的单词记忆方法，部分是由于受到了教学材料以及课时设置的制约。

首先是教学材料的制约。在教授词汇的过程中，大部分教师都是依托于教科书，资料的查阅也大多数来自教学参考书、网络英文词典，词汇的意思比较死板，例句一般比较陈旧，个别材料的词汇活动操作性不强，甚至有些过时的用法。教师受制于教材，甚至局限于教材，导致出现了处理好教材上的词汇练习就万事大吉的现象。这样做显然对于学生词汇的习得十分不利。

在当今科技迅猛发展的时代，局限于以上的教学材料远远不够。海量的英文原版网站，丰富的原汁原味的语料，以及层出不穷的词汇教学方法以及课堂活动设计，都为教师提供了新颖的、基于母语语境的素材。

其次是课时设置的制约。不管是大学英语还是英语专业，在进行课堂授课时，由于教学目标全面，教学任务繁多，导致部分教师将词汇的教学放到了课下自主学习部分，课上时间用在其他听、说、读、写、译语言技能的训练上。受到课时有限的制约，部分教师也逐渐认为，词汇学习就是学生个人的任务，学生课下自己记忆单词即可，不一定非要在课上单独拿出时间来学习。在英语基本能力的训练以及词汇教学的冲突下，部分教师自然而然地将词汇放到了课下由学生个人来进行学习。

1.1.3 忽视语境因素以及文化内涵

语言诞生并存在于文化当中，是文化的载体；而文化的重要组成部分就是语言，没有语言，文化将很难传承。语言和文化密不可分，相互制约和促进。因此，要想真正活学活用英语语言，必须依托于英语的文化背景，尤其是注意两种语言之间的文化差异，在这样的指导思想下，词汇教学才可能真正有效。

然而，在现实的词汇教学中，有一些脱离文化语境的做法，教师把单词孤立讲解，甚至在明知道单词有丰富的文化背景内涵的情况下，依然选择忽视文化背景，而只强调单词的意思。殊不知，脱离了文化内涵或者文化语境的单词，已经失去了它的灵魂和活力。

1.2 学生在词汇学习上的问题

目前，中国大学生普遍重视英语词汇的学习。这是因为词汇是语言的基石，词汇能力是妨碍学生语言运用能力提高的主要因素；阅读、听力、写作和翻译中出现的很多问题都是由词汇能力薄弱引起的。但是，中国大学生在记忆单词方面，投入了大量时间和精力，结果却收效甚微。这种"高投入，低收益"的反差背后的原因是什么呢？从学生的角度来讲，主要是在词汇学习的过程中存在如下问题：

1.2.1 词汇习得策略单一，方法不得当

首先，母语思维不利于单词的有效习得。一些学生在记忆单词的过程中，主要依赖于母语方式记忆，即在记忆该单词之前，先在脑海里把单词翻译成母语，再把母语转换为英语。不可否认，这是一种十分普遍的现象，甚至是教师本身也存在这个问题。这种记忆单词的方法，使得学生们在记忆的过程中，始终都要依赖母语的工具来辅助记忆，将会阻碍英语思维的形成以及良性发展，不利于英文思维的培养和建立，英语翻译成母语然后母语又翻译成英语的这种中式思维会限制英语表达的地道性和流利性。

其次，学习词汇没有掌握正确的方法。部分学生记忆单词的方法是死记硬背。对照课本上的单词表或者词汇书上的单词，按照顺序，枯燥机械地通过多次重复的方法来记忆。这样做的后果就是记忆不牢，记忆效果不好，遗忘速度快。还有一部分学生，词汇的输入主要依赖于课上教师的讲解，被动地学习词汇，自发主动地学习机会较少，自主输入词汇数量较少。

错误的方法带来的直接后果，除了词汇量增长缓慢，另一个后果就是拼写错误较多。英语是一种拼音文字，写错一个字母、颠倒了两个字母、漏掉了一个字母或者增加了不该增加的部分，都会导致单词拼写的错误。纵观各类考试以及平时学生作业中所犯的单词拼写错误可以发现，除了以上所提及的写错、颠倒、漏掉、增加等类型外，学生在词汇拼写上还经常犯的一类错误是自己造单词。比如，有的将 resolve 的名词形式写成 resolvement，将 embarrass 的名词形式写成 embarrassion 等等。这些都是学习策略单一和方法不得当造成的直接后果。

1.2.2 词汇习得的广度和深度不足

首先，词汇习得的广度不足。词汇习得的广度指的是学生习得的词汇的总数量。通过笔者十多年的教学观察发现，不少学生词汇量明显不足，导致口语以及书面表达过程中词汇贫乏、简单。学生词汇量的大小直接影响到学生语言输入和输出的质量，进而影响到他们的口头以及书面交际能力。专家

R. Anderson 和 P. Freebody 指出满足大学一年级流利阅读所需要的词汇量在 15,000~20,000 之间，这个数字比目前我国大学生实际掌握的词汇量要大得多（游玉祥，2002）。因此，学生要想顺利地进行听、说、读、写、译等各项活动，一定的词汇量的确是一个必要的前提。习得一门语言的核心就是习得它的词汇，词汇解决了，很多其他的语言问题会迎刃而解。对于学习者能掌握多少词汇量，甚至有学者指出，对于第二语言习得者来说，受过良好教育的本族语者掌握的词汇量大可作为学习者追求的目标（李广琴，2006）。也就是说，学生是有可能掌握等同于本族语者的词汇量的。

范琳等（2015）指出我国语言学习者的二语词汇学习策略，取得了不少重要研究成果，呈良性发展趋势，今后我国二语词汇学习策略研究将不断向纵深发展。词汇习得的深度指的是学生对于词汇的全方面掌握程度。部分学生在学习词汇时，只记忆该单词的某一个意思，大多采用"一对一"死记硬背的单词识记方式，即一个单词对应一个汉语意思，利用机械重复的方法记忆该单词的其中一个意思，而忽略了一个单词的其他多重丰富含义，更不去考虑这个单词的多重意思以及丰富含义之间的相互关联，或者词汇和词汇之间的相互关联。这种较为单一的机械式记忆方法，会影响学生词汇掌握的深度，不利于建立其语义网络，从而不利于长时记忆。

即使学生掌握了一定的词汇量，但是在听、说、读、写、译等语言应用活动中发现，自己所掌握的词汇量中，多为平时不经常用到的单词，然而一些必须掌握的、常用的单词，却并未习得。这种情况一般是由于学习者在学习词汇的过程中，词汇材料选取不合适或者学习者在习得过程中未注意词汇的实际意义或者脱离了现实生活实际。例如，bacon、hamburger、coca-cola 这些词汇对学生来说，可谓是得心应手，而对于日常生活经常用到的词汇，像油条、豆浆、白酒，却捉襟见肘。

1.2.3 词汇运用和输出能力不强

对于英语词汇的学习，很多学习者有一个普遍的误区，那就是他们认为词汇量越大，英语能力就越高，于是就有了学生每天抱着单词书按照字母表的顺序记单词的现象。学生学习很认真，但是遗忘也很快，到最后可能只记住了当天那些单词,之前记忆的单词都忘记了。或许也有同学通过这样错误的认知,积累了一些词汇,但是却发现在口语表达以及书面表达时,记忆过的词汇调不出来,很多单词想不起来也用不上。因此,在学习词汇的过程中,一定不要盲目追求词汇量的大小而忽视了词汇的运用和产出,忽视了对词汇意义的真正理解和正确的应用。只有坚持正确的学习规律,并加以练习和运用,这样才能最终有效地掌握词汇。

经过问卷调查发现,由于应试和升学压力的影响,绝大部分非英语专业学生采用的词汇输入方法主要是死记硬背教材和四、六级考试配套单词手册。他们很少通过多种渠道去接触真实的外语语言材料。词汇教学基本局限于教师讲解生词表或课文里遇到的词汇,采用的方法多是英汉对译、提供同义词或反义词、构词分析或演示词典例句等。这些做法无疑在一定程度上帮助学生学习了不少英语词汇,但是也带来了一些问题,因为这种强化式记忆孤立了词汇之间的关联,脱离了词汇出现的语境。如果依靠这样单一的输入方式,学生很难将新旧词汇之间建立联系,很难通过其背景知识来激活对新词的认知,很难建立起自己的词库。换言之,目前的大学词汇教学方法使得学生的词汇知识难以实现内化。

同时,词汇输出对于词汇习得的重要性被学生普遍忽略。由于不重视输出能力的培养,加之学生语言输出环境的局限,学生用英文写作或者口头交流的实践很少,学生用于积极表达的单词数量极其有限。也就是说,学生词汇的外化能力相当差,这种外化能力的欠缺反过来对词汇内化能力的提高带来明显的负面效应(曾维秀,2003)。

词汇能力包括学习者运用词义、同义词、派生词和搭配的接受性能力和产出性能力。在学习外语的早期阶段,词义知识发展极快,同时同义词、派生词和搭配词知识也有进步。但是随着总体语言水平向中级发展,词义知识的增长速度逐渐放缓,而增长较快的是同义词、派生词和搭配词知识。然而在外语学习者水平达到中级以后,各类词汇知识的增长都基本停滞不前,出现"高原现象"。濮建忠从类联接和搭配这两个方面入手,利用中国英语学习者语料库,发现了中国大学英语学习者对英语常用词深度知识的掌握程度还处在较低的水平,在掌握类联接和搭配这两个词汇知识的关键方面还存在着明显不足,对于常用词使用相关的典型词块的掌握还有欠缺(陈波,2012)。

　　由于学生在词汇习得上的各种问题,导致他们在书面以及口头表达中表现出了明显的词汇匮乏、用词单一、词汇搭配以及结构数量有限,其写作以及口语总体水平不高,直接影响到了交际的质量,学生交际能力的发展也因此受到了制约。随着英语学习的深入,语音语法问题已经基本不会阻碍学生的学习,但是词汇问题、词汇贫乏却会成为语言流利性以及准确性的障碍。

2 英语词汇习得的理论基础

针对目前大学英语词汇教学指导思想片面的问题,有必要从理论上深入系统地了解词汇习得的本质,从而运用更加科学有效的方法提高词汇习得效果。心理学和语义学的研究表明同外语词汇习得关系最为密切的理论主要包括记忆、加工层次、语义场、词汇"板块性"和"词汇附带习得"五大理论。

2.1 记忆理论

由于词汇知识不是单独存在的,它覆盖了词汇在口语以及书面语中的使用频率、句法行为以及与其他词的关联网络等内容,所以词汇并不是一个单独存在的个体,它拥有一系列的相互关联的内容体系,词汇习得的发生需要将语言意义以词汇的形式加以转换,从而帮助理解和认识。因此,词汇只能逐步地习得,进而将词汇的相关信息逐步整合入心理概念和记忆的词条,从而使学习者逐步获得词汇应用的能力。词汇的习得及记忆储存情况在很大程度上会影响语言的掌握和使用。

认知心理学对记忆的研究表明,信息加工模型中的信息处理过程包括感知、编码、意义建构和检索。从接收信息的角度看,信息加工过程主要呈现出三个阶段,即感觉记忆、工作记忆和长期记忆。首先,由于注意,有限的信息由感觉记忆进入大脑的工作记忆中。类似一个电话号码保存在大脑中直到把它拨出去,所以工作记忆也叫作短期记忆。同时保存在这个工作间里的信息的时间也不长，且容量有限。长期记忆才被认为是一个存档系统，它有极大的容量、持久的保存时间，它可以分为语义记忆和情境记忆。语义记忆是指对意义、理解和其他基于概念的与具体经历无关的知识的记忆；情境记忆是指与一定的时间、地点和具体情景相联系的记忆。语义记忆和情境记忆一起构成了大脑对陈述性知识（是有关"世界是什么"的知识，能够直接陈述）的记忆。关于大脑对知识的储存和提取，在心理语言学界比较有影响的是柯林斯的扩展激活模式。在这个模式中，心理词汇是以网络关系的形式为表征的，即以语义联系或语义相似性将概念组织起来，相互关联的各个节点之间的距离取决于它们之间的结构关系特征。节点之间的联结力度可以通过各种各样的激活方式得以加强。不同的加工水平引起了不同的信息储存和信息提取能力。一般而言，加工水平越高，加工深度越深，单词的记忆也就越牢固。经过加工复述的信息从短时记忆进入长时记忆系统。然而，长期记忆并不是所谓的永不遗忘。相反，它是一个从快速遗忘到永远不忘的区间状态。其实在信息加工模型的每一阶段，信息的传递都伴随着大量的信息丢失，在全部的感觉信息中能进入短时记忆的信息只有一部分，而短时记忆是从感觉到长时记忆的中转站。完成这一过程的必要条件是通过对材料加以有效的组织和深层次上的加工复述（王平，2008）。

从记忆理论（The theory of memory）的"注意"角度来讲，并不是所有的输入都有均等的价值，只有那些被特别注意的输入才能变成吸收，这是语言习得的必需条件；记忆需要注意，注意与产出具有紧密的联系。因此没有对生词的足够注意，习得就不可能发生。因此，在词汇教学的任务设计上，任务要求和感知的突显度（perceptual saliency）是决定注意的重要条件。教师可以设计不同的任务来促进学生词汇能力的提高，拓展学生的发音、拼写、意义、语法和联想等词汇知识。当然由于这些任务对不同词汇知识的注意要求不同，那么产生的词汇加工方法就不同，词汇记忆的效果也不同。增强输入的突显度指的是语言形式的突出性和重要性。突显输入的因素有很多，包括教师、学习材料、学习者自己等，也就是说，突显既可由内力、也可由外力驱动，而且两种驱动力都很重要。因此在词汇学习中，教师可以利用多种办法，提高输入的突显度，如使用粗体、斜体、下划线、大写等方式，还可以利用修改语篇、使用注释等加强手段，增强学生对于词汇的记忆。

因此，要达到对单词的长久记忆，对词汇进行组织编码和意义建构就显得非常重要。提高词汇的记忆效果必须创设良好的环境和条件，促进学生主动积极地选择适合自己的方式编码并且最大限度地提高提取信息的频度，保持词汇信息的新近性。同时，增强输入的突显度，既有内力的驱动，又有外力的驱动，以此增强词汇的记忆。词汇遗忘的归因主要是对认识主体的忽视，肤浅的意义编码、非充分的意义建构、复述的缺失以及凸显度不足等。

2.2 加工层次理论

Atkinson 和 Shifrin（1968）第一次提出一个系统全面的信息加工模式，即记忆信息三级加工模型：新信息要经过感觉记忆、短时记忆和长期记忆三个阶段。信息从短时记忆转入长时记忆是通过复述而实现的；复述时间越长，记忆保持越好。然而，Craik 和 Lockhart（1972）对此提出异议，提出加工层次理论（The theory of depths of processing），认为记忆的保持不在于复述时间的长短，而在于加工方式的差异，认为加工层次越深，记忆保持越好。记忆的保持取决于认知加工方式的差异，即加工层次越深，记忆保持越好。词汇认知加工分为两个层次——形式加工层次和语义加工层次：形式加工层次即复述，语义加工层次指建立词语之间的联想，建立词语与表象之间的联系，指一个词得到识别之后，还可以与其他词建立联想，与有关的表象和故事联系起来。Craik 和 Tulving 提出"精加工"的概念，指出习得词汇时需要对其进行全面的加工，包括单词发音、拼写、语法范畴、语境意义及其纵横聚合关系，等等。要对一个生词进行全面的加工，即包括单词发音、拼写、语法范畴、语境意义及其纵聚合关系等，而不只是加工其中的一个或两个方面。

在形式加工、语义加工和精加工的基础上，Wittrock（1974）提出产出性加工（generative processing），强调学生要主动建构信息，积极激活和利用原有知识、经验和能力，从而加深记忆。实验研究表明：经过语义加工比经过形式加工所记的单词更牢固；通过产出性任务所记的单词比使用非产出性任务所记的单词更牢固（张乃玲，2004）。学习者自己产出的含有目标词的句子与实验者给出的含有目标词句子相比，在前者中学习者更易记忆目标词，这说明学习要积极激活和利用原有知识、经验和能力对信息进行主动构建，这样记忆才会更加深刻（张庆宗，2002）。

Craik 提出的信息加工层次理论还从信息加工的纵向视角对信息加工和记忆过程进行了阐释。该理论认为，人类大脑对信息的记忆和存储是一个动态过程，它可以反映出大脑在信息加工时对信息感知和理解的程度。同时，不同加工层次和深度也会对信息记忆和存储产生影响。就词汇学习而言，对词汇的某单一维度知识的加工属于浅层次加工，对词汇各个维度（形式、意义、句法、功能等维度）的全方位加工属于深层次加工。基于这一论据，信息加工理论对刻意词汇学习和偶遇词汇学习的概念进行了重新定义。以往研究认为，区分刻意学习和偶遇学习的标尺是"注意"，即学习者是否有意识地学习该目标词。但持信息加工论的学者认为，能否习得词汇并不取决于学习者是否刻意去学，而取决于对词汇各维度知识的加工深度，对词汇知识各维度知识加工越全面、加工程度越深，对该词汇的习得和掌握情况越好（宋丽娟，2009）。

根据 Craik 和 Lockhart 的理论，记忆是从浅层次到深层次的连续活动。在学习一个目标词时，学习者在识别该词的语音、字形和意义之后，还会将其与其他词建立联想、与有关的表象和故事或情节或过去的经验联系起来。影响加工层次的是对目标词的关注时间、与学习者大脑中已有记忆结构的相容性，以及加工的时间。另外，学习者的"自我参照效果"（self-reference effect），即学习者将新信息与自我联系起来，使学习进入深层次加工，促进长时记忆。所以，在大学英语词汇学习中，除了理解意义、获取信息的间接学习，还应进行词汇的直接学习，即对词汇进行深层次加工，使识记的印象更深刻，保持的时间更长，保持效果更好，更准确运用语言（谭文辉，2005）。

2.3 语义场理论

语义场理论（The theory of semantic field）是现代语义学研究的重要成果

之一,由德国学者 J. Trier 在 20 世纪 30 年代首次提出。他认为语言词汇虽然浩如烟海,但并非杂乱无章;也就是说,一种语言所拥有的各个词并不是孤立存在的,词的概念在记忆中是通过一个广泛的关系网络来表征的,每个词的概念表征为网络中一个独特的节点,并借助各种关系与其他的词汇相互联系,构成完整的系统。语义场是词和整个词汇之间的现实存在。作为整体的一部分,它们具有与词相同的特征,即可以在语言结构中被组合,它们同时还具有词汇系统的性质,即由更小的单位组成。Cornu(1979)指出人们倾向于依据语义场来记忆单词。White(1988)发现优秀的学生按语义链记忆单词,而记忆效果较差的学生则根据声音群记忆单词(伍谦光,1995)。所以,从语义场出发,根据词汇上下义关联记忆并且逐渐扩充单词是一种非常可行的途径。

根据语义场内各个词位间的关系,可以把语义场划分为以下四种类型:上下义义场、同义义场、反义义场、整体与部分义场。

2.3.1 上下义义场

上下义义场是语义场中最常见的一类。在语言中,有些词表示总概念,而有些词表示具体概念,由总概念词汇和具体概念词汇的包含关系构成的语义场即为上下义义场。例如:animal 是表示总概念的上义词,那么 vertebrate(脊椎动物)和 invertebrate(无脊椎动物)就是下义词。而 vertebrate 下又有 amphibian、bird、fish、reptile、mammal 五大类。所以,上义词和下义词具有明显的相对性。

2.3.2 同义义场

由意思相同或相近的词构成的义场即为同义义场。同义义场分为两种:绝对同义义场和相对同义义场。绝对同义义场指的是该义场中的词意思完全相同,在任何语境下都可以替换。在英语语言中,绝对同义词数量不多,多数是关于一些特殊的专业术语,例如:scarlet fever 和 scarlatina,都是表示猩红热,任何场合下两个词都可以互换;相对同义义场指的是该义场中的词中心意思相同，但各词之间存在细微差别。比如 anger 和 rage，都有生气的意思，但是生气的程度不同，anger 意为普通的生气，没有具体的程度；rage 意为生气到失去控制，生气的程度很大。再比如 kick the bucket 和 pass away，都有死亡的意思，但是前者用于非正式的场合而后者常用于较正式的场合，两个词的语体风格有差异。

2.3.3 反义义场

反义义场是指由语义相反或相对的词构成的义场。反义义场分为三种：两极反义义场、互补反义义场和关系反义义场。两极反义义场是指该义场中的词意思相反，极性对立，称为两极反义词，例如：love 和 hate，hot 和 cold。互补反义义场指的是义场中的词意思互不相容，非此即彼，称为互补反义词，例如 male 和 female，sleep 和 awake。关系反义义场指的是义场中的词在意义上对称，双方都以对方的存在为前提，例如 husband 和 wife，lend 和 borrow 等。

2.3.4 整体与部分义场

整体和部分语义关系是指一个词的词义包含另一个词的概念意义。也就是说，后者词汇的意义是前者词汇意义的一个部分，两个词汇之间形成了整体和部分的关系。其中，表示整体含义的词汇被称之为整体词汇，表示部分含义的词汇被称为组成词汇。如 month 是整体词，而 January、February、March、April、May、June、July、August、September、October、November 和 December 则是组成词汇。整体与部分关系下的词汇又可分为顺序关系和分散关系。顺序关系表达的是整体词汇和组成词汇之间是按照一定顺序排列而成的，如上面提到的月份的例子。分散关系表达的是部分词汇无须按照一定的顺序排列，如 computer 作为整体词与 mouse、screen、keyboard 等词组成了一个分散关系义场。

2.4 词汇的"板块性"理论

词汇的"板块性"理论是由英国词汇学家 Michael Lewis 提出的。Michael Lewis（1993）在他的 *The Lexical Approach* 中提出词库（lexis）是语言的核心，它由各种类型的板块（chunk）组成，板块的不同组合再形成句子。词汇板块性，指的是语言中出现频率较高，形式和意义较固定，运用语境较确定，兼具词汇和语法功能，由多个词组成，以整体形式被记忆、加工、储存和提取的成串的语言结构。换言之，板块主要指的是词与他词的共现形式，尤指处于约定俗成的固定习语和自由词汇中间的半固定语言结构（如 have lunch/supper）。英语有四种板块：词和短语（如 wake up、check in），固定搭配（如 bad traffic、terrible weather），习惯用语（black sugar、long time no see、It's up to you.），句子框架（on the one hand, …on the other hand, …）。近几年，研究人员们逐渐意识到语言产出就是从记忆中取用短语单位（phrasal units）的过程。一些语言学家经过电脑数据统计分析发现，英语交际的自然语言中 90% 是由那些处于单词和固定短语之间的半固定板块结构来实现的（张乃玲，2004）。

语块理论认为，语言是语法化的词汇，也就是说，语块具有语法性，它表语义，也表结构，具备生成功能。这是语块最显著的一个特点。如短语类语块 "after a day" 可以扩张成：after an hour/a week/a month/a year；或 two hours/two weeks/two months/two years 等诸多含义不同但共享同一个语法结构的短语。再比如句子类语块 "I want my daughter to…" 既表达了一种语义，也表达 want+sb+ to do 这一语法结构。我们可以说 My father wants me to…/His teacher wants him to…/We want our government to…等。由此可见，一个语块构型能生成一批具有相同构造、表示同样功能的语块。因此，我们只要记住一个语块，再通过举一反三、触类旁通，就可以掌握一个语块群，极大地扩大词汇总量，提高英语应用能力。语块是记忆组织的一个理想单位，是集词汇、语法与语用为一体的词汇化板块，是有效建构语言的材料，可以通往记忆储存的最高层次组织，人们掌握的语块越多，语言使用将越灵活、越地道。外语教学应该利用语块的语法性，来加强系统性学习，强化学生语块的记忆储存与运用，促使他们更好地把语块内化为心理词块，进而提高学生的英语应用能力（齐晓星，2009）。

2.5 词汇附带习得

词汇附带习得（incidental vocabulary acquisition）最早是 Nagy、Herman 和 Anderson 在基于研究儿童学习母语词汇的基础上，于 1985 年提出的。他们认为，词汇附带习得是一种无意习得，是相对于有意学习（intentional learning）而言的。母语词汇的学习，除了小部分归功于有意学习外，其他大部分词汇是在学习听、说、读、写各种活动中无意习得的，其主要目的与注意力不在于词汇。有意学习是指学生刻意地背记单词，如通过背记单词、教师讲授、查阅字典、词汇活动和练习等记单词，学习者的注意力以及目标就是记忆单词；而词汇附带习得则是指学生在进行其他学习任务时，如阅读文章、听英文歌曲、看英文电影、听英文广播、读产品英文说明书、用英语交流等，其注意力并非在背记单词上，却附带习得了词汇，这种习得是在完成其他语言任务时附带收获的，具有"一举两得"的效果。以这种方法习得的单词可能仅仅是该词的部分语义，或者语音，并非全部意思，多次这种附带习得之后，效果会较好。附带习得一般发生在漫长的语言学习的过程中，通过大量反复接触新旧词汇从而不知不觉理解和掌握了大量词汇。根据 Nagy 等人的研究，不管是本族语还是二语，只有很小一部分归功于直接的词汇教学，大量词汇是通过附带习得的方式，比如泛读、泛听等，于无意间学会的，是一个缓慢渐进的过程，这就意味着学生需要在不同的语境中接触这个词才能掌握它。

学生在进行英语的听、说、读、写、译等各项活动时，都可以产生词汇的附带习得。比如"听"。在听力材料中，学习者会听到自己不熟悉、不认识的单词，结合听力材料的语境，以及过去的英语词汇基础，一般可以猜测出该词的意思或者通过该词的发音，构建出该词的词形，进而得到该词的意思。

这种猜词的方法，在阅读中应用的比较频繁。但是值得一提的是，阅读中附带习得词汇有一个前提，那就是有大约2,000到3,000的词汇量基础，大学阶段需要的更多。这样才可以利用语境等信息，猜测单词的意思，从而促进词汇的附带习得的发生。

综合五大理论，可以说提高学生外语词汇习得的关键是营造良好的习得环境，激发学生主动性，保证学生可以根据自身的记忆习惯，灵活便捷地选择丰富的词汇资源，进行全方位、深层次的词汇加工，掌握"词汇板块"的特征，发现"语义场"的规律，并且通过高频的词汇信息提取和产出性任务的完成来加强记忆，提高词汇习得效果。另外，还需要扩大阅读面，增加阅读量，创造词汇附带习得的环境，增加词汇习得的可能性。

词汇习得的目的，不是单纯地有一个数量，最主要的目的一定是在书面以及口头交际中运用。一般来说，学生对于接受型（receptive）技能上，比如阅读和听力，辨识单词相对比较容易；但是，在产出（productive）技能上，比如口语和写作，词汇的运用能力就相对更加需要提高。这除了跟学生的习得方法有关之外，也与教师的教学方法有关。因此，将词汇知识变成词汇运用能力，激活头脑中停留在认知层面的词汇，使其变成真正的工作词汇，活跃词汇，并且创造机会在使用中不断地复习和巩固已有词汇，不管对于学生的词汇习得还是对于教师的词汇教学，这都变得非常的重要。

3 运用词汇习得理论和策略，改善词汇教与学

教师应将词汇习得理论和策略科学合理地运用到教学实践中，根据学习者个体情况，不断改进教学方法，帮助学习者最大限度地提高英语词汇学习效果。同时，在教学实践中，设计并采取一系列手段和方法，充分调动学习者的积极性，及时获取学习者词汇习得中存在的问题、困难以及值得肯定的经验，改善词汇教与学，促进英语教学。

3.1 教师积极干预，设计丰富多样的词汇课堂活动

在词汇的课堂教学中，教师可以通过直接或者间接的干预，使得课堂的词汇输入过程变得更具可控性、趣味性，增强学生词汇习得的效果。比如，在阅读课程中，教师在进行阅读前的词汇指导时，可以将重点放在学生的根据上下文猜测词义的能力，以便帮助学生更好地掌握语境背景下词汇的具体含义以及其在语义场中的位置。教师也可以通过有意地介绍词源、词根、构词法、衍变、同义词、近义词、反义词、语义场、词族等方面，激发学生学习词汇的兴趣，使学生"知其然"，同时"知其所以然"。

影响学生词汇习得的因素有很多方面，比如，学生的词汇学习动机和态度、学习策略的运用等，但是不可否认，课堂上教师的讲解方式、词汇活动的设计也是不容置疑的影响因素。教师可以通过设计丰富多样的课堂词汇教学活动，使得词汇的学习有趣而且效果好。以下是几种有趣的词汇教学活动：

Bingo. 教师可以首先让学生画一个九宫格，学生把将要学习的词汇按照

自己喜欢的顺序随机放在九宫格里。第一遍活动,教师可以随机读单词,学生听到后就在自己的九宫格中将单词划掉,第一个划掉一横行、一竖行、一斜行的同学,大喊 Bingo。直到教师念完所有的单词,第一遍活动结束。第二遍时,教师可以说出单词的意思,学生听到单词的意思时,划掉相应的单词,第一个划掉一横行、一竖行、一斜行的同学,大喊 Bingo。直到教师说完所有的单词意思,第二遍活动结束。第三遍时,教师可以说出一个句子,但是关键词汇部分不念,要求学生仔细听辨,找出合适的词,并且在九宫格中划掉。第一个划掉一横行、一竖行、一斜行的同学,大喊 Bingo。直到教师念完所有的不完整的句子,第三遍活动结束。然后,教师可以把剩下的时间交给学生,两两一组或者四人一组,同学们之间相互进行这个活动。

单词接龙。教师以当日学习的一个词语为接龙的头,指定任意同学说出下一个单词,要求是下一个单词必须以上一个单词的末尾一个音节开头。比如,开头单词为 available,下一个同学可以接 blame,再下一个同学可以接 metonymy,以此类推。也可以将全班同学分成两组,以竞赛的形式进行。十秒钟接不上的组输了比赛,相应的惩罚可以是:每人下课自己进行接龙,每一串接龙必须满十个单词。

讲故事。教师可以在讲解完需要学习的单词后,要求学生写一段故事,要求是必须用上当堂所学的全部词汇。第一遍编故事的时候,可以不必有单词出现顺序的要求。第二遍编故事时,可以提高要求,要求学生必须按照先后顺序将当堂所学单词编进故事。学生故事完成后,教师可以先让学生对各自的搭档讲述一下自己的故事,然后再邀请几个代表分享自己的故事。较好的故事版本可以分享在班级微信或者 QQ 群里供全班同学学习。

唱单词。提供一个简单的歌曲旋律,比如字母歌、泥娃娃等的旋律。要求学生把当堂学习的词汇放到字母歌的旋律中唱出来。一般来讲,唱出来的时候会感觉特别怪异,因为单词的长短不一,不一定很合适,但是,会起到意想不到的活跃课堂氛围的效果。

你说我猜。在学习完部分词汇以后,教师可以让学生四人一组,其中一人负责用各种形式解释当堂学过的单词,其他三人猜并且将单词写下来。第一个人解释完了以后,第二名同学解释,剩下的同学猜测加拼写,直到所有人都完成了解释。

看图猜词。教师可以将学过的词汇，以图片的形式呈现出来，第一遍，可以在展示每一幅图片以后，全体同学一起，说出单词的意思。然后第二遍展示图片的时候，教师可以要求学生不要说话，自己写下每一幅图片对应的具体单词。

有趣的词汇课堂活动很多，只要教师足够用心，一定可以创造出五花八门丰富多样的活动，帮助学生以生动有趣的方式习得词汇。

3.2 结合信息加工理论，对词汇进行词形和语义的加工

根据心理学的信息加工理论可以得知，在词汇的学习过程中，编码、整合和单词有意义的构建对词汇记忆发挥着十分重要的作用（王平，2008），因为学习的发生是因为我们所学的新知识与我们的已有的认知概念产生了联系。根据这种说法，机械性的学习是一种相对独立的认知过程，在这个过程中，学习没有与其他材料建立意义关系，也就是说，在进行机械学习的过程是与现存的认知结构几乎没有联系的事物进行简单的储藏。在词汇的教学过程中，单纯地教授词汇的意义，把词汇孤立出来进行教学就是一种机械式的教学，学生以这种方式进行词汇学习也就是机械式的学习，效果可想而知。

然而，不同于机械性的学习，有意义的学习则发生在当前所学习的知识与认知结构中已经构建的相关知识建立相互联系的积极过程。如果把人们已有的认知结构比作一幢建筑物，那么机械性的学习就是获取这幢建筑物中独立的某一块砖的过程，而有意义的学习则是把砖块内化在整个建筑物中的过程，因此产生的记忆效果会更好。

基于以上说法，教师在词汇的教学过程中，应该对词汇进行词形的加工和语义的加工，以帮助学生在认知结构中建立广泛的连接。

首先，词形的加工。在进行词形加工的过程中，教师可以使用关键词技巧，也就是把将要学习的单词与读音相似的已经掌握的词建立联系。比如，tabloid 在英语中意为"小开的报纸；小报，花边消息报纸"。单独教授该单

词，学生很容易忘记。但是，如果将"tabloid"和"table"以及"void"联系起来讲解就容易得多。tabloid 小报就是桌子 table 很空虚 void，因为小报一般开小，放到桌子上铺不满，并且，由于并非正统报纸，人们可能喜欢随时随地阅读，不一定非要坐在桌前阅读，所以，桌子上没有放报纸，桌子很空虚。另外，词形的加工一般还与该词的读音有关系。众所周知，英语是拼音文字，单词是由字母组成的，字母代表音，单词的读音和拼写有密切的关系，大部分英语单词可以根据读音写出其形式，比如 congratulation，虽然单词较长，但是由于每个发音都对应某个或某组字母，词形的拼写相对好记忆。可是，当遇到词形和发音不太对应的时候，先要找出读音与词性结构的差异，这样，对整个词的记忆就减少为对差异部分的记忆。比如 schedule，按照美式发音，该单词念作/ˈskedʒuːl/。根据发音可以明显地观察到，字母 h 不发音。由于这个不发音字母的存在，导致该单词在拼写上，大部分学生犯错。这个时候，教师可以结合同学们过去学过的单词 school 来进行单词的词形加工。在 school 这个单词中，h 也不用发音，另外还有 scheme、scholar 等，这样进行词形加工之后，相信同学们在记忆该单词时效果会好一些。除此之外，教师也可以使用构词法进行词形加工，分析生词中学生认识的那一部分，使生词与旧词建立起联系，减轻记忆负担，从而有效提高词汇的教学效果以及学生的习得效果。

其次，词义的加工。教师可以通过适当的方式，构建语义网络，使学生将新习得的词汇汇入到原来的记忆网络中。语义网络的构建可以通过词汇之间的语义联系、搭配联系、主题联系等方法进行。例如年轻人通常比较喜欢的卫衣，用英语表示是"hoody"。为什么这个词是卫衣的意思呢？大家都知道，卫衣是一种连帽衫，而卫衣上的帽子，用英语表示就是"hood"，比如，"小红帽"的英文是 little red riding hood。hood 的意思是帽兜，一种帽子，覆盖大部分头部与颈部，有时甚至覆盖脸部。这样，把 hoody、hood，以及 little red riding hood 放在一起记忆，效果应该会比较好。再比如，overtake 这个单词，意为"超过、赶上"。运用单位分析法，发现该词由两部分组成：over 和 take。take 的意思不用多说，关键是学生如果能够理解 over 这一部分，将 overtake 这个单词与过去学过的单词建立起联系，记忆将可能变得轻松。跟

over 有关的单词有 overdo、overeat，意思都很简单，分别是"做的过火"和"吃多了"的意思。联系过去学过的这两个跟 over 有关的单词，结合新学习的 overtake，意思掌握起来就相对轻松一些了。

英语的单词具有较强的生成能力，需要记忆的单词数量也很大，因此，依靠附加到新词上的旧词知识是一个很好的意义编码的途径。教师应该适时地、系统地教给学生词缀、词根和词的组合等方面的基本知识（王平，2008），提供给学生较多的同类词、同族词等来促进学生对词的理解、接受和掌握，培养学生对词汇的合成与分解能力，提高词汇习得的效果。

3.3 运用语义场理论，提高学生词汇习得的效果

根据德国学者 J. Trier 的定义，语义场是"一组意义有关的词共同构成的一个集"，场内的组成成分的意义只有通过它与其他成分之间的关系和区别才能确定。几种常见的语义网络关系，即同义关系、反义关系、上下义关系、多义关系、搭配关系、局部和整体关系、联想关系等，对于教师的词汇教学，具体意义是什么呢？

在词汇教学中，教师在讲解某一个新词时，可以把与该词意义相近的其他词放在一起，与新词一起学习，因为意义相近的词放在一起时，教师带领学生分析这些词的相似之处和不同之处，就会引导学生发现词与词之间的细微差异与不同的应用场合，了解哪些词在哪些语境下可以互换，哪些词在哪些语境下不可以互换，从而更好地了解这些词的意思以及使用的场合。比如，如果教师要讲解的新词是 deceive（欺骗），那么可以一并给出如下表示欺骗的词：cheat、fool、betray、con 等，并引导学生体会这几个词不同的语境范围。五个词都有欺骗的意思，但是，cheat 一般指的是骗取钱财、考试作弊；fool 一般指的是嘲弄愚弄某人；betray 一般指的是不忠实，出卖或辜负了某人；con 一般指的是骗局，或与 pro 一起连用，表示反对。通过比较这些词语之间的细微差异，不但使学生学习了 deceive，而且还把同一语义场里的其他词汇一并进行了比较，形成了同义语义场网络，建立了词与词之间的联系，

扩大了词汇范围，帮助了记忆。

除了同义语义场之外，还有反义语义场。比如，学习 intrinsic 时，一并学习 extrinsic，类似的组合很多。如果新讲解的单词有上下义关系词，教师可以一并列出该词的上下义词，帮助学生习得词汇。如果新讲解的单词是个多义词，教师也可列出该词常用的一些意思，比如 magpie 是"喜鹊"的意思，同时还有"爱嚼舌的人"以及"爱收集东西的人"。后两个意思是基于喜鹊的基本特征而延伸出来的，这样学生在掌握一个基本的核心意思后，又掌握了其他的意思，丰富了词汇知识，同时基于核心意思的延伸，也帮助了学生掌握单词的核心意思。另外，根据整体部分语义场，还可以在讲解新词时向下找到该词的部分或者向上找到该词的整体。比如在学习 abstract 这个单词的时候，可以一并介绍该单词从属于学术论文（article、thesis 或 dissertation）的组成部分，组成部分除了 abstract（摘要）以外，还有 key words（关键词）、introduction（引言）、literature review（文献综述）、research question（研究问题）、methodology（研究方法）、conclusion（研究结论）、bibliography（参考文献）以及 acknowledgement（致谢），等等。运用整体部分语义场，帮助学生建立垂直的语义场网络，构建学生立体的词汇体系。搭配语义场一般比较适合用在搭配能力较强的单词讲解上。比如在学习 make a difference 时，可以找出常见的 make 的其他搭配，像 make face、make fire、make sense、make a decision、make out、make a promise，等等，由于语料库研究力度的加大，词汇搭配也变得越来越重要。最后还有联想语义场。比如教师在讲解一个新词的时候，可以引导学生发散思维，联想与该单词有关的任何词汇，以此调动学生的积极思考，激活大脑中的词汇储备并且通过联想，构建积极的语义场，建立单词之间的联系。

3.4 强化词汇的文化内涵，突出词汇的文化载体作用

教师在进行词汇教学时，不应仅是停留在词汇的读音、拼写、字面意义等表面层次，而应该重视词汇所负载的文化内涵，因为语言是文化的载体，

语言是由词汇构成的，从某种意义上来讲，词汇也是文化的载体，词汇与文化的关系密不可分。如果不注重词汇的文化含义，有可能引起学生对词汇理解的偏差，或者理解困难。

像英语中的颜色词，除了表示颜色之外，还有各自不同的内涵，如果在遇到颜色词，仅仅将其理解成颜色，会引起极大的意义偏差。比如，"Mary was blue about not being invited to the dancing party."（玛丽因为没有被邀请参加舞会而心情不好）。此处 blue 并不是"蓝色"的意思，而是"抑郁，心情不好"的意思。还有英语中的动物词汇，有的也有丰富的甚至不同于中国文化的内涵。比如，"She is a real old dragon."句中的 dragon 指的是"不友好、吓人的女性"，并非我们文化中能呼风唤雨、代表祥瑞的龙。再比如，as strong as a horse 是力大如牛的意思；a black sheep 是害群之马的意思；as stupid as a goose 是蠢得像猪的意思。"It rains cats and dogs."大雨倾盆而下，源于北欧神话。Moses, Solemn 源于《圣经》。如果教师不讲解这些单词背后的文化内涵，极有可能引起学生的理解偏差。

一个国家的历史越久远，其文化越浓厚，相对应的该国语言中词汇的文化内涵也比较丰富。英语的历史可以追溯到公元前 5 世纪，悠久的历史造就了词汇中的文化负载含义的丰富。这对于词汇教学的启示是：首先，教师在进行词汇教学时，应当优先选取具有文化内涵的词汇进行讲解学习，一方面可以帮助学生较容易地掌握该单词，另外还可以附带习得文化，同时还增加了学习的趣味性。其次，应当深入挖掘单词的文化内涵。有的词汇，看似平常，可能其背后还有丰富的文化含义。教师需要有探寻奥秘的好奇心以及对于英语文化的适当的敏感，这样就可以在讲解单词的时候，向学生传递单词所负载的文化内涵。学生只有在掌握了单词的表面意义，即发音、拼写和意思，再掌握单词的文化内涵，这才能称得上真正理解了单词的意思。

3.5 提供丰富的语料库，利用网络资源促进学生词汇习得

"板块性"理论表明词汇习得过程一定要注重习惯搭配等板块的分析和记

忆。网络技术提供了丰富的语料库，可以帮助学生快捷全面地了解词汇板块知识。而且，多媒体网络语料库是动态的语料库资源，它通过收集自然语言的发展确定新增语义，让学生摆脱词典和权威的束缚，合理建构词汇认知意义，与语言发展现实同步（冯青来，2004）。

随着信息技术、互联网的快速发展，语料库语言学已经成为一门学科，其在语言教学中的实际作用也越来越明显。基于语料库的数据驱动学习理念，宗旨是鼓励学生主动从真实的语料中观察、概括和归纳语言事实，符合以学生为中心的学习理念。因为学生可以利用语料库，在教师的指导下，运用检索软件在语料库中进行检索，搜索、提取、处理语料，从中探索、发现、归纳语言使用的规律，并通过练习提高学习者的语言应用能力。在大学英语的词汇教学中，如果使用语料库，有利于学生主动学习词汇，加深对于所学词汇的认知并能够比较真实语境中词汇的使用，有利于学生真正地掌握词汇，将学生对词汇的认知，从认知词汇，即仅记住了单词的意思，上升到工作词汇，即知道如何运用词汇。

基于 Sinclair 在 20 世纪 80 年代提出的词汇语法理论，词汇学习是不能脱离了语境而单独进行的，而大型语料库抽样得出的批量实例或通过语料库定位索引技术可呈现出某一搜索词的语法、语义和语用共现语境，就能表现出该搜索词在真实语言环境中的使用范式和准确意义（何安平，2009）。

目前网络上有很多大型的、各种类型的、面对不同学科分支的语料库，以美国当代英语语料库（Corpus of Contemporary American English，简称 COCA）为例，它不仅界面友好，而且完全免费，由包含 5.2 亿词的文本构成，这些文本由口语、小说、流行杂志、报纸以及学术文章五种不同的文体构成。从 1990 年至 2015 年间语料库以每年增加两千万词的速度进行扩充，以保证语料库内容的时效性（刘安洪，2014）。因此，以美国当代英语语料库为例，看一下语料库是怎样在教学中辅助学生进行词汇习得的。

首先教师本人要首先熟悉语料库的操作，然后再培训学生。学生掌握了语料库的基本界面、符号意义、功能作用等使用方法之后，教师可以结合要教授的教学材料，挑选出将要教给学生的词汇，也可以让学生自己挑选出对他们来说，认知上比较有挑战的词汇。教师通过使用 COCA 语料库向学生展示某一单词的真实使用语境，跟学生一起总结该词汇在不同语境的意思以及主要核心意思。然后让学生自己操作，把要学习的词汇输入语料库，通过观察排名在前十的共现语境，归纳总结词汇的意思、用法、搭配等，让学生自主探索、发现和总结，这样不但可以习得词汇的意思，还可以增强学生探索的热情以及自主学习词汇的能力。

3.6 提供灵活多元的词汇输入渠道，虚拟现实语言输出环境

根据"语义场"理论，学生词汇习得必须通过不断建立和扩大语义网络来实现。然而，在传统词汇教学中，学习材料封闭，输入方式单一。在网络环境下，词汇信息的输入渠道呈现多元化的特征。在建立和扩大语义网络方面，电脑网络搜索引擎（Net Search Engine）能够提供全面、快捷的帮助。例如，http：//www.lexfn.com/这个网页为学生提供了方便的上下义词搜索功能。Lexical Free Net这个程序可以搜索词汇之间的关系。总之，利用网络搜索引擎功能，可以大大拓宽学生的词汇信息认识渠道，从根本上摆脱传统词汇教学认知方式单一的弊端。

信息加工层次理论提倡把词汇放进特定的阅读情境中理解：首先通过联系具体情境猜测词义，然后再依靠不同情境给予验证，确定其意义，之后联系情境回忆提取词汇信息。这一积极建构意义的过程被认知心理学认为是最有效的学习方法。在网络环境下，超文本跳岔特点设计出无数条阅读路径供读者选择，突破了传统的单一直线式的阅读模式，可以保证学生根据需求灵活地按照不同顺序自由地阅读文档，显著地提高学生通过上下文情境来拓展词汇的效率。

心理语言学家对记忆的研究表明信息提取的频率与记忆效果关系密切，即提高编码信息输出的频度可以增进记忆。相关的研究还表明产出性任务可以使单词记忆得更牢固（Salthouse, 1985）。在传统的词汇学习环境下，学生缺乏互相交流的机会和环境，缺乏词汇输出的意识和条件。

相比之下，网络虚拟现实功能可以创造相对真实的外语输出环境。例如，

学生可以参加网上在线英语学习小组，通过 Email 的形式彼此保持交流，通过交流巩固储存在短时记忆中的词汇，并逐渐地转变为长时记忆信息。在书面交际的过程中，学生可以通过 POETS 网站提供的 EVA（English Vocabulary Assistant）程序分析某个词汇的使用准确性，进一步学习词汇（冯青来，2004）。此外，学生还可以利用 Internet 上的聊天室来提高词汇能力和口语交际能力。在"在线英语"聊天室，学生在通过键盘输入话语进行交流的同时，还可以通过话筒直接对话，听到对方的声音；而且，如果在电脑上加载了摄像头，学生还可以通过屏幕看到对方的形象。在这样虚拟现实的语言环境下，学生的积极性和主动性可以得到更大的激发，通过相对真实的交际活动促进自己的词汇习得、语言能力和交际能力。

4　遵循英语词汇习得规律，提高词汇习得效果

总而言之，英语词汇的习得是有规律可循的。其关键是要营造良好的习得环境，激发学生主动性，保证学生可以根据自身的记忆习惯，灵活便捷地选择丰富的词汇资源，进行全方位、深层次的词汇加工，掌握"词汇板块"的特征，发现"语义场"的规律，并且通过高频的词汇信息提取和产出性任务的完成来加强记忆，提高词汇习得效果。在外语教学中，我们应该认识和运用词汇习得的规律并根据学习者学习外语的内在化过程，努力创造适应语言习得的课内、课外环境，培养和调动他们的主观能动性，并采取各种刺激手段（即教学法）去激发释放学生头脑内的巨大潜能，使他们在学习外语过程中获得语言习得的效应，从而真正学好外语，达到事半功倍的教学效果。

参考文献

[1] SALTHOUSE T A. A Theory of Cognitive Aging [M]. Amsterdam：Elsevier Science Publishers B. V. , 1991.

[2] STAHL S A. Vocabulary Development [M]. Cambridge, MA：Brookline Books, 1999.

[3] 陈海庆，徐金荣. 外语教学中的主体动力因素及其培养 [J]. 山东外语教学, 1994 (3-4)：7-10.

[4] 陈斌. 词汇知识以及认知加工理论对词汇教学的启示 [J]. 昆明大学学报（综合版），2005 (1)：9-10, 11.

[5] 陈波. 二语词汇习得中的问题与思考 [J]. 齐齐哈尔师范高等专科学校学报, 2012 (6): 140-141.

[6] 戴聪腾. 对增加英语词汇量教学规律的探讨 [A]. 郑声滔, 吴国良, 李鲁. 全国优秀英语学术论文集 (上卷) [C]. 北京: 中国国际广播出版社, 1997.

[7] 堵楠楠. 近十年国内二语词汇习得研究回顾 [J]. 教育教学论坛, 2015 (13): 90-92.

[8] 范琳, 夏晓云, 王建平. 我国二语词汇学习策略研究述评: 回顾与展望——基于 23 种外语类期刊 15 年文献的统计分析 [J]. 外语界, 2014 (06): 30-37, 47.

[9] 冯青来. 多媒体及网络技术在词汇拓展策略中的应用研究 [J]. 外语电化教学, 2004 (2): 45-49.

[10] 桂诗春. 应用语言学 [M]. 长沙: 湖南教育出版社, 1988.

[11] 何安平. 辛格莱的词汇语法理论应用解读 [J]. 外语研究, 2009 (5): 52-57.

[12] 李广琴. 词汇量对第二语言习得的影响和词汇习得策略研究 [J]. 西安外国语学院学报, 2006 (1): 65-68.

[13] 刘安洪, 谢柯. 基于语料库的大学英语专业词汇课堂教学模式及效果 [J]. 重庆文理学院学报 (社会科学版), 2014 (1): 81-86.

[14] 齐晓星. 语块理论在大学英语教学中的运用 [J]. 湖南工业大学学报 (社会科学版), 2009 (3): 121-122.

[15] 宋丽娟. 认知理论视角下的二语词汇学习模式研究 [D]. 上海: 上海外国语大学, 2009.

[16] 谭文辉. "认知加工"大学英语词汇教学模式研究 [J]. 湖南税务高等专科学校学报, 2005 (3): 45-47.

[17] 王平. 认知心理学理论与词汇记忆教学策略 [J]. 太原大学教育学院学报, 2008 (1): 89-92.

[18] 王寅. 语义理论与语言教学 [M]. 上海: 上海外语教育出版社, 2001.

[19] 伍谦光. 语义学导论 [M]. 长沙：湖南教育出版社, 1998.

[20] 夏慧言, 郑希. 十五年来我国二语词汇习得研究述评 [J]. 重庆交通大学学报（社会科学版）, 2015 (13)：121-124, 129.

[21] 游玉祥. 谈大学生英语词汇习得存在的问题及对策 [J]. 武汉科技大学学报（社会科学版）, 2002 (2)：82-85.

[22] 曾维秀. 外语词汇教学中存在的问题及其解决策略 [J]. 重庆交通学院学报（社会科学版）, 2003 (6)：74-76.

[23] 张乃玲. 大学英语词汇教学方法及其理据 [J]. 太原师范学院学报（社会科学版）, 2004 (3)：146-147.

[24] 张庆宗, 吴喜燕. 认知加工层次与外语词汇学习——词汇认知直接学习法 [J]. 现代外语（季刊）, 2002 (2)：176-186.

[25] 赵艳芳. 认知语言学概论 [M]. 上海：上海外语教育出版社, 2001.

[26] 朱一楠. 现代教育技术及其对英语教学模式改革的支持 [J]. 天津大学学报（社会科学版）, 2003 (5)：289-292.

第二部分 02
英语词汇习得实践篇

1　A，B

1.1　A

ambassador /æmˈbæsədər/ *n.* 大使，使节；代表；特使；[比喻] 使者

【例句】As the ambassador of Spain he shoulders great responsibility of promoting the friendly exchanges between the two countries. 作为西班牙大使，他肩负着促进两国友好交流的重要使命。

【拓展】ambassadorial *adj.*

ambition /æmˈbɪʃn/ *n.* 抱负；渴望得到的东西；追求的目标；夙愿；*vt.* 追求；有……野心

【例句】①He never achieved his ambition of becoming a famous film star. 他想要成为明星的愿望一直没有实现。②She is intelligent but has little ambitions. 她很聪明，却没什么远大志向。

【拓展】ambitious *adj.*

【近义词】aspiration

ambulance /ˈæmbjələns/ *n.* 救护车

【例句】Call an ambulance the moment you find an old man without consciousness on the street. 当发现路上有老人失去意识，马上叫救护车。

amid /əˈmɪd/ *prep.* 在其间；在其中

【例句】Berkeley event was canceled amid protests due to security reasons. 安

全考虑，伯克利的演讲活动在众多抗议声中被取消了。

【近义词】in the mist of; among

amount /əˈmaʊnt/ ***n***. 数量；总额；全部含义；***vi***. （在意义、价值、效果、程度等方面）合计，总计；接近；发展成

【例句】As a billionaire, he possesses a great amount of wealth. 作为亿万富翁，他拥有一笔巨额的财富。

【用法】amount to 等于；相当于；意味着

【例句】China's tariffs amount to about three-tenths of a percent of our GDP. 中国的关税收入大约是我们 GDP 的 0.3%。

【近义词】aggregate; number; sum; total

amuse /əˈmjuːz/ ***vt***. 使人发笑；逗乐；使消遣；娱乐

【例句】Surely some people won't be amused. 当然有些人根本逗不乐。

【拓展】amusing ***adj***. →amusement ***n***.

analyze /ˈænəlaɪz/ ***vt***. 分析；解析；研究

【例句】The software analyzes and identifies fake reviews, helping you out when you buy stuff online. 这种软件可以分析和识别虚假的评价，在你网购的时候帮你的忙。

【近义词】examine

【拓展】analysis ***n***.

【用法】in the final (last, ultimate) analysis 总之，归根结底

【例句】The fertilizer can be of great help to young plants in the final analysis. 总之，这种肥料对于幼苗的成长有极大的帮助。

ancestor /ˈænsestər/ ***n***. 祖宗；祖先；原种

【例句】In some free genealogy databases online you can search for your ancestors and locate your family surnames. 在网上的一些免费宗谱数据库里，你可以寻找你的祖先，找到你的家族姓氏。

anchor /ˈæŋkər/ ***n***. 锚；锚状物；靠山；压阵队员；***vt***. 抛锚，抛锚泊船；使固定，使稳固；使稳定；在……任节目主持人；***vi***. 抛锚，停泊；固定；[体] 任主要运动员；主持节目；***adj***. 最后一棒的，末棒的

【例句】①Anchor away! 锚离底！②He is the anchor of the family. 他是整个家的靠山。③The ship was anchored in the harbor. 船停靠在海港。

ancient /ˈeɪnʃənt/ *adj*. 古代的；古老的，老式的；年老的；*n*. 古代人；古文明国的国民

【例句】①The city boasts its ancient city wall. 这座城市以它古老的城墙而自豪。②Ancient Indian people are said to be the original inhabitants here. 据说这个地方的原始居民是古印第安人。

【拓展】anciently *adv*.

angel /ˈeɪndʒl/ *n*. 天使，天使般的人；守护神；善良可爱的人；安琪儿

【例句】In folklore, angels are thought to be very friendly to the common people. 在民间传说中，天使对普通老百姓是很友爱的。

angle /ˈæŋgl/ *n*. 角；[比喻]（考虑、问题的）角度；观点；轮廓鲜明的突出体；*vt*. 使形成（或弯成）角度；把……放置成一角度；调整（或对准）……的角度；使（新闻、报道等）带有倾向性；*vi*. 垂钓；斜移；弯曲成一角度；从（某角度）报道

【例句】That house was leaning at a low angle after earthquake. 地震过后，房子倾斜得很厉害。

【用法】at an angle 以一定的角度，斜着

【例句】You might need a line at an angle to work the problem out. 要解出这个题目你可能需要一条角度线。

ankle /ˈæŋkl/ *n*. 踝，踝关节；脚脖子

【例句】His ankle was badly hurt after landing awkwardly. 由于落地不当，他的脚踝受伤严重。

anniversary /ˌænɪˈvɜːrsəri/ *n*. 周年纪念日；*adj*. 周年的；周年纪念的；年年的；每年的

【例句】It is the wedding anniversary of my parents next week. 下周是我父母的结婚周年纪念日。

annoy /əˈnɔɪ/ *vt*. 打扰；干扰；使烦恼；使恼怒；*vi*. 惹恼，令人讨厌，打搅；*n*. 烦恼

【例句】①I'm really annoyed at this mess. 这一团糟着实让我恼火。②It annoys me that I don't have time for a gathering of old friends. 没有时间参加老朋友的聚会让我很烦。

【用法】be annoyed with 对（某人）生气

【例句】Have you ever been annoyed with yourself when you forget something important? 当你忘记一些重要事情的时候，是不是对自己很生气？

【近义词】bother; disturb; irritate; trouble

annual /ˈænjuəl/ ***adj.*** 年度的；每年的；***n.*** 年鉴，年刊

【例句】The old couple always travel around to celebrate their annual wedding anniversary. 这对老夫妻每年都是四处游玩以庆祝他们的结婚纪念日。

ant /ænt/ ***n.*** 蚂蚁

【例句】My son spent a good hour observing a colony of ants. 我儿子花了足足一个小时观察一群蚂蚁。

anticipate /ænˈtɪsɪpeɪt/ ***vt.*** 预感；预见；预料；先于……行动；***vi.*** 过早地考虑（或说、做）一件事；过早地提出

【例句】①We didn't anticipate any trouble in raising money for the homeless. 我们没料到给无家可归者募捐会遇到麻烦。②They have been anticipating the day of their reunion. 他们一直在期待重聚的那一天。

【拓展】anticipatory ***adj.*** →anticipation ***n.***

【近义词】expect

antique /ænˈtiːk/ ***adj.*** 古老的，古代的；过时的，古董的；古时制造的；古风的；***n.*** 古玩，古董；古风，古希腊和古罗马艺术风格；***v.*** 仿古制作；使显得古色古香；寻觅古玩

【例句】①Luck discovered the true value of some antique china. 卢克发现了一些古董瓷器的真正价值。②Roses drape on the antique brick walls. 蔷薇覆盖在古老的城墙上。

【近义词】old; ancient

anxiety /æŋˈzaɪəti/ ***n.*** 焦虑，忧虑；渴望；令人焦虑的事；挂念

【例句】①Anxiety can be experienced occasionally or as a persistent condition that can interfere with your life. 焦虑感可能偶尔出现，也可能持续存在影响你的生活。②The book mainly tells us people's anxiety to end the war in Iraq. 这本书主要讲述了人们对于结束伊拉克战争的渴望。

【拓展】anxious *adj*.

【近义词】worry

anyhow /ˈenihaʊ/ *adv*. 总之；无论如何；不管怎样；随随便便

【例句】He's asleep now. Anyhow, he is quiet now. 他现在睡着了，不管怎样，他现在安静了。

anyway /ˈeniweɪ/ *adv*. 无论如何；而且；尽管；至

【例句】①But old men who think they're going to die anyway aren't very effective activists. 但是，有些老人认为自己无论如何都会死去，因此不会积极地参与进去。②Playing football was always what I wanted to do anyway. 而且，踢足球一直是我想做的事。

apart /əˈpɑːrt/ *adj*. 分离的，隔离的；*adv*. 相隔，相距；分散地，分开地；成部分，成碎片；分辨

【例句】①The two big trees stood 100 meters apart. 两棵大树相距 100 米。②To take better care of the grandchildren, they are now living apart. 为了更好地照顾孙子们，他们现在分开居住。

【用法】apart from 除了；tell...apart 区分

【例句】①Apart from the assignment teachers left yesterday, we are also occupied with the review work. 除了老师们昨天布置的作业，我们还忙着复习。②Even the parents sometimes fail to tell the twins apart. 即便是他们的父母，有时候也难以区分这两个双胞胎。

apartment /əˈpɑːrtmənt/ *n*. 一套公寓房间

【例句】She bought an apartment in the downtown last year. 去年她在市中心买了一套公寓。

apology /əˈpɑːlədʒi/ *n*. 道歉认错，愧悔；正式辩解，（口）临时凑合的代用品

【例句】He lodged a complaint and has now received a formal letter of apology.

他提出投诉，现在已经收到一封正式的道歉信。

【拓展】apologize *v*.

【用法】make an apology 道歉

apparent /əˈpærənt/*adj*. 易看见的，可看见的；显然的，明明白白的；貌似的，表面的

【例句】It is apparent that she does not want to tell the truth and just conceals it. 很明显她不想说实话，只想掩盖。

【近义词】clear; evident; obvious; plain; distinct; manifest

appeal /əˈpiːl/*n*. 上诉；呼吁；要求，恳求；*vi*. 呼吁；要求；有吸引力；求助（于）；提请注意；*vt*. 指控；将……上诉

【例句】①He is currently appealing against his sentence. 目前他正对他的判罚提出上诉。②This option is especially appealing to people who buy from more than one website. 这个选择对于经常从多个网址买东西的人来说尤其有吸引力。

【用法】appeal for 呼吁；appeal to 对……有吸引力

【例句】①He appeals for world peace on his first day as the Secretary General of the United Nations. 担任联合国秘书长的第一天他就呼吁世界和平。②Toyota's Kirobo Mini is designed to appeal to childless women. 丰田制造商发明创造出机器人孩童的目的是吸引那些没有孩子的女性。

【近义词】plead; entreat

appearance /əˈpɪərəns/*n*. 外貌，外观；出现，露面；[哲]现象

【例句】He resembled his father in appearance. 他长得像父亲。

【近义词】face; feature; look

appetite /ˈæpɪtaɪt/*n*. 欲望；胃口，食欲；嗜好，爱好

【例句】Due to her illness, she doesn't have any appetite for meals. 由于生病她没有胃口吃饭。

【用法】spoil one's appetite 坏了胃口，影响食欲

【例句】Young children are often advised not to spoil their appetite by eating sweets. 大人经常劝告小孩子们不要因为吃甜食影响食欲。

applause /əˈplɔːz/*n*. 热烈鼓掌；喝彩；掌声

【例句】There is a burst of applause in the hall after her excellent performance. 她精彩的演出之后大厅里爆发出一阵热烈的掌声。

【拓展】applaud *v*. 鼓掌；喝彩；applausive *adj*. 赞赏的；拍手欢呼的

appliance /əˈplaɪəns/ *n*. 器具，器械，装置；家用电器

【例句】①Under no circumstances can you touch the appliances with bare hands. 任何情况下不可以光用手触碰这些器具。②Dish washer is one of the appliances in our family now. 洗碗机现在是我家的家用电器之一。

【近义词】instrument；device；equipment；tool；implement；facilities

applicable /ˈæplɪkəbl/ *adj*. 适当的；可应用的；可实施的

【例句】①That is internationally applicable. 那是全球适用的。②Applicable Chemistry is an optional course in their college. 应用化学在他们学院是选修课。

【用法】applicable to 适用于，能应用于

【例句】This theory is also applicable to non-vacuum environment. 这一理论同样适用于非真空环境。

【拓展】applicant *n*. 申请人；application *n*. 申请；apply *vt.*&*vi*. 申请

【用法】apply for 申请

【例句】I do not knowhow to apply for a non-immigrant visa for a travel to the United States. 我不知道如何申请去美国旅行的非移民签证。

appoint /əˈpɔɪnt/ *vt*. 任命，委派；约定，指定；装设，布置

【例句】The University of Oxford is to appoint its first female vice-chancellor since its records began nearly 800 years ago. 牛津大学计划任命一位女性副校长，这是有史记载八百年来第一次。

【近义词】designate；elect；name；nominate

【拓展】appointment *n*. 约定，约会；任命，委派

appreciate /əˈpriːʃieɪt/ *vt*. 感激；欣赏；领会；鉴别；*vi*. （使）增值，涨价

【例句】Foreign people can not appreciate Chinese poem exactly and completely. 外国人很难准确完全的欣赏中国诗歌。

【近义词】comprehend；understand；apprehend；grasp

【拓展】appreciative *adj*.

approach /əˈproʊtʃ/ *vi*. 接近，走近，靠近；*vt*. 接近；着手处理；使移近；*n*. 方法；途径；接近

【例句】①The boy sat down on a big stone and took a pebble out of his shoe when a strange young man approached. 男孩坐在大石头上，从鞋子里倒出一颗石子，这时一个陌生的年轻人走了过来。②So how do we approach this situation? 那么我们怎么处理这种局面？③The four-step approach is a friendly and informative guide with practical advice to help you tackle these problems. 四步法使用便利，信息量大，方法实用，有助于帮你解决这些问题。

【近义词】method；way；means

appropriate /əˈproʊpriət/ *adj*. 适当的；恰当的；合适的；*v*. 盗用；侵吞；拨（专款等）

【例句】①For a moment she thought of giving the money to an appropriate charity. 有那么一会儿她考虑把钱捐给一家合适的慈善机构。②It is illegal for a civil servant to appropriate the fund of the government. 公务员擅自挪用政府资金是非法的。

【近义词】proper；suitable

approval /əˈpruːvl/ *n*. 同意；批准；赞成

【例句】You can not work here without your parent's approval. 没有你父母的批准你不能在这里工作。

【用法】meet with sb's approval 得到某人的赞许，得到某人的认可

【例句】Does the schedule meet with your approval? 这份日程安排您满意吗？

【近义词】agreement；assent；consent

【拓展】approve *vt*. & *vi*.

【例句】We would not approve of such abortion. 我们不会赞成堕胎。

approximate /əˈprɑːksɪmət/ *adj*. 近似的，大概的；极相似的；［植］相近但不连接的 *vi*. 接近于；近似于；*vt*. 靠近；使接近；使结合

【例句】Grace asked me where I was and I gave her my approximate whereabouts. 格丽斯问我在哪，我给了她一个大体的位置。

【拓展】approximately *adj*.

arbitrary /ˈɑːrbɪtreri/*adj*. 随意的，任性的；主观的，武断的；霸道的

【例句】United Nations officials condemned the arbitrary detention of Palestinian children by Israel. 联合国官员谴责以色列任意拘禁巴勒斯坦儿童。

【近义词】tyrannical

architect /ˈɑːrkɪtekt/*n*. 建筑师，设计师；创造者，缔造者；造物主

【例句】He is a well-known architect in the world thanks to his achievements. 他由于自己杰出的成就成为一名世界知名的建筑师。

【拓展】architecture *n*. 建筑学

argument /ˈɑːrgjumənt/*n*. 争论，争吵；论据；[数] 幅角；主题，情节

【例句】The opposing argument in Joseph's new book received more supports. 约瑟夫新书中提出的相反论据得到了更多的支持。

【近义词】controversy; dispute; quarrel

arise /əˈraɪz/*vi*.&*vt*. 产生；出现；起身，起立；起源于，产生于

【例句】Green house effect arises from negligence of the environmental protection. 温室效应起因于对环境保护的疏忽。

【用法】arise from 产生于，起因于

【近义词】originate; spring; stem

arithmetic /əˈrɪθmətɪk/*n*. 算术，计算；算法

【例句】To this day his mental arithmetic cannot be faulted. 至今他的心算能力完美无缺。

arouse /əˈraʊz/*vt*. 引起；唤醒；激起性欲；使行动起来；惹怒，激怒

【例句】His speech arouses people's patriotism. 他的演讲唤起了人们的爱国心。

【近义词】wake; waken

arrange /əˈreɪndʒ/*vt*. 布置，整理；改编（剧本等）；安排；*vi*. 达成协议，商定（某事）；[音乐]（尤指专业）改编乐曲

【例句】His relatives and friends have arranged a bridal chamber for his wedding. 他的亲戚朋友为他的婚礼安排了一间新房。

【用法】arrange about/for 为……做准备；安排

【例句】There are a multitude of ways in which a teacher can arrange for the students to take part in group work in class. 老师可以有很多方式安排学生参与到课上的活动中。

【拓展】arrangement *n.*

arrest /əˈrest/ *vt.* 逮捕；阻止；吸引（注意）；*vi.* 心跳停止；*n.* 拘留；停止；监禁

【例句】①That young man who committed chain homicides in a clown's mask has been arrested by the police. 那个戴着小丑面具的连环杀手已经被警方抓捕。②I failed to arrest his taking risks. 我没能阻止他冒险。

【近义词】apprehend；detain；capture；catch

【辨析】arrest、apprehend、detain 均有依法"逮捕""拘押""监禁"的意思。arrest 可用于刑事案件，也可用于民事案件，如债务等；而 apprehend 只用于刑事案件；detain 则是为了询问或审查而拘留或监护，不是严格的法律术语。

【例句】①He never expected that he would one day be arrested for plagiarism. 他从没想到过有一天会因为剽窃罪被捕。②The police have apprehended the killer. 警方已经抓捕了杀人凶手。③You might get detained if you don't carry any identification with you. 如果你不携带任何证件的话可能会被拘留起来。

arrow /ˈæroʊ/ *n.* 矢，箭；箭状物；箭头记号

【例句】Follow the arrows and you will find the restroom. 按照箭头方向走，你就能找到洗手间。

arrogant /ˈærəgənt/ *adj.* 傲慢的；自大的；妄自尊大的

【例句】He was anything but an arrogant twit. 他绝不是一个傲慢自大的讨厌鬼。

【近义词】conceited；proud

【反义词】humble；modest

【拓展】arrogance *n.*

artificial /ˌɑːrtɪˈfɪʃl/ *adj.* 人造的，不自然的；虚伪的；武断的，随意决定的；矫揉造作的

【例句】①Our drink is free from any artificial coloring and flavorings. 我们的饮料不含有任何人工色素和调味品。②Artificial emotion won't fool anyone in the long run. 时间久了虚伪的情感骗不了任何人。

【近义词】synthetic; man-made

artistic /ɑːrˈtɪstɪk/ *adj.* 艺术的；有艺术天赋的；精美的，别致的

【例句】She had a great artistic taste for architect. 她对建筑有极高的艺术品位。

【拓展】art *n.* →artist *n.* →artless *adj.*

ash /æʃ/ *n.* 白蜡树；白蜡木；灰；灰烬

【例句】After a day, their house has been burned down to ashes. 烧了一天，他们的房子已经变为灰烬。

aside /əˈsaɪd/ *n.* 旁白；顺便说的话；*adv.* 在一边；另外；离开

【例句】①In an aside to his wife, he roared, "Leave me alone." 在他对母亲的一段旁白中，他大叫道："不要管我。"②Stand aside, it's dangerous! 危险，站一边去！

【用法】aside from 除……之外；set aside 留出；驳回

【例句】①Aside from doing schoolwork, American children are supposed to take part in various extra-curricula activities. 除了做学校作业，美国孩子也要参加各种各样的课外活动。②Extra funds are set aside for the medical assistance of the victims in the conflicts. 另行拨款以对冲突中的受害者实施医疗救助。

aspect /ˈæspekt/ *n.* 方面；方位；外观；外貌

【例句】The skills you learn from sports can be used in many aspects of your life. 你在体育活动中学到的技能可以用到你生活中的很多方面。

【近义词】phase; side; appearance

aspiration /ˌæspəˈreɪʃn/ *n.* 强烈的愿望；吸气，吸入；发送气音

【例句】①Dream and aspiration are driving force for a better life. 梦想和渴望是更好生活的推动力。②The effectiveness of the medicine on the treatment of aspiration pneumonia has been proved to be true. 这种药对吸入性肺炎的效用已被证实。

【近义词】ambition

assemble /əˈsembl/ *vi.* 集合；收集；*vt.* 装配，组合

【例句】Directions on how to assemble the product can be found in the box. 可以在箱子里找到组装这个产品的说明。

【近义词】collect; congregate

【拓展】assembly *n.*

assert /əˈsɜːrt/ *vt.* 断言；主张，坚持；生效；维护

【例句】He asserted that what the doctor had done was wrong. 他断言医生做错了。

【用法】assert oneself 表达自己，坚持自己主张

【例句】The way how you assert yourself contributes to the current partnership with your teammates. 你表达自己主张的方式促成了你跟队友目前的伙伴关系。

【近义词】affirm; allege; maintain

assess /əˈses/ *vt.* 评定；估价；对（财产、收入等）进行估价（作为征税根据）；确定（损害赔偿金、税款、罚款等）的金额

【例句】That old house was assessed at 60,000 dollars. 那栋老房子估价60,000美元。

【近义词】appraise; evaluate

asset /ˈæset/ *n.* 资产，财产；有价值的人或物；有用的东西；优点

【例句】①You need professional suggestions on asset management. 你需要资产管理方面的专业建议。②The famous soccer player is a great asset to the club. 这名著名的足球运动员是这家俱乐部的宝。

assign /əˈsaɪn/ *vt.* 分配；指定；指派；归因；确定；*n.* 受让人

【例句】He assigned them tasks for the day. 他分给他们当天的任务。

【近义词】allot; distribute; appoint; designate

【拓展】assignment *n.*

assist /əˈsɪst/ *vt.* 帮助；协助；*vi.* 帮助；出席；*n.* 帮助；协助；助攻；

协助的器械

【例句】She assisted her mother with the meal. 她帮妈妈做饭。

【用法】assist with 帮助；照料；做；在……给予帮助

【近义词】aid; help

【拓展】assistance *n.*

associate /əˈsoʊsieɪt; əˈsoʊsiət/ *vt.* 联想；联合；*vi.* 交往；*n.* 伙伴；同事；同伴；*adj.* 副的；共事的；有联系的

【例句】We find it quite remarkable that one's level of happiness is captured by the three words a person chooses to associate with happiness. 我们发现值得注意的是，一个人的幸福指数可以通过他选择的跟幸福有关的三个字来获得。

【用法】associate with 与……交往，联系

【近义词】connect; link; attach

【拓展】associative *adj.* →association *n.*

assume /əˈsuːm/ *vt.* 假定；设想；承担；（想当然的）认为；假装

【例句】①Let's assume first he is innocent before more evidence comes out. 首先在出现更多证据前让我们假定他是无辜的。②Our website won't assume any liability of your speech. 我们的网站不会因为你们的言论承担任何责任。

【近义词】presume; suppose; postulate

【拓展】assumable *adj.* →assumption *n.*

assure /əˈʃʊr/ *vt.* 向……保证；使……确信

【例句】We assure you a most fruitful, exciting and educational meeting. 我们向你们保证这将是一次收获满满，激动人心并有教育意义的会议。

【用法】assure of 对……放心

【例句】The airline stewardess tried to assure the old lady of the safety of air traveling. 空姐试图让那位老妇人放心，坐飞机出行是安全的。

【近义词】guarantee

【拓展】assurance *n.*

astonish /əˈstɑːnɪʃ/ *vt.* 使惊讶；使吃惊

【例句】His cycling around the world astonished everyone at that time. 他骑车

周游世界的壮举让当时的人们都很惊讶。

【近义词】amaze; surprise; astound; startle; stun

athlete /ˈæθliːt/ *n*. 运动员

【例句】That girl finally falls in love with an athlete. 那个女孩最后爱上了一位运动员。

【拓展】athletic *adj*.

atmosphere /ˈætməsfɪr/ *n*. 大气，空气；大气层；风格，基调，情调；气氛

【例句】①Meteoroids burn up as they pass through Earth's atmosphere. 流星体穿越地球大气层的时候燃烧起来。②Many students choose this university in view of its academic atmosphere. 许多学生因为它的学术氛围而选择这所大学。

atom /ˈætəm/ *n*. 原子；原子能；微粒，微量

【例句】Particles revolve around atoms. 粒子围绕原子旋转。

【拓展】atomic *adj*.

attach /əˈtætʃ/ *vt*. 使依附；贴上，系上；使依恋；*vi*. 从属；附着；伴随而来；联在一起

【例句】①There is a middle school attached to the famous university. 这所知名大学有一所附属中学。②Attach the coupon to the front of the receipt. 在收据的正面贴上优惠券。③Children are deeply attached to their mothers. 孩子们都深深地依恋自己的母亲。

【用法】attach to 使相关；使牵连；使依附

attain /əˈteɪn/ *vt*. 达到，实现；获得；到达；*vi*. 达到；获得；到达

【例句】As you strive to attain your American Dream, consider first what success is. 当你努力实现自己的美国梦的时候，首先考虑一下什么是成功。

【近义词】achieve; earn; gain; obtain; win

【拓展】attainable *adj*. →attainment *n*.

attend /əˈtend/ *vt*. 出席；上（大学等）；照料；陪伴；*vi*. 出席；致力于；照顾

【例句】①The meeting was attended by scholarship winners. 获得奖学金的学

生出席了这次会议。②We later found that we attended the same school. 后来我们发现我们上的是同一所学校。③Are you being attended to, this young lady? 这位小姐，有人招待你吗？

【拓展】 attendance *n*.

attitude /ˈætɪtuːd/ *n*. 态度；看法；姿势；意见，倾向

【例句】 Attitude is everything. 态度决定一切。

【近义词】 posture; stand

attorney /əˈtɜːrni/ *n*. （辩护）律师

【例句】 Jefferson claimed to be the most distinguished attorney of his century. 杰斐逊声称自己是他那个世纪最杰出的辩护律师。

【近义词】 counselor; lawyer; solicitor

attract /əˈtrækt/ *v*. 吸引；引起

【例句】 ①People usually first get attracted to his sense of humor. 人们首先被他的幽默感吸引。②His comment will certainly attract criticism. 他的评论一定会引起批评。

【拓展】 attraction *n*. →attractive *adj*. →attractiveness *n*. →attractively *adv*.

attribute /ˈætrɪbjuːt; əˈtrɪbjuːt/ *vt*. 把……归于；认为……是某人所做，认为是……所为；*n*. 属性；标志；象征；特征

【例句】 ①His lack of sympathy is attributed to his miserable childhood. 他缺乏同情心，这被认为跟他悲惨的童年有关。②Diligence is considered to be one of the most valuable attributes of a man. 勤奋被认为是一个人最重要的品质之一。

【用法】 attribute to 认为某事（物）属于某人（物）

【近义词】 ascribe; quality; characteristic; trait

【拓展】 attributable *adj*.

audience /ˈɔːdiəns/ *n*. 听众；观众；读者；倾听；拥护者；正式会见

【例句】 There are two additional methods we use to understand our target audience better. 我们还有两个方法来更好地理解我们的目标听众。

audio /ˈɔːdioʊ/ *adj*. 声音的；成音频率的；*n*. 音频；音响设备

【例句】 We do everything from the simplest recording and editing to the most sophisticated audio processing and restoration. 从最简单的录音和剪辑到复杂的音频处理和恢复，我们什么都能做。

author /ˈɔːθər/ *n*. 作家；作者；*vt*. 编写；创作

【例句】Jane Austine is the author of *Pride and Prejudice*. 简·奥斯丁是《傲慢与偏见》的作者。

authority /əˈθɔːrəti/ *n*. 权力；官方；当局；职权；权威

【例句】There is very strong evidence that having more women in authority would improve business performance more generally. 有力的证据表明，更多的女性当权会广泛地提高企业绩效。

【用法】in authority 掌权

automatic /ˌɔːtəˈmætɪk/ *adj*. 自动的；无意识的；必然的；*n*. 自动装置；半自动武器

【例句】①This machine has an automatic temperature control. 这台机器有自动控温系统。②Fear is an automatic feeling in danger. 害怕是身处危险时的一种下意识感觉。

【拓展】automatically *adv*. →automotive *adj*.

automobile /ˈɔːtəməbiːl/ *n*. 汽车；*adj*. 汽车的；自动的；机动的

【例句】As the largest automobile manufacturer in India, the company leads the industry in technological innovation and scale of production. 作为印度最大的汽车制造商，这家公司在科技创新和生产规模上都处于行业领先位置。

auxiliary /ɔːgˈzɪliəri/ *n*. 助动词；辅助物；帮助者；附属组织，附属机构；*adj*. 辅助的；附加的；备用的，预备的

【例句】An auxiliary policeman was killed in a fight with two muggers. 一名协警在与两名劫匪的斗争中牺牲了。

available /əˈveɪləbl/ *adj*. 可利用的；可获得的，可得到的；有空的；有效的

【例句】①Facilities of a university available to students are one of the major concerns for applicants. 一所大学里学生能使用的公共设施情况是申请者们主要关心的事之一。②Will the professor be available tomorrow for a meeting? 教授明

天有时间参加会议吗？

【拓展】availability *n*.

avenue /ˈævənuː/ *n*. 林荫道；大街；途径手段

【例句】The avenues are crowded with shoppers on Sundays. 每逢星期天大街上到处都是购物的人。

【近义词】road；street；lane；boulevard；alley

【辨析】上述单词均可表示道路。avenue 指两边住宅或建筑物林立的繁华大街；road 使用范围比较广，通常指车辆和人可以通行的大路；street 主要指路边有房屋的街道；lane 指的是胡同、小巷、车道等；boulevard 指林荫大道，大马路；alley 也指小巷、小路，还可以指花园里的小径。

【例句】①The Fifth Avenue in New York attracts millions of visitors and shoppers every year. 纽约的第五大道每年都吸引着数以百万计的游客和购物者。②All roads lead to Rome. 条条大路通罗马。③Keep an eye on your child and keep him away from the street. 盯紧孩子，不要让他跑到大街上玩。④Which lane were you in when the accident took place? 车祸发生的时候你在哪个车道？⑤Go straight ahead and turn right at the University Boulevard. 径直朝前走，在大学路右转。⑥I walked my dog along the alley in the park. 我沿着公园的小径遛狗。

avoid /əˈvɔɪd/ *vt*. 避开，避免，预防；［法］使无效，撤销，废止

【例句】Take the box away to avoid damage to its outside. 把箱子拿开以防磨损到外层的包装。

【近义词】evade；shun；keep away from

【拓展】avoidable *adj*. →avoidance *n*.

await /əˈweɪt/ *v*. 等候；期待；将降临于

【例句】On screen a message glows："Stay indoors and await further instructions." 屏幕上一条信息在闪现："待在家里不要外出，等候进一步的指示。"

award /əˈwɔːrd/ *vt*. 授予，奖给，判给；判归，判定；*n*. 奖品；（仲裁人、公断人的）裁定；（法院、法官的）判决；裁定书

【例句】①I was awarded damages of ￥30,000. 我得到了3万元的损害赔偿金。②She won an Academy Award as Best Actress for her first American movie. 她

的第一部美国电影为她赢得了奥斯卡最佳女演员奖。

【近义词】confer; give; grant; present

【拓展】awarding *n*.

【辨析】give、present、grant、award、confer 均有"给予"的意思。give 是最普通用语。present 较正式，指以一定的形式或程序赠给，并暗示所给的物品有一定的价值。grant 指依照对方的希望或要求给予，有权者以正式手续给予。award 指有充分理由给予奖赏。confer 指地位较高者把名誉或地位授予地位较低者。

【例句】①On his retirement, his colleagues presented him with a painting. 退休那天，同事们送了他一幅油画。②The bank finally granted him a 4 million dollar loan. 银行最终给了他4百万贷款。③The president of our university will confer a doctor degree on you on your graduation day. 你毕业那天，咱们学校的校长会颁发你博士学位。

aware /əˈwer/ *adj*. 知道的，明白的；意识到的；明智的

【例句】He did his best to explain at an interview that he is well aware of the importance of the third party support. 在一次采访中他努力解释道，他很明白第三方支持的重要性。

【拓展】awareness *n*.

【近义词】conscious

awful /ˈɔːfl/ *adj*. 糟糕的；可怕的；充满敬畏的；难受的；*adv*. 极其，十分

【例句】①After an awful night alone on the mountain, the girl finally got rescued. 一个人在山上度过了可怕的一晚后，女孩最终获救了。②It was absolutely awful to say goodbye. 说再见的感觉很糟糕。

awkward /ˈɔːkwərd/ *adj*. 尴尬的；笨拙的，不熟练的；（设计）别扭的；棘手的；难操作的

【例句】It was an awkward Christmas when the whole family was tangled in a web of dramas from financial issues to relationship. 那是一个让人尴尬的圣诞节，一家人因为财务问题、恋爱关系问题等乱成一团。

【近义词】clumsy

【拓展】awkwardly *adv*. →awkwardness *n*.

ax /æks/*n*. 斧子；解雇；（吉他等）乐器；*vt*. 削减；用斧砍；<口>解雇；削减

【例句】The old man cleft a wood in two with an ax. 那个老人用斧头把木头一劈为二。

axe /æks/*n*. 斧；解雇；倒闭；撤销，砍掉；*vt*. 用斧砍；解雇；大量削减；去掉

【例句】①Axes were often used to cut trees. 过去人们经常用斧头砍树。②I asked for a raise, only to get the axe from my boss. 我要求加薪，结果老板把我解雇了。

1.2 B

blade /bleɪd/*n*. 刀片，剑；（壳、草等的）叶片；桨叶；浮华少年

【例句】The blade of leaf on the wall will never be shriveled up and fall. 墙上那片树叶将永远不会枯萎飘落。

【拓展】bladed *adj*.

blank /blæŋk/*adj*. 空白的；未填写的；空虚的；*n*. 填空处；空白；*vt*. 使……无效；不理睬某人；*vi*. 消失

【例句】①I totally blanked on hearing the horrible news. 听到噩耗我大脑一片空白。②Please write down your name on this blank sheet of paper and print it out. 请在这张空白的纸上写上你的名字然后打印出来。

【近义词】empty

blast /blæst/*n*. 爆炸；一阵（疾风等）；响声；*vt*. 击毁，摧毁；尖响；裁判高声吹哨；*vi*. 爆炸；攻击；严厉批评或猛烈攻击

【例句】① More than 100 people died in Srilanka's blast. 在斯里兰卡爆炸事件中已经有100多人丧生。②The articles blast the government for its oppression.

这些文章严厉抨击政府的压榨。

bleed /bliːd/ *vt.* 使出血；勒索；*vi.* 给（某人）放血；长期榨取（某人的钱）

【例句】①The pilot made her leave the plane after her congested ears began to bleed. 她充血的耳朵开始流血后飞行员要求她离开飞机。②The subsidies needed to keep the trains operating would bleed the funds available for more productive transportation services. 维持火车运行会耗掉所有的资金，这些资金本可以用于更有成效的交通运输业。

【拓展】bleeding *adj.*

blend /blend/ *vt.* 混合；协调；*vi.* 掺杂；结合；相称；*n.* 混合；混合物

【例句】The trick is to blend the industry's more cautious, subtle, and private views into the random time segments. 方法就是在任意时间段都融入更谨慎、更精细、更清静地行业观点。

【用法】blend into（两样以上的东西）融为（一体）

blog /blɑːg/ *n.* 博客，网志；*vi.* 维护网志

【例句】She has endless fan sites and blog posts devoted to her. 她有无数喜欢她的粉丝网址和粉丝博客。

bloodshed /ˈblʌdʃed/ *n.* 流血；屠杀，杀戮；流血事件

【例句】In a detective novel there was a bloodshed and all the passengers on that train were murderers. 在一部侦探小说中，发生了一起残忍的杀戮，车上所有的乘客都是凶手。

bloody /ˈblʌdi/ *adj.* 血腥的，残忍的；血一样的；嗜杀的，残忍的

【例句】They were bruised and bloody. 他们浑身淤青，血淋淋的。

bloom /bluːm/ *n.* 花，最盛期；*vi.* 开花；使植物繁盛；变得健康

【例句】①It's perfect time for picture taking when flowers are in bloom. 花开的时候是拍照的最佳时间。②Cherry trees begin to blossom from early April in Zhongshan Park. 中山公园的樱花树从四月初开始开花。

【用法】in (full) bloom 正在开花

blouse /blaʊs/ *n.* 宽松的上衣；女衬衫；工装；*vt.* 使……宽松下垂

【例句】But they were displeased by her presence in a torn blouse. 穿了件破烂的衬衫，她的出现让他们不太高兴。

boast /boust/ *vt*. 自夸，自吹自擂；自负；*n*. 夸口，自负；自负的事物

【例句】①It is almost needless to say that these three films boast the most wonderfully intoxicating music. 无须多说，这三个电影都有最令人陶醉的音乐。② I feel disgusted when he boasts about his achievement in university. 当他自吹读大学时的成就时，我感到很厌烦。

【用法】boast about（of）夸耀，吹嘘

【近义词】brag

boost /buːst/ *vt*. 促进，提高；*n*. 提高，增加帮助

【例句】Here are tutorials to boost your computer skills. 这些教程可以提高你的计算机使用能力。

【近义词】elevate; enhance

bold /bould/ *adj*. 明显的，醒目的；勇敢的，无畏的；*n*. 粗体字；黑体字

【例句】①The left parenthesis at the beginning of the word is not in bold. 单词开头左边的括号没有黑体。②This is a bold move. 这是大胆的举动。

【近义词】brave

bolt /boult/ *n*. 螺栓，螺钉；闪电，雷电；*vt*.（把门、窗等）闩上

【例句】They bolted the door, and put the furniture against it. 他们插上门，并用家具抵住。

【用法】bolt out of the blue 晴天霹雳

【例句】His father fainted suddenly and had been kept in ICU, which for her was like a bolt out of the blue. 他的父亲突然晕倒后一直待在特护病房，这对她来说简直是晴天霹雳。

bomb /bɑːm/ *n*. 炸弹；彻底的失败；高压贮罐；*v*. 轰炸，投弹于

【例句】①They just want to make Wall Street's life really miserable, hit like a bomb. 他们只是想让华尔街的日子不好过，就像是一枚炸弹重重一击。②An hour later they would bomb the other side without looking out for civilians. 一小时之后他们将会轰炸另一边，也不管那里是否有平民。

bond /bɑːnd/ *n.* 纽带，联系；债券；*v.* 使结合；建立互信关系；与……紧密联系

【例句】①The bond crash has been an accident waiting to happen for months. 几个月来一直都有可能发生债券崩盘。②Bosnia and Croatia endeavors to play the role of a mediator to bond the two countries together. 波斯尼亚和克罗地亚致力于做一个调停者，在两个国家间建立紧密联系。

boom /buːm/ *n.* 隆隆声；繁荣；激增；*v.* 发出隆隆声；使繁荣；使迅速发展

【例句】①Despite prospects of an economic boom in the next few years, the Northern industrial states face a creeping erosion. 尽管未来几年有希望出现经济腾飞，北部的工业州正面临发展缓慢问题。②Downstairs, the machine boomed and kept us awake the whole night. 楼下机器一直轰鸣，吵得我们整晚没睡。

boot /buːt/ *vt.* 穿（靴）；踢；启动；*n.* 长靴，皮靴

【例句】The first time you boot the system, it checks your disk and asks if you want to create a system backup. 当你第一次启动系统时，它会先检查你的硬盘，并问你是否需要建造一个系统备份。

【拓展】bootless *adj.*

border /ˈbɔːrdər/ *vt.* 沿……的边，环绕……，给……镶边；*n.* 边，镶边；包边；边界

【例句】①Australian shrubs and two large willows will also border the new lake. 新建的湖边也会种上澳大利亚灌木丛和两棵大柳树。②It is difficult to imagine how American soldiers defend this border. 很难想象美国大兵们如何守卫这条边境。

【近义词】boundary；frontier

bore /bɔːr/ *vt.* 令人厌烦；钻孔；*n.* 使人讨厌的人；膛径，口径；钻子

【例句】Don't bore me with ancient ghost stories. 不要用那些老掉牙的鬼故事烦我。

【近义词】dull

【拓展】boring *adj.*

bounce /baʊns/ *v*. 跳，反弹；急促地动；拒付；*n*. 弹跳；弹性；活力

【例句】①It does not take as much of a jolt to bounce the heads. 不需要使劲就可以晃动头。②He does not rule out a trading bounce. 他没有排除贸易反弹这个可能性。

bound /baʊnd/*adj*. 有义务的；必定的；被束缚的；*vi*. 跳，弹跳；限制；*vt*. 给……划界，限制；使弹回；*n*. 界限，限制；跃起

【例句】①You are bound by the contract to submit design proposals before May. 根据合约要求，你必须在五月份前提交设计方案。②The test is bound to be a failure with so many uncertainties. 有那么多的不确定性，这次实验注定会失败。

【用法】be bound to 注定，一定

【近义词】boundary；limit

【拓展】boundless *adj*.

boundary /ˈbaʊndri/*n*. 分界线；范围；（球场）边线

【例句】There is no certain boundaries between different oceans. 大洋之间没有明确的边界。

bow /baʊ；boʊ/*vi*. 弯腰，鞠躬；*vt*. 低头；俯首；*n*. 弓；鞠躬；船头

【例句】The Japanese obsession with exchanging business cards is part of a subtle effort to determine who ranks higher and who should bow the lowest. 日本人热衷于见面的时候相互交换商业名片，这是一种比较微妙的确定谁的地位更高，谁应该更深鞠躬的方式。

【近义词】bend

brake /breɪk/*v*. 刹车；*n*. 制动器，闸；刹车

【例句】To brake the dollar's recent rise, the United States has to lower its interest rates. 要抑制最近的美元升值，美国需要降低利率。

brand /brænd/*vt*. 铭刻于；加商标于；打烙印于；*n*. 牌子；烙印

【例句】①Refusing to pay would brand the United States as an international deadbeat. 不交钱的话就会给美国冠上国际赖账者的名号。②Del Monte was adopted as the premier brand. 德尔蒙特被一致认为是一流品牌。

brass /bræs/ *n*. 黄铜；铜管乐器；钱；黄铜饰品

【例句】Russians' special strengths in the strings with the Americans' virtuosity in winds and brass is part of the message. 俄国在管弦乐方面的独特优势和美国在风管乐和铜管乐方面的精湛技艺是想要传递的信息。

【拓展】brassy *adj*.

breadth /bredθ/ *n*. 宽度；宽容；(知识、兴趣等的) 广泛

【例句】It is easy to calculate the area with a certain length and breadth. 有了一定的长度和宽度，就很容易计算出面积。

breast /brest/ *n*. 乳房，乳腺；胸脯，胸部；*vt*. 与……搏斗；挺胸迎……而上

【例句】Breast cancer is the second most common cancer in women after skin cancer. 对女性来说最常见的癌症除了皮肤癌，就是乳腺癌。

【近义词】bosom；chest

breed /briːd/ *vt*. 产，生；养育，训练；*vi*. 产仔；繁殖；*n*. 属；种类；类型

【例句】Malaysia is sharing its prawn-spawning prowess so other nations can learn how to breed the big shrimp. 马来西亚正在分享对虾大量产卵的优良技术，因此其他国家就可以学习如何养殖对虾。

【近义词】reproduce

breeze /briːz/ *n*. 微风；轻而易举的事；*vi*. 吹微风

【例句】Examples might be a battery that was mostly discharged, or a solar panel with low insolation, or a wind generator with a gentle breeze. 比如说，一块几乎没充电的电池，没有足够日晒的太阳电池板，或是风力微弱的风力发电机。

【近义词】blast；wind

brick /brɪk/ *n*. 砖，砖块；砖块状物体；一块砖的厚度；*vt*. 用砖建造、砌或铺；*adj*. 用砖做的；似砖的

【例句】They dismantled the house board by board and brick by brick. 他们一砖一瓦地把房子拆了。

【用法】make bricks without straw 做无米之炊

bride /braɪd/ *n*. 新娘，即将（或刚刚）结婚的女子；姑娘

【例句】The bride and the bridegroom are grinning like mad in every photo. 新娘和新郎在每一张照片里都笑得很灿烂。

【拓展】bridegroom *n*.

brief /briːf/ *adj*. 短暂的；简洁的；简明的；*vt*. 向……介绍基本情况；简要指明；*n*. 概要；简短声明；要点摘录

【例句】We would then frankly brief the people on all details. 之后我们会简要地向人们介绍所有细节。

【用法】in brief/to be brief 简而言之

【例句】In brief, no tests or exams should be ignored. 简而言之，不应忽视任何测验或考试。

【近义词】concise

【拓展】brevity *n*. 短暂；简明；简洁，简短

brilliant /ˈbrɪliənt/ *adj*. 明亮的；美好的；才华横溢的

【例句】Everybody who becomes a member of that undergraduate club, remains for ever beautiful and brilliant. 任何能成为那所本科生俱乐部成员的人，都会永远保持他们的美丽和优秀。

【拓展】brilliantly *adv*. 辉煌地，灿烂地；brilliancy *n*. 光辉；耀度；brilliance *n*. 光辉；才华

brow /braʊ/ *n*. 眉，眉毛；前额；山脊

【例句】Montana raised a brow and now didn't seemed like a good time for an argument. 蒙大拿挑了一下眉毛，现在似乎不是争吵的时候。

browse /braʊz/ *vt.&vi*. 浏览；吃草；随意翻阅；*n*. 浏览；吃草；放牧

【例句】You can browse the internet for the relevant information instead of asking around. 你可以浏览网页查询相关信息，不用四处打听。

brutal /ˈbruːtl/ *adj*. 野蛮的；残忍的；不讲理的；无情的

【例句】①Her name and history will consistently serve as a brutal reminder of Japan's past. 她的名字和生平会一直残忍地让人们想到日本的过去。

【近义词】inhuman; savage; barbarous; ruthless

【拓展】brute *n*. →brutality *n*.

bubble /ˈbʌbl/ *vi*. 使冒泡，发出冒泡的声音；*n*. 泡，水泡；泡影，妄想

【例句】It was also necessary to dispose of issues left as a result of the bursting bubble. 解决泡沫破灭遗留下的问题也是非常有必要的。

【用法】the bubble bursts 成为泡影

bucket /ˈbʌkɪt/ *n*. 水桶；一桶；*v*. 用桶装，用桶运；倾盆而下

【例句】After a couple of years, the income from purchasing business is a drop in the bucket to them. 几年后，代购收入对他们来说只是杯水车薪。

budget /ˈbʌdʒɪt/ *vt*. 在预算中拨款给；按预算拨（款）；规划；*n*. 预算；预算拨款

【例句】We travelled in summer holiday on a tight budget. 暑假里我们很节俭地出门游玩了一次。

bulb /bʌlb/ *n*. 球茎，块茎植物；电灯泡

【例句】Be sure you know how deep and how far apart to plant each kind of bulb. 种这些块茎植物，一定要清楚每种要种多深、隔多远。

bulk /bʌlk/ *v*. 形成大块；堆积起来；*adj*. 大批的，大量的；*n*. 大量；主体

【例句】Wheat germ and bean curd are sold in bulk. 麦芽与豆腐都是批量售卖的。

【用法】in bulk 整批，不加包装

bullet /ˈbʊlɪt/ *n*. 子弹，弹药；弹丸

【例句】After the war, a small fragment of the bullet still remained in his head. 战后他的头部依然留有一小块子弹碎片。

bump /bʌmp/ *vi*. 颠簸着前进；*n*. 碰撞，撞击；肿块；*adv*. 突然地，猛烈地

【例句】①You do not need to bump into new words and look them up in a dictionary at once. 你不必碰到生词就马上查字典。②He came down with a forcible bump on a huge rock. 他落下的时候猛地撞到了一块巨石上。

【用法】bump into 偶然碰见

【拓展】bumpy *adj.*

bunch /bʌntʃ/ *n.* 束，捆；一帮，一伙；*vt.* 聚成一串，聚成一组；*vi.* 形成一串，形成一组

【例句】①Yesterday he presented his teacher with a bunch of flowers. 昨天他送给了老师一束花。②Don't bunch the flowers up so tightly. 不要把花绑得那么紧。

bundle /ˈbʌndl/ *n.* 一捆；一批；一大笔钱；*vi.* 匆匆送走；赶

【例句】His wife came into the room with a bundle of clothes. 他妻子拿着一包衣服走进屋内。

【近义词】bunch；pack；packet

burden /ˈbɜːrdn/ *n.* 负担，包袱，责任，义务

【例句】Dismayed by her financial burden and the bleak job prospects, Susan decided to move into translational medicine. 经济负担重，找工作无望，苏珊灰心丧气，决定转而研究转化医学。

【拓展】burdensome *adj.*

【近义词】load

bureau /ˈbjʊroʊ/ *n.* 局；（提供某方面信息的）办事处；（美国政府部门）局

【例句】Wells is a staff reporter in *The Wall Street Journal's* San Francisco bureau. 威尔斯是《华尔街日报》旧金山分局的记者。

【拓展】bureaucratic *adj.* →bureaucracy *n.*

butterfly /ˈbʌtərflaɪ/ *n.* 蝴蝶；蝶泳；举止轻浮的人

【例句】I sometimes find it hard to tell butterflies and moths apart. 有时候我觉得很难区分蝴蝶和蛾子。

2 C，D

2.1 C

conceal /kənˈsiːl/ *vt.* 隐藏，隐蔽，隐瞒

【例句】①The listening device was concealed in a pen. 窃听器藏在笔里。②I tried to conceal my surprise when she told me her age. 当她告诉我她的年龄时，我尽力掩饰自己的惊讶。

【用法】conceal sth from sb 对某人隐瞒某事

【辨析】conceal、hide 均有"隐藏"的意思。conceal 常与 hide 通用，但比 hide 正式些，多指有意将某事物隐藏起来或不予以泄露，只做及物动词；hide 指有意或无意地将某物（或人）藏在人们不易看到或发现的地方。可作及物动词和不及物动词。

concede /kənˈsiːd/ *vt.* 承认（为真或正确），让；让与，容许

【例句】①The government has conceded that the new tax policy has been a disaster. 政府承认新的税收政策是彻底失败的。②He kept on arguing and wouldn't concede defeat. 他不停地争论，不肯认输。

【用法】concede to sb 对某人让步

【拓展】concession *n.* 让步，（退一步）承认；特许，特许权

concentrate /ˈkɑːnsntreɪt/ *v.* 专注，专心，全神贯注，集中（注意力）；集中，聚集，会集，集结；*n.* 浓缩物，浓缩液

【例句】①Most of the country's population is concentrated in the North. 该国大部分人口集中在北部。②Come on, concentrate! We don't have all day to do this. 来吧，集中精神！我们没有一整天的时间来做这件事。③The company is concentrating on developing new products. 公司正集中精力开发新产品。

【用法】concentrate on/upon 集中，全神贯注

【辨析】concentrate、focus 均有"集中（精力，注意力等）"之意；focus 一般不以具体事物做宾语，而 concentrate 既可以具体事物做宾语，又可以抽象事物做宾语。

concern /kən'sɜːrn/ ***vt.*** 使担忧，使挂念，使焦虑；对……很重要，与……相关，关于，影响；（故事、电影或文章）涉及，是关于……的；***n.*** 担心，忧虑，挂念，忧虑的事情；重要的事，关心的事，关切的事

【例句】①The state of my father's health concerns us greatly. 我父亲的健康状况让我们非常担心。②It concerns me that he hasn't been in contact. 还没有联系到他，我很担心。

【用法】concern yourself 关心，关注，担心；to whom it may concern（用于正式信函开头处）敬启者；be of concern 很重要，有重大影响

【拓展】concerned ***adj.*** 有关的；关切的；担心的

confess /kən'fes/ ***v.*** 承认（错误、罪行等），供认，坦白；（不情愿地）承认

【例句】①She confessed to her husband that she had sold her wedding ring. 她向丈夫承认她把结婚戒指卖了。②I have to confess that when I first met Reece I didn't think he was very bright. 我得承认，当我第一次见到瑞斯时，我觉得他不是很聪明。

【拓展】confession ***n.*** 招供，认错

confidence /'kɑːnfɪdəns/ ***n.*** 信任，信赖；自信，相信，信心；秘密，私事，私房话

【用法】in confidence 私下地，秘密地；take sb into your confidence 向……透露自己的心事，将秘密告诉……

【例句】①She had complete confidence in the doctors. 她对医生完全有信

心。②She's completely lacking in confidence. 她完全缺乏信心。③They talked endlessly, exchanging confidences. 他们聊个不停，互诉心事。

【拓展】confident *adj*. 自信的；有信心的；确信的；有把握的；信任的；confidential *adj*. 机密的，秘密的

confine /kənˈfaɪn/ *vt*. 限制；禁闭；*n*. （常用 pl.）范围；界限

【用法】confine...to...把……限制在……

【例句】①Let's confine our discussion to the matter in question, please! 请把讨论集中在正题上！②The hostages had been confined for so long that they couldn't cope with the outside world. 人质被囚禁了这么久，以致他们无法应付外面的世界。

【拓展】confined *adj*. 有限的，受限的，幽禁的；confinement *n*. 监禁，禁闭；分娩，生育

confirm /kənˈfɜːrm/ *vt*. 确认，确定；证实，肯定

【例句】①Six people have confirmed that they will be attending and ten haven't replied yet. 六个人已经确认他们将出席，还有十个人还没有答复。②The smell of cigarette smoke confirmed what he had suspected: there had been a party in his absence. 烟味证实了他的猜疑：他不在时有一个聚会。

【拓展】confirmation *n*. 证实，确认；confirmed *adj*. 证实了的

conflict /ˈkɑːnflɪkt; kənˈflɪkt/ *n*. 冲突，分歧，争论；战斗，斗争；*vi*. 不一致；发生抵触；相矛盾；冲突

【用法】conflict with sb (sth) 与……冲突；in conflict with 与……冲突

【例句】①There was a lot of conflict between him and his father. 他和他父亲之间有很多冲突。②We wish to avoid conflict between our countries if at all possible. 我们希望尽可能避免两国间的战争。

conform /kənˈfɔːrm/ *v*. （与 to, with 连用）符合，顺应，相配

【例句】①At our school, you were required to conform, and there was no place for originality. 我们学校要求每个人循规蹈矩，容不得创新求变。②Students can be expelled for refusing to conform to school rules. 学生拒绝遵守校规可被开除。

confront /kənˈfɔːrm/ *vt*. 面对，面临；遭遇；直面，正视

【例句】①We try to help people confront their problems. 我们试图帮助人们面对他们的问题。②It's an issue we'll have to confront at some point, no matter how unpleasant it is. 不管它有多讨厌，我们终究要面对这个问题。③I thought I would stay calm, but when I was confronted with the TV camera, I got very nervous. 我以为我会保持冷静，但当我面对电视镜头时，我变得非常紧张。

【拓展】confrontation *n*.（尤指敌对国家的）对抗；面对；对峙

confuse /kənˈfjuːz/ *vt*. 使混乱，使迷惑；混淆，混同

【用法】confuse A with B 把 A 误当作 B

【例句】①Stop confusing the issue! 别再把事情越搞越乱！②It's easy to confuse his films, because he tends to use the same actors. 很容易混淆他的电影，因为他倾向于使用相同的演员。

【拓展】confusion *n*. 混乱，混淆，困惑；confused *adj*. 混乱的，糊涂的；confusing *adj*. 令人困惑的，混乱的，混淆的

conscience /ˈkɑːnʃəns/ *n*. 良心

【例句】You didn't do anything wrong and you should have a clear conscience. 你没有做错任何事，你应该问心无愧。

【用法】be on one's conscience 因为某事而内疚；in all conscience 当然，一定；凭良心说，公开地说

【例句】①Yesterday I ignored an old woman who asked me for money in the street, and it's been on my conscience ever since. 昨天我没理会在街上向我讨钱的那个老妇人，但随后一直觉得良心不安。②You couldn't, in all conscience, ask her to pay the whole bill! 凭良心说，你不能叫她一个人付所有的账！

【拓展】conscientious *adj*. 认真的，凭良心做的

conscious /ˈkɑːnʃəs/ *adj*. 意识到，察觉到，感觉到；有意识的，神志清醒的，有知觉的；故意的，存心的，刻意的

【例句】①He's still conscious but he's very badly injured. 他仍然清醒，但伤得很重。②I think she's very conscious of being the only person in the office who didn't have a university education. 我想她很清楚自己是办公室里唯一没有受过

大学教育的人。③It wasn't a conscious decision to lose weight. It just happened. 我没有刻意减肥，就瘦下来了。

【拓展】subconscious *adj*. 下意识的，潜意识的；unconscious *adj*. 失去知觉的，无意识的，无意的；consciousness *n*. 意识，觉悟

consent /kənˈsent/ *vi*. 同意，答应，允许；*n*. 同意，允许

【用法】consent to do sth 同意做某事；by common consent 大多数人同意，普遍认可；informed consent 知情同意；by mutual consent 经双方同意

【例句】①They can't publish your name without your consent. 没有你的同意他们不能公布你的名字。②Her latest novel, by common consent, is her best yet. 她最新一本小说被普遍认为是她迄今最好的作品。

【拓展】consensual *adj*. 经双方同意的，一致同意的

considerable /kənˈsɪdərəbl/ *adj*. 相当大的，相当多的

【例句】①Michael has already spent considerable time in Barcelona. 迈克尔已经在巴塞罗纳待了相当长的时间。②The fire caused considerable damage to the church. 大火对教堂造成了相当大的破坏。

【拓展】consideration *n*. 考虑，照顾；inconsiderable *adj*. 不值得考虑的，小的，无足轻重的；considerate *adj*. 体贴的，体谅的；深思熟虑的

consideration /kənˌsɪdəˈreɪʃn/ *n*. 深思，考虑；考虑的事；设想周到，体谅

【用法】under consideration 在考虑中；give something careful/full etc. consideration 仔细考虑某事；deserve/merit consideration 值得考虑；take something into consideration 把……考虑进去

【例句】①After some consideration, we've decided to sell the house. 经过考虑，我们决定把房子卖掉。②We would have to give serious consideration to banning it altogether. 我们必须认真考虑全面禁止它。③You have no consideration for others! 你不考虑别人！

conspicuous /kənˈspɪkjuəs/ *adj*. 显眼的，显著的，显而易见的

【例句】①In China, her blonde hair was conspicuous. 在中国，她的金发很显眼。②The temple's grand white arches rose conspicuously over the dirty decaying city. 这座寺庙的白色大拱门十分显眼地耸立在这座肮脏腐朽的城市上空。

constitute /ˈkɑːnstɪtuːt/ *vt*. 组成，构成；被视为；设立

【用法】constitute a threat to sb 形成对某人的威胁

【例句】①This latest defeat constitutes a major setback for the Democrats. 最近的失败对民主党来说是一个重大的挫折。②We must redefine what constitutes a family. 我们必须重新定义家庭的构成。③Nitrogen constitutes 78% of the earth's atmosphere. 氮占地球大气的78%。

consult /kənˈsʌlt/ *vt*. 参考，查阅，咨询；*vi*.（常与 with 连用）商量，请教

【例句】①If the symptoms get worse, consult your doctor. 如果症状恶化，请咨询医生。②Why didn't you consult me about this? 你怎么没跟我商量这件事？

【拓展】consultation *n*. 咨询，商量；consultant *n*. 顾问，咨询者；consulting *adj*. 咨询的，商议的，顾问的

consume /kənˈsuːm/ *v*. 吃，喝；消耗，消费，花费；毁灭，烧毁；充满，使着迷

【例句】①He consumes huge amounts of bread with every meal. 他每顿饭都要吃大量的面包。②Our high living standards cause our current population to consume 25 percent of the world's oil. 我们的高生活水平导致我们现在的人口消耗世界25%的石油。③He was consumed with jealousy. 他充满了嫉妒。

【拓展】consumption *n*. 消费，消耗；consumer *n*. 消费者，顾客，用户

contemporary /kənˈtempəreri/ *adj*. 当代的，现代的；同时期的，同时代的；*n*. 同时代的人；同年龄的人，同辈

【例句】①Although the play was written hundreds of years ago, it still has a contemporary feel to it. 虽然这出戏是几百年前写的，但它仍然具有当代的感觉。②Almost all of the contemporary accounts of the event have been lost. 几乎所有关于这一事件的同时期的报道都已遗失。

contend /kənˈtend/ *vi*. 争夺，竞争；*vt*. 声称，断言，主张

【例句】①He's contending against someone with twice his experience. 他在和一个有他两倍经验的人竞争。②The lawyer contended (that) her client had never

67

been near the scene of the crime. 律师辩称她的当事人从未靠近过犯罪现场。

content /ˈkɒntent; kənˈtent/ *adj.* 满足的，满意的，甘愿的；*vt.* 满足，满意；*n.* 目录；内容；所容纳之物；容量，含量

【用法】be content with 满足于；be content to do 愿意做；content oneself with...满足于……

【例句】①He seems fairly content with his life. 他似乎对自己的生活相当满意。②It's a very stylish and beautiful film, but it lacks content. 这是一部非常时尚漂亮的电影，但缺少内容。③He didn't need to open the letter because he already knew the contents. 他不需要打开信，因为他已经知道信的内容了。④My explanation seemed to content him. 我的解释似乎使他满意。

context /ˈkɒntekst/ *n.* 背景，环境；上下文，前后关系

【用法】place/put/see etc. something in context 把某事放在特定背景下看待；in the context of something 在……情况下，在……的背景下

【例句】①This small battle is very important in the context of Scottish history. 在苏格兰历史的背景下，这场小战斗是非常重要的。②In this exercise, a word is blanked out and you have to guess what it is by looking at the context. 在这个练习中，一个词被删去了，你必须通过观察上下文来猜测它是什么。③The reporter took my remarks completely out of context. 记者引用我的话完全是断章取义。

contract /ˈkɒntrækt; kənˈtrækt/ *n.* 合同，契约；*v.* 签订（合同）；缩小，收缩；患上，感染（疾病）

【用法】be under contract 签订合同（为某公司或某人工作）；有合同约束；contract with/between 与……签订合同

【例句】①They could take legal action against you if you break the contract. 如果你违反合同，他们可以对你采取法律行动。②As it cooled, the metal contracted. 金属冷却后收缩了。③He contracted malaria while he was travelling. 他旅行时感染了疟疾。④Our company was contracted to build shelters for the homeless. 我们公司签约为无家可归者建造庇护所。

contrary /ˈkɒntreri/ *adj.* 相反的，对立的，完全不同的；乖戾的，故意作

对的；*n*. 相反，对立面

【用法】quite the contrary 恰恰相反；on the contrary 正相反；to the contrary 正相反的，恰恰相反的

【例句】①Contrary to all our expectations, he found a well-paid job and a nice girlfriend. 出乎我们的意料，他找到了一份报酬不菲的工作和一个不错的女友。②He doesn't really mean it—he's just being contrary. 他不是真的这么想的——他只是在故意作对。

contrast /kən'træst; 'kɑːntræst/*v*. 对照，对比；*n*. 对照，对比，对立

【例句】①I like the contrast of the white trousers with the black jacket. 我喜欢白色裤子和黑色夹克的对比。②If you contrast some of her early writing with her later work, you can see just how much she improved. 如果你把她早期的一些作品与后来的作品进行对比，你就能看出她进步了多少。③The styles of the two film makers contrast quite dramatically. 两位电影制片人的风格形成了鲜明的对比。

contribute /kən'trɪbjuːt/*v*. 捐献，贡献；投稿，撰稿

【例句】①Her family has contributed ＄50,000 to the fund. 她的家人向基金捐款5万美元。②She contributes to several magazines. 她为几本杂志撰稿。

【拓展】contribution *n*. 贡献；contributor *n*. 贡献者，投稿者；contributory *adj*. 捐助的，贡献的

convert /kən'vɜːrt/*v*. （常与 into 连用）转变，变换，改变信仰；兑换；*n*. 改变信仰（或习惯、生活方式）的人

【例句】①I used to hate exercise, but my sister has converted me to it. 我以前讨厌运动，但我姐姐改变了我。②The stocks can be easily converted to cash. 股票很容易兑换成现金。

【拓展】convertion *n*. 变换，转化

convey /kən'veɪ/*vt*. 表达，传达；运送，运输

【例句】①His poetry conveys a great sense of religious devotion. 他的诗表达了强烈的宗教信仰。②The goods are usually conveyed by rail. 货物通常由铁路运输。

【拓展】conveyance *n*. 运输，搬运；conveyor *n*. 搬运者

convince /kənˈvɪns/ *vt*. 使相信，信服，说服

【用法】convince sb of sth 使某人相信……；convince sb that… 使某人相信……

【例句】①The defence lawyer managed to convince the jury of his innocence. 辩护律师设法使陪审团相信他是无辜的。②I hope this will convince you to change your mind. 我希望这能说服你改变主意。

【拓展】convinced *adj*. 被说服的；convincing *adj*. 令人信服的

coordinate /koʊˈɔːrdɪneɪt/ *vt*. 使相配合，协调；相配，相称；*adj*. 同等的，并列的；*n*. 坐标

【例句】①We need someone to coordinate the whole campaign. 我们需要有人来协调整个竞选活动。②The bed linen coordinates with the bedroom curtains. 床单和卧室的窗帘很相配。

【拓展】coordination *n*. 同等，配合；coordinator *n*. 协调人；coordinated *adj*. 协调的

correspond /ˌkɔːrəˈspɑːnd/ *vi*. 相似，相等；符合；通信

【用法】correspond to 相当于……，符合于……；correspond with 符合，与……通信

【例句】①The money I've saved corresponds roughly to the amount I need for my plane ticket. 我省下的钱大致相当于我买机票所需的钱。②I've been corresponding with several experts in the field. 我一直在与该领域的几位专家保持通信往来。

correspondence /ˌkɔːrəˈspɑːndəns/ *n*. 关联；通信联系；信件，信函

【用法】（be in）correspondence with sb 与……有通信联系；correspondence between… ……之间的对应关系

【例句】①Any further correspondence should be sent to my new address. 以后来信请寄到我的新地址。②Her correspondence with Jim lasted many years. 她与吉姆的通信持续了许多年。③The survey found no correspondence between crime and unemployment rates. 调查发现犯罪率和失业率之间没有对应关系。

corruption /kəˈrʌpʃn/ *n*. 贪污，腐败，堕落；（语言）变体

【例句】①It is reported that he has been put in prison because of his economic corruption. 据报道，他因经济腐败而入狱。②The word 'Thursday' is a corruption of 'Thor's Day'. "星期四"这个词是"雷神节"的变体。

courage /ˈkɜːrɪdʒ/ *n*. 勇气，胆量

【用法】lose courage 失去勇气；take up courage 鼓起勇气，奋勇

【例句】①People should have the courage to stand up for their beliefs. 人们应该有勇气捍卫自己的信仰。②Gradually I lost the courage to speak out about anything. 渐渐地，我失去了说出任何事情的勇气。

【拓展】courageous *adj*. 勇敢的，有胆量的

cover /ˈkʌvər/ *vt*. 盖，覆盖；包含，包括；走完；涉及，处理；考虑；报道；支付，付费；保险，承保；*n*. 覆盖物，遮盖物；封面，封底

【用法】from cover to cover 从头到尾；be covered with…覆盖着……

【例句】①Snow covered the hillsides. 山坡上覆盖着雪。②This leaflet covers what we've just discussed in more detail. 这本小册子详细介绍了我们刚才讨论的内容。③She's covering the American Election for BBC Television. 她正在为英国广播公司电视台报道美国大选。④We covered 400 km in three hours. 我们在三小时内赶了400千米。⑤Who should we put on the cover of the magazine this month? 这个月我们该把谁登上杂志的封面？

【拓展】coverage *n*. 所包括的范围，新闻报道；covered *adj*. 有盖的，隐蔽着的；covering *n*. 掩蔽物，遮盖物

create /kriˈeɪt/ *vt*. 创造，创作，创建；产生，引起

【例句】①He created a wonderful meal from very few ingredients. 他用很少的原料做了一顿美餐。②Her behaviour is creating a lot of problems. 她的行为造成了许多问题。

【拓展】creation *n*. 创造，创作；creative *adj*. 有创造力的；creativity *n*. 创造力；creator *n*. 创造者

【辨析】create、invent、discover 均有"创造"的意思。creat 意为"创造、创作"，指产生出新的东西，其对象往往是精神上的，如艺术、文学作品

中的人物及新的科学领域等。也可指创造出新的具体事物；invent 指通过研究和实验发明前所未有的新产品；discover 指"发现或找到"某种自然界本来已存在，但以前未被人类发现或认识的事物。

credit /ˈkredɪt/ ***n***. 赞扬，赞许，荣誉；赊购，赊账，贷款；学分；***vt***. 相信，信任；给银行账户上存钱

【用法】be a credit to sb/sth 是……的骄傲，是……的光荣；do your family, parents, teacher, etc. credit 为家庭（父母、老师等）增光；all credit to sb 值得大加称赞

【例句】①She got no credit for solving the problem. 她解决了这个问题，没有得到任何表扬。②They decided to buy the car on credit. 他们决定赊购这辆车。③Each of these classes is worth three credits. 每门课都有三个学分。

【拓展】creditable ***adj***. 可信的；creditor ***n***. 债权人

criticize /ˈkrɪtɪsaɪz/ ***v***. 批评，批判；指责；评论

【例句】We'll get nowhere if all you can do is criticize. 如果你所能做的就是批评，我们就什么也做不了。

cultivate /ˈkʌltɪveɪt/ ***vt***. 准备（土地）耕种，种植，栽培；培养；修习，培育

【例句】①Most of the land there is too poor to cultivate. 那里的大部分土地太贫瘠，无法耕种。②She has cultivated an image as a tough negotiator. 她树立了一个强硬谈判者的形象。③The new prime minister is cultivating relationships with East Asian countries. 新总理正在与东亚国家建立关系。

【拓展】cultivated ***adj***. 栽培的；有修养的，文雅的；cultivation ***n***. 培养，耕作

current /ˈkɜːrənt/ ***adj***. 当前的，现时的；通用的，流通的，广泛流传的；***n***. （水、空气等的）流动；水流，气流，电流；趋势，潮流

【用法】current money 通用货币；the current of public opinion 舆论的动向；the warm/cold current in the sea 海洋中的暖（寒）流

【例句】①The word is no longer in current use. 这个词现在不再使用了。②He was swept out to sea by the strong current. 他被强流冲到海里去了。③There is a growing current of support for environmental issues among voters. 选民对环境问题的支持日益增多。

【拓展】currently *adv*. 目前，当时，现在

custom /ˈkʌstəm/ *n*. 风俗，习俗；个人习惯，惯例；光顾，惠顾；（pl.）海关，关税

【用法】the Customs 海关

【例句】①In my country, it's the custom for women to get married in white. 在我的国家，妇女结婚时穿白色衣服是一种习俗。②He left the house at nine exactly, as is his custom. 他九点准时离开家，这是他的习惯。③If we don't give good service, people will take their custom elsewhere. 如果我们不能提供良好的服务，人们就会光顾别处。

【拓展】customer *n*. 顾客；customary *adj*. 通常的，习惯的；customize *v*. 定制

2.2 D

detail /ˈdiːteɪl/ *n*. 消息，细节；细微特征；细枝末节，无足轻重的事；*v*. 详述，详记；指派，派遣

【例句】①We don't know the full details of the story yet. 我们还不知道故事的全部细节。②A police officer took down the details of what happened. 一名警官记下了发生的事情的细节。③It's his eye for detail that distinguishes him as a painter. 他细致入微的观察能力使其成为一位与众不同的画家。④We haven't discussed the matter in detail yet. 我们还没有详细讨论这件事。⑤Tony says, he's going to get the car, and finding the money to pay for it is just a minor detail. 托尼说，他要去买车，找到买车的钱只是小事一桩。⑥Can you produce a report detailing what we've spent on the project so far? 你能写一份报告详细说明我们迄今为止在这个项目上花了多少钱吗？⑦Four soldiers were detailed to check the road for troops. 四名士兵被派去为部队检查道路。

【用法】in detail 详细地，详尽

detect /dɪˈtekt/ v. 发现，察觉；探测，检测，测出

【例句】①Some sounds cannot be detected by the human ear. 有些声音不能被人的耳朵察觉。②High levels of lead were detected in the atmosphere. 大气中检测到高含量的铅。

【拓展】detectable *adj*. 可发觉的，可看穿的；detection *n*. 察觉，发现，侦破（案件）

determine /dɪˈtɜːrmɪn/ v. 确定，决定，影响；下决心；查明

【例句】①Eye color is genetically determined. 眼睛的颜色是由基因决定的。②She determined that one day she would be an actor. 她决心有一天她会成为一名演员。③The police never actually determined the cause of death. 警方从未真正确定死因。

【拓展】determination *n*. 决心；determiner *n*. <语言>限定词；determined *adj*. 坚定的，毅然的，确定的

develop /dɪˈveləp/ v. 发展，发育，成长；制定；发生，出现；患上，患病，逐渐形成；开发，建设；洗印，显影

【例句】①It became clear that he wasn't developing like all the other little boys. 很明显，他并不像其他小男孩那样成长。②We have to develop a new policy to deal with the problem. 我们必须制定一项新政策来解决这个问题。③Large cracks began to develop in the wall. 墙上开始出现大裂缝。④She's developed some very strange habits lately. 她最近养成了一些很奇怪的习惯。⑤They're planning to develop the whole site into a shopping complex. 他们计划把这整块地皮开发建设成购物中心。⑥We developed some old negatives from my parents' wedding day. 我们冲洗了一些父母结婚那天拍的底片。

dictate /ˈdɪkteɪt/ v. 命令，决定，影响，要求；口述，口授；n. 命令，要求

【例句】①The rules dictate that only running shoes must be worn on the track. 规则规定，在跑道上只能穿跑鞋。②The party's change of policy has been dictated by its need to win back younger voters. 该党改变政策的原因是它需要重

新赢得年轻选民的支持。③I dictated my order over the phone. 我在电话里口述了我的命令。④Individual EU countries are free to follow their own dictates on matters concerning the economy. 个别欧盟国家可以在有关经济的问题上自行决定。

differ /ˈdɪfər/ *vi.* 相异，不同；意见分歧

【用法】differ from 不同于；differ between 区别于

【例句】①His views differ considerably from those of his parents. 他的观点与他父母的大不相同。②The twins look alike, but they differ in temperament. 这对双胞胎长得很像，但性格不同。③Economists differ on the cause of inflation. 经济学家们在通货膨胀的原因上意见不同。④I beg to differ with you on that point. 在那一点上，我与你意见不同。

digest /daɪˈdʒest/ *v.* 消化；领会，领悟；整理，做摘要；容忍，甘受（侮辱等）；*n.* 文摘，摘要；文汇，简报

【例句】①I find that I don't digest meat easily. 我发现我不容易消化肉。②This chapter is so difficult to digest, I'll have to read it again later. 这一章太难消化了，我之后还得再看一遍。③The company publishes a monthly digest of its activities. 该公司每月出版一份其活动摘要。

dignity /ˈdɪɡnəti/ *n.* 庄重，端庄，尊严；自尊，自尊心

【例句】①He is a man of dignity and calm determination. 他是个沉稳、冷静而果断的人。②How could you wear something so indecent? Have you no dignity? 你怎么能穿这么不雅观的衣服？你没有自尊心吗？③Patients should be allowed to die with dignity. 病人应该被允许有尊严地死去。

dilemma /dɪˈlemə/ *n.* 左右为难，两难境地

【用法】in a dilemma 进退两难，左右为难；face a dilemma/be faced with a dilemma 面临进退两难的境地

【例句】①The president is clearly in a dilemma about how to tackle the crisis. 总统显然在如何应对危机方面进退两难。②She faces the dilemma of disobeying her father or losing the man she loves. 她面临着不服从父亲或失去所爱之人的两难境地。

diminish /dɪˈmɪnɪʃ/ *v.* （使）减少，（使）缩小，降低；贬低

【例句】①These memories will not be diminished by time. 这些记忆不会随着时间而减少。②Don't let him diminish your achievements. 别让他贬低你的成就。

disagree /ˌdɪsəˈgriː/ *v.* 不同意，持异议，反对；有不同，有差别，不一致

【用法】disagree with sb（食物）使……感到不适；disagree about/on/over 对……有不同意见

【例句】①I profoundly disagree with the decision that has been made. 我对已经做出的决定表示强烈反对。②Spicy food disagrees with me. 辛辣的食物不适合我。③The statements of several witnesses disagree. 几个证人的证词不一致。

【拓展】disagreement *n.* 分歧，意见不合，不一致；disagreeable *adj.* 不合意的，令人不快的

disapprove /ˌdɪsəˈpruːv/ *v.* 反对，不赞成

【例句】①I knew my parents would disapprove, but I went anyway. 我知道我父母会反对，但我还是去了。②I strongly disapprove of underage drinking. 我强烈反对未成年饮酒。

【拓展】disapproval *n.* 不赞成，反对；disapproving *adj.* 不满的，反对的

disaster /dɪˈzæstər/ *n.* 灾难，大祸

【例句】①An inquiry was ordered into the recent rail disaster. 对最近的铁路事故进行了调查。②It would be a disaster for me if I lost my job. 如果我丢了工作，那对我来说将是一场灾难。

【辨析】disaster、misfortune 和 calamity 均含有"灾难"的意思。disaster 普通用词，指大灾难、痛苦或伤亡。misfortune 普通用词，多指较为严重的不幸，强调不幸多由外界因素所致。calamity 语气最强，指可怕的灾难，强调最终的结局。

【例句】①Heavy and prolonged rain can spell disaster for many plants. 大雨和持续的降雨会给许多植物带来灾难。②It will be a calamity for farmers if the crops fail again. 如果农作物再歉收，对农民来说将是一场灾难。

【拓展】disastrous *adj.* 灾难性的，损失惨重的

discard /dɪˈskɑːrd/ *v.* 抛弃，丢弃；出（牌）；*n.* 出掉的牌，被抛弃的人

（物）

【例句】①Discard any old cleaning materials. 丢弃所有旧的清洁材料。②Discarded food containers and bottles littered the streets. 丢弃的食品容器和瓶子散落在街道上。

discover /dɪˈskʌvər/ *v*. 发现；找到；发现并培养（人才）

【例句】①Who discovered America? 谁发现了美洲？②Scientists have discovered how to predict an earthquake. 科学家们已经发现如何预测地震。③Los Angeles is full of young actors working as waiters, hoping to be discovered by a movie agent. 洛杉矶到处都是年轻的演员在做服务员，希望能被电影经纪人发现并提携。

【拓展】discoverer *n*. 发现者；discovery *n*. 发现

discriminate /dɪˈskrɪmɪneɪt/ *v*. 歧视；区别对待；区分，区别，辨别出；*adj*. 能识别的，有分辨能力的

【用法】discriminate against 歧视（某人）；discriminate between 区别，找出（非常相似的两人或物）之间的微小区别；对（两物）进行分辨；discriminate sth from sth 将……与……区别开

【例句】①She felt she had been discriminated against because of her age. 她觉得她因年龄而受到歧视。②Police dogs can discriminate between the different smells. 警犬可以辨别不同的气味。③The parties have become so similar it is difficult to discriminate Republicans from Democrats. 各党派变得如此相似，很难区别共和党和民主党。

【拓展】discrimination *n*. 歧视，区别；discriminatory *adj*. 歧视性的

disgust /dɪsˈɡʌst/ *n*. 厌恶，憎恶，反感；*v*. 令人厌恶，令人反感

【例句】①She walked out in disgust. 她厌恶地走了出去。②Joan looked at him with disgust. 琼厌恶地看着他。③Beresford, much to his disgust, was fined for illegal parking. 令贝雷斯福德十分反感的是，他因违章停车而被罚款。

【拓展】disgusting *adj*. 令人厌恶的，令人作呕的，讨厌的

dismiss /dɪsˈmɪs/ *v*. 对……不予理会，摒弃，去除；将……免职，解雇，开除（学生、工人等）；遣散，解散；驳回，不受理

77

【例句】①Let's not just dismiss the idea before we've even thought about it. 我们还是别不假思索就把这种想法排除在外。②He has been dismissed from his job for incompetence. 他因不称职而被解雇了。③The professor dismissed the class early because she had a meeting. 教授因为开会而提前下课。④The defending lawyer asked that the charge against his client be dismissed. 辩护律师要求撤销对他的当事人的指控。

disrupt /dɪsˈrʌpt/ *v.* 打断，中断，扰乱

【例句】①Heavy snow disrupted travel into the city this morning. 今天早上大雪打乱了进城的交通。②Climate change could disrupt the agricultural economy. 气候变化可能会扰乱农业经济。

distinct /dɪˈstɪŋkt/ *adj.* 显著的，明显的，确定无疑的；明显不同的，差别明显的

【例句】①There's a distinct smell of cigarettes in here. 这里有一股明显的烟味。②The two concepts are quite distinct. 这两个概念截然不同。

【拓展】distinction *n.* 区别；特质；荣誉，勋章

distinguish /dɪˈstɪŋɡwɪʃ/ *v.* 辨别，区分；使有别于，有……特点

【用法】distinguish between 辨别，识别（两者）之间的不同；distinguish sb/sth from 区别某人/某物；distinguish yourself 使自己出类拔萃，表现突出

【例句】①He's color-blind and can't distinguish between red and green easily. 他是色盲，很难区分红色和绿色。②He distinguished himself as a writer at a very early age. 他很小就以作家的身份出名。

【拓展】distinguished *adj.* 卓越的，著名的

distribute /dɪˈstrɪbjuːt/ *v.* 分发，散发，分配

【例句】①The books will be distributed free to local schools. 这些书将免费分发给当地学校。②Make sure the weight of the load is evenly distributed. 确保负载的重量均匀分布。

【拓展】distribution *n.* 分发，分配；distributor *n.* 分销商；配电器；distributive *adj.* 分发的，分配的，分部的

diverse /daɪˈvɜːrs/ *adj.* 多种多样的，形形色色的；不同的，相异的

【例句】①New York is a very culturally diverse city. 纽约是一个文化非常多元的城市。②We hold diverse views on the topic. 我们对这个问题持有不同的看法。

doubt /daʊt/ *n*. 怀疑，疑惑，疑问；*v*. 怀疑，不确定，不肯定

【用法】without doubt 必定，无疑

【例句】①I'm having doubts about his ability to do the job. 我对他的工作能力表示怀疑。②Witnesses have cast doubt on the accused's innocence. 证人对被告的清白表示怀疑。③The future of the stadium is in doubt because of a lack of money. 由于缺乏资金，体育场的未来令人怀疑。④She is without doubt the best student I have ever taught. 她无疑是我教过的最好的学生。⑤They had begun to doubt that it could be done. 他们开始怀疑能否做到。⑥He's never lied to me before, so I have no reason to doubt his word. 他以前从来没有骗过我，所以我没有理由怀疑他的话。

【拓展】doubter *n*. 持怀疑态度的人；doubtful *adj*. 不大可能的，不确定的；doubtless *adv*. 很可能地，无疑地；undoubted *adj*. 不容置疑的

durable /ˈdʊrəbl/ *adj*. 持久的，耐久的

【例句】①The machines have to be made of durable materials. 机器必须由耐用材料制成。②His poetry has proved durable. 他的诗经得起考验。

【拓展】durability *n*. 耐久性，持久性

3 E, F, G, H

3.1 E

encounter /ɪnˈkaʊntər/ *vt.* 遭到，遇到；*n.* 遭遇，冲突

【例句】①As I have learned in my career, there is no correlation between an individual's scientific achievement and his or her ethical behavior. I routinely encounter individuals who are or were great scientists but remain flawed in regard to their thinking about race. 正如我在职业生涯中所学到的，个人的科学成就与他或她的道德行为之间没有相关性。我经常遇到那些曾经或者都是伟大科学家的人，但他们对种族的思考仍然存在缺陷。②I'm thinking that this might be the best chance I ever get to have a casual encounter with someone new and exciting. 我认为这可能是我与一个陌生的且令人兴奋的人偶然相遇的最佳机会。

endure /ɪnˈdʊr/ *vt.* 忍受，容忍；持续，持久

【例句】①You should learn to endure the misery of homesickness when you stay far away from your hometown. 当你远离家乡时，你应该学会忍受乡愁的痛苦。②The political system established in 1400 endured until about 1650. 1400 年建立的政治制度持续到 1650 年左右。

enforce /ɪnˈfɔːrs/ *vt.* 实施，执行；强制，强迫

【例句】①Drug addicts are enforced to get them off the drug through some strict measures. 通过一些严格的措施强制吸毒成瘾者戒毒。②The policy calls for all police to strictly enforce the laws and arrest all drug dealers. 该政策要求所有警察严格执行法律并逮捕所有毒贩。

engage /ɪnˈgeɪdʒ/ *vt.* 使从事于（多用被动语态，搭配介词 in）；聘用

【例句】①However, just because girls, on average, are less likely to want to engage in rough-and-tumble play than boys, it does not mean that any one girl is less likely to want to rough-and-tumble play than her boy peers. 然而，仅仅因为平均而言，与男孩子相比，女孩子不想参加打闹游戏，这并不意味着任何一个女孩子都不太可能和男孩子一样想玩打闹游戏。②Our company is going to engage you as a legal adviser. 我们公司准备聘请你当法律顾问。

enhance /ɪnˈhæns/ *vt.* 提高，增加；增进

【例句】Your chances for promotion in this department will be enhanced if you take more courses in evening school. 如果你在夜校再学一些课程，那你在这个部门获得提升的机会就会增加。

enthusiasm /ɪnˈθuːziæzəm/ *n.* 热情，热心

【例句】Young people showed little interest in past media and much enthusiasm for contemporary media. 年轻人对过去的媒体没什么兴趣，而对当代媒体充满了热情。

【拓展】enthusiastic *adj.* 热情的，热心的；be enthusiastic about 对……热心；热衷于……，对……充满热情

entitle /ɪnˈtaɪtl/ *vt.* 给……权利（资格）；给（书或文章）……题名，给……称号

【例句】①A doctrine of the American way of life is that all persons are entitled to an education. 美国人生活方式的信条是：一切人都有权受教育。②After reading an article entitled "*Cigarette Smoking and Your Health*", I lit a cigar to calm my nerves. 读完一篇题为《吸烟与您的健康》的文章后，我点燃了一支香烟来镇定我的神经。

envy /ˈenvi/ *vt.* 妒忌，羡慕；*n.* 妒忌（的对象），羡慕（的目标）

【例句】①I so envy the people I meet who command a range of skills. 我非常羡慕那些能够掌握一系列技能的人。②I know I should be mature and sensible and rise above any feelings of petty envy. 我知道我应该成熟和理智起来，并且要摆脱任何嫉妒的感觉。

【拓展】feel envy at 对感到妒忌（羡慕）；out of envy 出于妒忌

【例句】He felt envy at my success. 他羡慕我的成功。

envious /ˈenviəs/ *adj.* 羡慕的，嫉妒的

【例句】Mary would always be envious of her sister's beauty. 玛丽总是嫉妒她妹妹的美丽。

equivalent /ɪˈkwɪvələnt/ *adj.* 相等的，相当的；等量的，等值的；*n.* 相等物

【例句】①His behavior is equivalent to treason. 他的行为等于背叛。②An equivalent amount of energy would be necessary to split the atom apart. 将原子分开需要等量的能量。③The difference between the expected value and the certainty equivalent is the risk premium for the gamble. 预期价值与确定性等价物之间的差异是赌博的风险溢价。

essential /ɪˈsenʃl/ *adj.* 必要的，主要的，本质的

【例句】Language is an essential ingredient of abstract thought. 语言是抽象思维的主要构成要素之一。

establish /ɪˈstæblɪʃ/ *vt.* 建立，设立；确立

【例句】He called on non-government organizations to establish contact with the families of the infected children and find a way to help them. 他呼吁非政府组织与受感染儿童的家属建立联系，并找到帮助他们的方法。

estimate /ˈestɪmət；ˈestɪmeɪt/ *vt.* 估计，估价；*n.* 估计，估价

【例句】Some researchers have estimated that obesity causes about 300,000 deaths in the U.S. annually. 一些研究人员估计，每年美国肥胖导致约 30 万人死亡。

【拓展】estimate...at 估计……为，estimate for 为……估价，by estimate 做估计，form an estimate of 对……做估计，at a rough estimate 大略估计，大略说来

evaluate /ɪˈvæljueɪt/ *vt.* 评价，估价

【例句】I have no idea how to evaluate these factors so I'm just going to concentrate on the moral issue. 我不知道如何评价这些因素，所以我只关注道德问题。

eventually /ɪˈventʃuəli/ *adv.* 终于；最后

【例句】She eventually married the most persistent of her admirers. 她终于嫁给了最执着追求她的人。

evident /ˈevɪdənt/ *adj.* 明显的，明白的

【例句】The impact of modern technology on the biosphere is evident worldwide. 现代技术对生物圈的影响在全世界是明显的。

evolve /iˈvɑːlv/ *v.* （使）进化，（使）演化；发展，演变

【例句】①Because one's place and status matter so much in Japan, the Japanese have evolved an elaborate system to attend to these things. 因为在日本一个人的地位和身份如此关系重大，日本人已经发展了一种顾及这些事情的精心筹划的体系。②Models of how volcanoes work and evolve have become important tools in mineral exploration. 关于火山是怎样活动和演化的模型，已成为矿物勘探的一个重要工具。

evolution /ˌiːvəˈluːʃn/ *n.* 进化，演化；发展，演变

【例句】①The 1890s witnessed wholesale acceptance of the theory of evolution by liberal theologians. 十九世纪九十年代，进化论被开明的神学家们全盘接受。②The world monetary climate has been changing in a way parallel to the evolution of national money. 世界货币的趋势同一国货币的演变相类似，一直在变化。

exaggerate /ɪɡˈzædʒəreɪt/ *vt.* 夸大，夸张

【例句】The possibility of making distinct races by crossing has been greatly exaggerated. 对于杂交可能产生特殊品种一说，实在是夸张过甚。

exceed /ɪkˈsiːd/ *vt.* 超过，胜过，越出

【例句】I tried to carry on a conversation in English, but it far exceeded my ability. 我想用英语来谈话，但是力不从心。

【拓展】exceedingly *adv.* 极端地，非常

【例句】Sometimes he instantly approved a proposal whose prospects seemed exceedingly slight. 有时他立刻就批准了一项建议，但这项建议的前景却似乎是非常渺茫的。

exclude /ɪkˈskluːd/ *v*. 把……排除在外，排斥

【例句】①One cannot exclude the possibility of a fall in house prices. 人们不能排除房价下跌的可能性。②This policy excludes people who have a criminal record from entering the country. 该政策不允许有犯罪记录的人进入该国。

【拓展】exclusive *adj*. 排外的；独占的，唯一的

【例句】These three mechanisms, while independent, are not mutually exclusive. 这三种机制虽然是互相独立的，但并不互相排斥。

execute /ˈeksɪkjuːt/ *v*. 处死，处决；实施，执行

【例句】①He is executed for a murder that he committed and yet did not commit. 他还是因为杀人未遂而被处决了。②I do solemnly swear that I will faithfully execute the office of president of the United States. 我郑重宣誓我必忠实地执行美利坚合众国总统的职务。

【拓展】executive *adj*. 执行的，行政的；*n*. 执行者，行政官

【例句】①The president of the united states is the executive head of the government. 美国总统是政府的行政首脑。②In her case, as a professional, her mothering instincts overcame her desire to become a high-flying business executive. 就她而言，虽是一名专业人士，但她的母性本能克服了她想成为一名有雄心壮志的商业主管的愿望。

exert /ɪɡˈzɜːrt/ *v*. 尽（力）；运用，施加

【例句】①The new government should win the public trust by exerting itself to attain tangible results in its efforts to translate the promise into action. 新政府应该通过努力来赢得公众信任，要尽力将承诺变为行动并取得实际成果。②He has been exerting a great influence on me to change my mind. 他一直在施加很大影响要我改变主意。

【拓展】exert…on/upon 对……施加……，使受（影响等）；exert oneself 尽力，努力

expand /ɪkˈspænd/ *vt*. &*vi*. 扩大，膨胀，扩张，张开

【例句】It is through education that we expand the frontiers of knowledge and improve our cognitive ability. 正是通过教育，我们拓展了知识的前沿，提高了我们的认知能力。

【拓展】expansion ***n***. 扩大，扩张，膨胀

exploit /ɪkˈsplɔɪt；ˈeksplɔɪt/***vt***. 剥削；利用；开采，开发，开拓

【例句】①The workers in capitalist countries are cruelly exploited by the capitalists. 资本主义国家的工人受资本家的残酷剥削。②The contemporary unrest is no doubt exploited by some whose purposes are all too clear. 当今世界上的动乱，无疑在被某些人利用，这些人的目的是显而易见的。③We shall try our best to exploit the oil under the sea. 我们要努力开发海底石油。

exterior /ɪkˈstɪrɪər/***adj***. 外部的，外表的；***n***. 外部，外表

【例句】We are painting the exterior wall of the house. 我们正在给房子的外墙涂漆。

external /ɪkˈstɜːrnl/***adj***. 外部的，表面的；***n***. 外部，外表；外观

【例句】①Wireless connectivity and some features may require you to purchase additional software, services or external hardware. 无线连接和某些功能可能需要您购买其他软件、服务或外部硬件。②The external of the book looks very nice. 这本书的外表看起来很漂亮。

extreme /ɪkˈstriːm/***adj***. 极度的，极端的；尽头的，末端的；***n***. 极端

【例句】①He said the world was facing a new threat from 'brutal states' armed with weapons of mass destruction, and from extreme terrorists. 他说，世界正面临着来自装备大规模杀伤性武器的"野蛮国家"和极端恐怖分子的新威胁。②After spending lavishly for years, the company has now gone to the opposite extreme and has cut expenses drastically. 经过多年的奢侈消费，该公司现在已经走向了相反的极端，并大幅削减了开支。

【用法】in the extreme 极端，非常；go to extremes 走极端

3.2　F

flexible /ˈfleksəbl/ *adj*. 易弯曲的，柔韧的；灵活的

【例句】①Those who come to Yoga learn ways to breathe, stretch and become more flexible. 那些来练瑜伽的人学习呼吸和伸展的方法，身体变得更加柔韧。②The best teachers are creative and flexible in their thinking. 最优秀的教师思维上具有创造性和灵活性。

flourish /ˈflɜːrɪʃ/ *vi*. 繁荣，茂盛，兴旺；*n*. 繁荣，兴旺

【例句】①Indigenous people are proud of the fact they survived the colonial era and they are determined to flourish, continue their traditions and assert their rights. 土著人民为自己在殖民时代幸存而自豪，他们决心繁荣、延续自己的传统并维护自己的权利。②The quarterly was in full flourish then. 这份季刊当时盛极一时。

【用法】in full flourish 在全盛时；a flourish of trumpets （重要事情开始前的）大肆宣扬；with a flourish of trumpets 自吹自擂地，耀武扬威地

fluent /ˈfluːənt/ *adj*. 流利的，流畅的

【例句】Living in a foreign land, not being fluent in the language, yet still being able to communicate can be quite an accomplishment. 生活在异国他乡，语言虽不流利，但仍然能够沟通，这可能是一个很大的成就。

forecast /ˈfɔːrkæst/ *n*. 预测，预报；*vt*. 预报，预示

【例句】①Together the two firms can provide financial forecasts for virtually every listed company in the world. 这两家公司可以为世界上几乎所有上市公司提供财务预测。②The national metrological center forecast that heavy snows and rains would continue to hit central and eastern China in the next two days. 国家测量中心预测在未来两天里大雪和大雨将会继续袭击中国的中部和东部地区。

【辨析】forecast、forctell 和 predict 均有"预言"之意。forecast 与 predict 更加相近，通常指对一般或特殊事件的预测，现在主要指预报天气；foretell

较普通，着重指对未来事件的预见，不注重其准确性及根据。predict 较正式，指根据已知事实或自然规律来推断未来的事情，带有科学准确的意味。

former /ˈfɔːrmər/ ***adj***. 从前的，以前的，先前的；前任的，前者的；***n***. [the former] 前者

【例句】①He has taken up his former post again. 他重新担任原职。②Of the two opinions, I prefer the former. 这两种意见中我倾向于前一种。

【辨析】former、preceding、previous 和 prior 均有"以前的""先前的"之意。former 指属于过去某一段时间的，有"从前的""前任的"之意；preceding 指时间、位置或顺序上居先，与定冠词连用，含有"前一个""前几个"之意；previous 指在时间或顺序上"在前的""早先的"的意思；prior 除有 previous 的意义，还有"更重要的""优先的"的意思。

formerly /ˈfɔːrmərli/ ***adv***. 以前

【例句】The girl was formerly a waitress and she is now a manager in a large restaurant. 这个女孩以前是服务员，现在是一家大餐馆的经理。

frequent /ˈfriːkwənt; friˈkwent/ ***adj***. 时常发生的；经常的

【例句】①These recitations must be roughly repeated at frequent intervals if they are not to be lost. 背诵内容要想不被遗忘，就需要时常重复。②He was a frequent visitor to Dawros, where he stayed and enjoyed meeting the neighbours, especially the late Jim Feehily, who practically lived on the same street. 他是道罗斯的常客，他在那里住过，喜欢与邻居见面，特别是已故的 Jim Feehily，他几乎住在同一条街上。

【拓展】frequent *adj*. →frequently *adv*. →frequency *n*.

frown /fraʊn/ ***vi***. 皱眉，蹙额，表示不满

【例句】His wife frowns on/upon his smoking and drinking. 他的妻子对他的吸烟和饮酒表示不满。

fulfill /fʊlˈfɪl/ ***vt***. 履行；满足；完成

【例句】①Some officials were dismissed because they could not fulfill their duties. 一些官员被解雇是因为他们未能履行职责。②He does not feel really fulfilled in his present job. 他对目前的工作没有感觉真正的满足。③I feel quite ashamed that I have not fulfilled the task. 未能完成任务，为此我感到很惭愧。

fundamental /ˌfʌndəˈmentl/ ***adj.*** 基础的，基本的；［pl.］基本原则，基本法则

【例句】①Respect for law and order is fundamental to a peaceful society. 尊重法律和秩序是和平社会的基础。②It is essential to teach small children the fundamentals of road safety. 教小孩子道路安全基本规则是必须的。

【拓展】fundamental ***adj.*** →fundamentally ***adv.***

【例句】The facts show that the Computer Revolution may well change society as fundamentally as did the Industrial Revolution 事实表明，像工业革命一样，计算机革命也会给社会带来根本性的变化。

furnish /ˈfɜːrnɪʃ/ ***vt.*** 供应，提供；装备

【例句】Nine hundred men were furnished with arms and from time to time were drilled in secret. 有900人给配备了武器，他们还常常秘密操练。

furthermore /ˌfɜːrðərˈmɔːr/ ***adv.*** 而且，此外

【例句】①The parents should furthermore be vigilant and cautious in viewing programmes on cable TV. 此外，在观看有线电视节目时，父母应该保持警惕和谨慎。②I said that there are costs to democracy; furthermore, they are quite high. 我说过，民主是有代价的，而且很高。

fuss /fʌs/ ***n.*** 忙乱，大惊小怪；过度体贴；大惊小怪的人；***vt.*** 使烦恼，使烦忧；***vi.***（为小事）烦恼，过于忧虑

【例句】①Do not make so much fuss over the children. 不要对孩子们这么大惊小怪。②Do not fuss me while I am driving. 我开车的时候不要一惊一乍的。③She's always fussing about her food. 她总是在为她的食物烦恼。

3.3 G

glare /gler/ ***n.*** 耀眼的光；怒视，瞪眼；***vi.*** 瞪眼，怒目而视；发出耀眼的光

【例句】①The glare of the sun on the water gives his eyes a feeling of discomfort. 水面上耀眼的阳光使他眼睛感到不舒服。②I can't endure his glare at me in public. 我不能忍受他当众对我怒视。③He glared at everyone in the room as if expecting a challenge. 他怒视着房间里的每个人，好像在期待着挑战。④The sun glared down on us. 刺眼的阳光照在我们身上。

glimpse /glɪmps/ *n*. 一瞥，一看；短暂的感受，短暂的体验；*v*. 瞥见（of/at）

【例句】①They caught a glimpse of a dark green car outside the door. 他们瞥见门外有一辆深绿色的汽车。②The purpose of this activity is a glimpse of what life might be like in the future. 这次活动的目的是对未来生活可能是什么样子的一次短暂体验。③She glimpsed at the children playing in the park, then continuing her housework. 她瞥见孩子们在公园里玩，然后继续做家务。

glitter /ˈglɪtər/ *vi*. 闪光，闪烁；闪现，流露

【例句】①All is not gold that glitters. 闪光的未必都是金子。②His blue eyes glittered with anger. 他的蓝眼睛里流露着愤怒。

gloom /gluːm/ *n*. 阴暗，昏暗，忧郁

【例句】①He peered into the increasing gloom. 他凝视着渐深的夜色。②A gloom fell over her family when her father lost his job. 父亲失业后，她的家里笼罩在一片愁云惨雾之中。

【拓展】gloom *n*. →gloomy *adj*.

glory /ˈglɔri/ *n*. 光荣，荣誉；荣耀的事；壮丽，壮观

【例句】①You must love everything that contributes to the glory of the motherland. 你必须热爱一切为祖国争光的东西。②These churches are the glory of this city. 这些教堂是这座城市的荣耀。③The rose garden is in a glory of color now. 玫瑰园现在一片缤纷的色彩。

【拓展】glory *n*. →glorious *adj*.

glow /gloʊ/ *n*. 光亮，光辉；兴高采烈；*vi*. 发光，发热，脸红；（感情等）洋溢

【例句】①The oil lamp gives a soft glow. 油灯发出柔和的光。②The child

showed the glow of happiness together with his parents. 孩子和父母在一起流露出幸福的光彩。③His face glowed with delight. 他高兴得满脸通红。④He glowed with health. 他容光焕发。

glue /gluː/ *n*. 胶，胶水；*vt*. 胶合，粘贴

【例句】①You can fix the toy plane's tail with this glue. 你可以用这种胶水把玩具飞机的尾部粘好。②We must glue the mat down at the edges to stop it curling. 我们必须用胶水把席子的边缘粘住，以免卷起来。

grace /greɪs/ *n*. 优美，优雅；［常 pl.］风度，魅力；*vt*. 使优美；使增光

【例句】①So far the girls have handled it all with grace and enthusiasm. 到目前为止，女孩们都以优雅和热情来处理这一切。②Hua Chunying, spokeswoman of Chinese foreign ministry, answered all the questions from reporters with social graces. 中国外交部发言人华春莹彬彬有礼地回答了记者的所有提问。③Will you grace the occasion by your presence. 如蒙光临，不胜荣幸。

【用法】with good/bad grace 欣然地/勉强地

【拓展】grace *n*. →graceful *adj*.

grand /grænd/ *adj*. 宏伟的，壮丽的；重大的，重要的；绝佳的，极好的；总的，全部的

【例句】①The grand building polarizes a deep local pride. 这座宏伟的建筑集中体现了当地人深切的自豪感。②This is one of the grand challenges of our time. 这是我们这个时代面临的重大挑战之一。③It is a grand opportunity for you to learn English. 这是你学习英语的大好机会。④See whether the grand total of pleasures is greater than the grand totals of pain. 看快乐的总数，是否大于痛苦的总数。

grant /grænt/ *vt*. 授予，同意；*n*. 拨款，授予物

【例句】①You could grant limited access to certain users. 可以向特定用户授予有限访问权限。②Through the grant, India will improve its ability to streamline electricity demand. 印度将利用这项拨款改善其电力需求合理化的能力。

【用法】take...for granted 认为……是理所当然的；granting/granted that... 假定……

【例句】①We take it for granted that we get help from our parents when we are in trouble. 遇到困难时，我们认为从父母那里得到帮助是理所当然的。②Granting/Granted that you've made some progress, you should not be conceited. 即使已经取得了一些进步，你也不应该自负。

grateful /ˈgreɪtfl/*adj*. 感激的，感谢的

【例句】We are particularly grateful to him for his timely help. 我们特别感谢他的及时帮助。

【拓展】gratefully *adv*. →gratitude *n*.

greed /griːd/*n*. 贪婪，贪心；贪食

【例句】①Some people think that most of the crime comes from money greed. 有些人认为大部分的犯罪来自对金钱的贪婪。②The beggar was looking at the newly baked cakes with greed. 乞丐贪吃地看着新出炉的蛋糕。

【拓展】greedy *adj*. 贪婪的，贪心的；贪食的，嘴馋的；渴望的

【用法】be greedy for/of; be greedy to do sth

【例句】①Elders are not to be greedy for money. 老年人是不可以贪财的。②Do not eat with the wicked man or be greedy for his choice of food. 不要与恶人同吃，也不要贪他挑选的美食。③The pupils in the area of mountain are greedy for knowledge. 山区的小学生渴望知识。

grill /grɪl/*v*. 烧烤；拷问，盘问；*n*. 烤架；烧烤食物

【例句】①You can fry, bake, grill, or roast potatoes. 土豆你可以炸、烘、烧、烤。②He grilled candidates for the job seriously. 他严肃盘问求职者。③You can put it in your oven, in your frying pan, on your grill. 你可以把它放在烤箱里，煎锅里，烤架上。④The host treated us with a plate of mixed grill. 主人用一盘混合烤食招待我们。

groan /grəʊn/*vi*. 呻吟；*n*. 呻吟，抱怨

【例句】The people groan under the burden of taxes. 人民在赋税的重压下呻吟。

gross /grəʊs/*adj*. 总的，毛的；显著的，严重的；粗俗的，粗野的

【例句】①No country has yet managed to reduce energy use while raising gross domestic product（GDP）. 目前还没有一个国家在提高国内生产总值（GDP）的同时设法减少能源。②Some businesses have very high costs of revenue and very low gross margins. 有些企业收益成本很高，毛利却很低。③He is a gross bookworm. 他是个不折不扣的书虫。④Don't speak gross language before the elderly. 不要在老人面前说粗话。

guarantee /ˌgærənˈtiː/ ***vt.*** 保证，担保；***n.*** 保证，担保；保证书，担保人

【例句】①This watch is guaranteed for two years. 这块手表保修两年。②Wealth is no guarantee of happiness. 财富并不能保证幸福。③With that guarantee in her pocket, she gave the go-ahead. 保证书落进口袋之后，她没话了。

guilty /ˈgɪlti/ ***adj.*** 内疚的；有罪的

【例句】①He still feels quite guilty when he looks back on the past. 回顾过去时，他仍然感到内疚。②The court adjudged her to be guilty. 法院判她有罪。

3.4　H

highlight /ˈhaɪlaɪt/ ***vt.*** 突出，强调，使显著；***n.*** 最精彩的部分，最重要的事情

【例句】①Highlight only those achievements that make you the best candidate for the job. 只强调那些让你成为这份工作的最佳候选人的成就。②The match between China and America is likely to prove one of the highlights of the tournament. 中美之间的比赛很可能成为本届世界杯的一大亮点。

hinder /ˈhɪndər/ ***vt.*** 阻碍，妨碍

【例句】Further investigation was hindered by the loss of all documentation on the case. 有关此案所有文件的丢失阻碍了进一步的调查。

hitherto /ˌhɪðərˈtuː/ ***adv.*** 到目前为止，迄今

【例句】This is a species of fish hitherto unknown in the West. 这是一种迄今为止在西方还不为人所知的鱼。

homogeneous /ˌhoʊməˈdʒiːniəs/ ***adj.*** 同种类的，同性质的，有相同特征的

【例句】The unemployed are not a homogeneous group. 失业者不是一个同质的群体。

honorable /ˈɑnərəbəl/ *adj*. 光荣的，荣誉的；可敬的，高尚的

【例句】①He is our honorable member. 他是我们的荣誉会员。②Working hard to enter an honorable profession should make any loving family proud. 努力去从事一份高尚的职业应该会让任何一个有爱的家庭感到很骄傲。

hook /hʊk/ *n*. 钩，钩状物；*vt*. 钩住

【例句】①Tom hung his coat on the hook behind the door. 汤姆把外套挂在门后的挂钩上。②Paul hooked his tractor to the car and pulled it to safety. 保罗把拖拉机挂在汽车上，把它拖到安全的地方。

【用法】hook up to 将（与）……连接起来；off the hook 脱离困境

【例句】①The new product has a pair of small loudspeakers fitted inside, which you can easily hook up to your computer's sound card. 新产品有一对内置的小喇叭，你可以很容易把它接到电脑的声卡上。②So I often encourage people to let themselves off the hook, cut themselves some slack. 因此我经常鼓励人们让自己脱离困境，放自己一马。

horizon /həˈraɪzn/ *n*. 地平线；[pl.] 眼界，见识

【例句】In the distance, the dot of a boat appeared on the horizon. 远处小黑点般的一条小船出现在地平线上。

【用法】on the horizon 在地平线上；即将发生的

①The sea and sky seemed to blend on the horizon. 海天似乎在地平线上融为一体。②As rescue efforts continued and with rebuilding efforts on the horizon, it appeared that government officials began to acknowledge that overdevelopment may have contributed to the disaster. 随着救援工作继续、重建工作即将开始，看起来政府官员们开始承认过度开发可能是导致这场灾难的原因之一。

【拓展】horizon *n*. →horizontal *adj*.

hospitality /ˌhɑːspɪˈtæləti/ *n*. 好客，殷勤

【例句】Every visitor to Georgia is overwhelmed by the kindness, charm, and hospitality of the people. 格鲁吉亚的每一位游客都被当地人民的善良、魅力和

好客所折服。

hostile /ˈhɑːstl/ *adj.* 敌对的，敌意的，不友善的；敌方的

【例句】The city is encircled by a hostile army. 该市被敌军包围。

【拓展】hostile *adj.* →hostility *n.*

humble /ˈhʌmbl/ *adj.* 谦逊的；简陋的；（级别或地位）低下的；*vt.* 使谦恭，使卑下

【例句】①He started his career as a humble farmer and now he has become the boss of a big company. 他从一个卑微的农民起家，现在他已成为一家大公司的老板。②Her words and action have humbled me, so I decide to try my best to realize my dream. 她的言行让我谦卑，所以我决定尽我最大的努力去实现我的梦想。

humidity /hjuːˈmɪdəti/ *n.* 湿度，潮湿，湿气

【例句】The heat and humidity were insufferable. 炎热和潮湿令人难以忍受。

【拓展】humid *adj.* →humidity *n.* →humidify *v.*

humiliate /hjuːˈmɪlieɪt/ *vt.* 羞辱，使……丢脸，使蒙羞

【例句】Her boss humiliated her in front of all her colleagues. 她的老板当着所有同事的面羞辱她。

hypothesis /haɪˈpɑːθəsɪs/ *n.* 假说，假设

【例句】These are arguments in favor of this hypothesis. 这些是支持这个假设的论据。

hysterical /hɪˈsterɪkl/ *adj.* 歇斯底里的

【例句】Janet became hysterical and began screaming. 珍妮特歇斯底里地尖叫起来。

4 I, J, K

4.1 I

injection /ɪnˈdʒekʃn/ *n.* 注射；注射剂；[医] 充血；（卫星等的）入轨

【例句】①Execution by lethal injection is scheduled for July 30th. 定于7月30日执行注射死刑。②It has to be given by injection, usually twice daily. 它必须通过注射摄入，通常一天两次。③He was executed by lethal injection earlier today. 他于今天早些时候被注射处死。

injure /ˈɪndʒər/ *vt.* 损害，毁坏；伤害（名誉、自尊等）；（尤指事故中）伤害

【例句】①I can say, with absolute truthfulness, that I did not injure her. 我可以绝对坦率地说，我没有伤害她。②You do not go out to injure opponents. 你并非蓄意伤害对手。③It can be no light matter for the local government that so many young prisoners should have wanted to kill or injure themselves in that district. 在那个地区竟然有那么多的年轻囚犯试图自杀或自残，当地政府决不可等闲视之。

injury /ˈɪndʒəri/ *n.* 伤害，损害；受伤处；伤害的行为

【例句】①The victim suffered a dreadful injury and lost a lot of blood. 受害者受了重伤，大量失血。②He made a remarkable recovery from a shin injury. 他的胫骨伤恢复得相当不错。③He needed surgery to cure a troublesome back injury.

他需要做手术来治好烦人的背伤。

【用法】add insult to injury 伤害之余又侮辱（使原本不好的关系更加恶化）

innocence /ˈɪnəsns/ *n*. 清白；天真无邪；无罪的人

【例句】①Her wide-eyed innocence soon exposes the pretensions of the art world. 她的天真烂漫很快就暴露了艺术界的矫揉造作。②Nowadays that sort of innocence is in short supply. 现在那种天真烂漫很少见。

innocent /ˈɪnəsnt/ *adj*. 天真无邪的；无知的；无辜的，无罪的，清白的；*n*. 天真无邪的人；无辜者

【例句】①He was innocent and the victim of a frame-up. 他是清白的，是受人诬陷的。②Under all the innocent fun, there are hidden dangers, especially for children. 在所有简单无害的娱乐项目背后都隐藏着危险，特别是对儿童而言。③Both groups on either side are just picking off innocent bystanders. 对峙双方都只是在瞄准射击无辜的旁观者。

【用法】presumed innocent 推定无罪；innocent bystander 无辜的旁观者

inquire /ɪnˈkwaɪr/ *vt. & vi*. 打听，询问；查究

【例句】①Inspectors were appointed to inquire into the affairs of the company. 督查员受委派调查该公司的事务。②Elsie called to inquire after my health. 埃尔茜打电话来问候我。③You can inquire of your new neighbors where the post office is. 你可以问问你的新邻居邮局在哪儿。

【用法】inquire after 问候；问好

inquiry /ˈɪnkwəri/ *n*. 调查，审查；询问，质问，质询，追究；探究；打听

【例句】①The government ordered an independent inquiry into the affair. 政府下令对该事件进行独立调查。②They needed more time to consider whether to hold an inquiry. 他们需要更多的时间来考虑是否进行调查。③The allegations against them were made in sworn evidence to the inquiry. 在调查取得的宣誓证词中对他们提出了指控。

insert /ɪnˈsɜːrt; ˈɪnsɜːrt/ *vt*. 插入；嵌入；（在文章中）添加；加插；*n*.

添入物（尤指一页印刷品图中插入或套印的小图）；（书报的）插页；插入物；添加物

【例句】①Insert coins into the slot and press for a ticket. 把硬币插进投币口，然后按一下买票。②The newspaper had an insert of pages of pictures. 该报带有数页插图。

【用法】insert sth（in/into/between sth）插入；嵌入；insert sth（into sth）（在文章中）添加，加插

【例句】Position the cursor where you want to insert a word. 把光标移到你想插入字词的地方。

insight /'ɪnsaɪt/ *n.* 洞察力，洞悉；直觉，眼光；领悟；顿悟

【例句】①He got his first insight into how inhumane employers can be. 他对雇主的冷酷无情第一次有了深刻认识。②His exploration of the myth brings insight into the American psyche. 他对这个神话的探讨揭示了美国人的心理。③His autobiography provides an illuminating insight into his mind. 他的自传可以让读者深入洞察他的精神世界。

【用法】insight（into sth）洞悉；了解

【例句】The book gives us fascinating insights into life in Mexico. 这本书生动地表现了墨西哥的生活。

insist /ɪnˈsɪst/ *vt. & vi.* 坚持；强调；坚决要求；坚决认为

【例句】①They insist on tastier chocolate than the anaemic British stuff. 他们坚持要做比淡而无味的英国货味道更好的巧克力。②The psychologists insist, however, that they are not being prescriptive. 然而，心理学家坚称他们并非一味灌输。③Our buyers insist on high standards of workmanship and materials. 我们的买主对工艺和材料坚持要高标准。

【用法】insist（on sth）坚决要求；坚持

【例句】I didn't really want to go but he insisted. 我并不真的想去，但他硬要我去。

【辨析】insist 指坚持认为某种想法正确或坚称某种说法属实，尤指与他人的想法或说法相左，也可指坚决要求做某事。adhere 指坚守规则、信仰、

协定等。persist 指不顾困难或他人的反对而坚持做某事。

【例句】①She insisted on her innocence. 她坚称自己无罪。②We should adhere to the traffic rules. 我们应该遵守交通规则。③He persisted in his refusal to apologize. 他坚持不道歉。

inspect /ɪnˈspekt/ ***vt***. 检查，检验；视察；***vi***. 进行检查；进行视察

【例句】①They have the right to come in and inspect the meter. 他们有权进来查表。②Elaine went outside to inspect the playing field. 伊莱恩走到外面查看操场。③The captain wants to inspect your kit. 船长想检查你的行装。

【用法】inspect damage 检查（或审查）损失；inspect sites 检查（或视察）场地

inspection /ɪnˈspekʃn/ ***n***. 检查；检验；视察；检阅

【例句】Whether the authorities will allow inspection is highly doubtful. 当局是否允许检查还是个大问号。

inspire /ɪnˈspaɪər/ ***vt***. 鼓舞；激励；赋予灵感；启迪；***vi***. 吸，吸入

【例句】①Our challenge is to motivate those voters and inspire them to join our cause. 我们面临的挑战是如何调动那些选民的积极性并鼓励他们加入我们的事业。②These caves cannot but inspire wonder in the beholder. 这些洞穴让观者无不叹为观止。

【用法】inspire sb（with sth）| inspire sth（in sb）使产生（感觉或情感）

【例句】Her work didn't exactly inspire me with confidence. 她的工作并没有真正地使我产生信心。

install /ɪnˈstɔːl/ ***vt***. 安装；安顿，安置；任命；使……正式就职

【例句】①Another change that Sue made was to install central heating. 苏做的另一个改变是安装中央供暖系统。②The army has promised to install a new government within a week. 军队已经许诺在一周内任命新一届政府。③The unit is comparatively easy to install and cheap to operate. 这种设备比较容易安装而且用起来便宜。

【用法】install sb（as sth）使就职，任命

【例句】He was installed as President last May. 他于去年五月份正式就任

总统。

【拓展】installment *n.* 分期付款；安装

installation /ˌɪnstəˈleɪʃn/ *n.* 安装；装置；永久性军事基地；就职

【例句】Installation of the new system will take several days. 新系统的安装需要几天时间。

instance /ˈɪnstəns/ *n.* 例子，实例；情况；要求，建议；[法]诉讼手续；*vt.* 举……为例

【例句】①The rally was organised at the instance of two senior cabinet ministers. 集会是应两位资深内阁大臣的要求组织的。②It is not a unique instance, but has its counterpart. 无独有偶。

【用法】in the first instance 第一；首先

【例句】In the first instance, notify the police and then contact your insurance company. 首先是报警，然后与你的保险公司联系。

instant /ˈɪnstənt/ *n.* 瞬间，顷刻；立即；*adj.* 立即的；迫切的；目前的；即食的；速溶的

【例句】①In the same instant he flung open the car door. 与此同时，猛地推开了车门。②I had bolted the door the instant I had seen the bat. 我一看到蝙蝠就把门闩上了。③At that instant the museum was plunged into total darkness. 就在那时，博物馆陷入了一片漆黑。

【辨析】instant 指极短的时间，如转瞬即逝的刹那间，通常用单数。moment 指很短的一段时间，多用于日常口语。second 指极为短暂的一段时间，常可与 moment 换用。

instantly /ˈɪnstəntli/ *adv.* 立即，马上；即刻地；*conj.* 一……就

【例句】In a pinstriped suit he instantly looked like a stuffed shirt. 穿上一套细条纹西装后，他马上就显得一本正经起来。

instead /ɪnˈsted/ *adv.* 代替，顶替；反而；反倒

【例句】Instead of moving at his usual stately pace, he was almost running. 他没像平时那样优雅庄重地走着，而是几乎跑了起来。

instinct /ˈɪnstɪŋkt/ *n.* 本能，天性；冲动；天资，天才；*adj.* 深深地充

满着

【例句】①His instinct would be to seek a new accommodation with the Nationalists. 他本能的反应会是寻求与民族主义者取得新的和解。②She hadn't followed her instinct and because of this Frank was dead. 她没有听从自己心里的话，弗兰克因此死了。③Farmers are increasingly losing touch with their instinct for managing the land. 农民正在逐渐丢失经营土地的本领。

【用法】basic instinct 基本本能；maternal instinct 母性本能；natural instinct 自然本能；survival instinct 生存本能

institute /ˈɪnstɪtuːt/ *vt.* 建立；制定；开始；着手；*n.* 协会；学会；学院；（教育、专业等）机构

【例句】①He visited the Institute of Neurology in Havana where they both worked. 他访问了两人都曾工作过的哈瓦那的神经病学研究所。②At the Curtis Institute he studied conducting with Fritz Reiner. 在柯蒂斯学院，他师从弗里茨·莱纳学习指挥。

institution /ˌɪnstɪˈtuːʃn/ *n.* （大学、银行等规模大的）机构；惯例，制度，规定，建立；社会事业机构

【例句】The woman will be confined to a mental institution. 这个女人将被关进精神病院。

instruct /ɪnˈstrʌkt/ *vt.* 教，讲授；教导，指导；通知；命令

【例句】①We should instruct the passengers what customs regulations are. 我们应该向乘客说明海关规则是什么。②You can instruct your bank to allow a third party to remove money from your account. 你可以通知银行，允许第三方从你的账户取款。

【用法】instruct sb (in sth) 教授，传授（技能等）

【例句】All our staff have been instructed in sign language. 我们的员工都接受过手语训练。

instruction /ɪnˈstrʌkʃn/ *n.* 授课；教诲；传授的或获得的知识，课程

【例句】①This technique brings life to instruction and eases assimilation of knowledge. 这一方法给教学带来了活力，也使知识的吸收变得容易了。②The worst part of the set-up is the poor instruction manual. 安装时最糟糕就是操作指南讲述不够清楚。

【用法】instruction（to do sth）| instruction（that...）指示；命令；吩咐；explicit instruction 清楚明白的命令（或指导）

【例句】I'm under instructions to keep my speech short. 我接到指示，讲话要简短

instrument /ˈɪnstrəmənt/ *n*. 仪器；手段，工具；乐器；法律文件；*vt*. 用仪器装备；为演奏谱曲；向……提交文书

【例句】①An instrument called a trocar makes a puncture in the abdominal wall. 一种叫作套管针的工具在腹壁上刺了一个孔。②The veto has been a traditional instrument of diplomacy for centuries. 几个世纪以来否决权一直是外交上惯用的手段。③There is an internal circuit breaker to protect the instrument from overload. 内置有断路器，防止设备过载。

insufficient /ˌɪnsəˈfɪʃnt/ *adj*. 不足的，不够的；绌；亏短；支绌

【例句】①The judge finally concluded there was insufficient evidence of premeditation. 法官最终做出判定，没有足够证据证明那是有预谋的。②There is insufficient space for enlargement of the buildings. 没有足够的空间扩建这些建筑。

【用法】insufficient（to do sth）| insufficient（for sth）不充分的；不足的；不够重要的

【例句】His salary is insufficient to meet his needs. 他的薪水不够应付需要。

【拓展】insufficiently *adv*.；insufficiency *n*.

insult /ɪnˈsʌlt, ˈɪnsʌlt/ *vt*. 侮辱，凌辱；辱骂；损害；*n*. 侮辱，凌辱；损害；无礼

【例句】①She spat the name out like an insult. 她像骂人似的说出了那个名字。②Forgive me, I don't mean to insult you. 请原谅，我并非意侮辱你。③He felt the smart of their insult for many days. 他受到他们的侮辱后好多天都感到难受。

【用法】add insult to injury 伤害之余又侮辱（使原本不好的关系更加恶

101

化）

insurance /ɪnˈʃʊrəns/ *n*. 保险，保险业；保险费；预防措施

【例句】①She learned her insurance had been canceled by Pacific Mutual Insurance Company. 她得知自己的保险已经被太平洋互助保险公司中止了。② The country needs a defence capability as insurance against the unexpected. 国家需要有一定的防御能力，以应对不可预知的情况。

【用法】insurance coverage 保险范围；insurance payments 保险费

insure /ɪnˈʃʊr/ *vt*. 保证；确保；为……保险；投保；*vi*. 买卖或卖保险

【例句】①—"One thing you can never insure against is corruption among your staff."—"Agreed."——"永远也防不胜防的就是员工内部的贪污腐败。"——"同意。" ② Think carefully before you insure against accident, sickness and redundancy. 在为意外事故、疾病与失业投保之前一定要考虑清楚。③Will it insure success to you? 这将保证你成功吗？

【用法】insure (yourself/sth) (against/for sth) 投保；给……保险

【例句】Having a lot of children is a way of insuring themselves against loneliness in old age. 养很多孩子是他们预防老年孤寂的一种办法。

integrate /ˈɪntɪɡreɪt/ *vt*. 使一体化；使完整；使整合；*vi*. 成为一体；结合在一起；合并；求积分；*adj*. 完整的；整体的；综合的

【例句】The way Swedes integrate immigrants is, she feels, 100% more advanced. 她觉得瑞典人帮助移民适应当地生活的方式百分百地更为先进。

【用法】integrate efforts 协同努力；integrate information/knowledge 整合信息/知识

intellectual /ˌɪntəˈlektʃuəl/ *adj*. 智力的；理智的；聪明的；*n*. 知识分子；有极高智力的人；凭理智办事的人

【例句】①Upbringing is also of vital importance to the intellectual development of children. 后天培养对儿童的智力发展也至关重要。②As intellectuals, we should shoulder the responsibility to educate more useful talents for our nation. 作为知识分子，我们应该肩负起为国家培养更多有用人才的责任。

【用法】intellectual ability 智力；intellectual interests 智识兴趣

intelligence /ɪnˈtelɪdʒəns/ *n*. 智力；聪颖；情报；情报机构

【例句】Too bad he used his intelligence for criminal purposes. 他把聪明都用在了犯罪上，太可惜了。

【辨析】mind 指人的思维或感知、想象等能力，无褒贬之意。brain 指能理解思考和快速学习的能力，通常用复数。intelligence 指学习、理解、思维、判断等的能力，也指聪明、聪慧。wit 指思维敏捷并能做出正确判断的能力，强调机敏，通常用复数。

【例句】①His brilliant mind contributed to his great success. 他非凡的智慧助他取得巨大的成功。②He wanted to find a job that didn't require too much brains. 他想找一份不需要动太多脑筋的工作。③Did your child show high intelligence from an early age? 你的孩子从小就显示出了很高的智力水平吗？

intelligent /ɪnˈtelɪdʒənt/ *adj*. 聪明的；理解力强的；有智力的；[计] 智能的

【例句】①She was thin and spare, with a sharply intelligent face. 她又高又瘦，一副精明过人的模样。②An intelligent computer will be an indispensable diagnostic tool for doctors. 智能计算机将成为医生不可或缺的诊断工具。

【拓展】intelligently *adv*.

intend /ɪnˈtend/ *vt*. 意欲，计划；为特殊目的而设计；为特定用途而打算；意指或意味；*vi*. 怀有某种意图或目的

【例句】England intend fielding their strongest team in next month's World Youth Championship. 英格兰意欲在下月的世界青年锦标赛中推出他们的最强阵容。

【用法】intend sth (by sth) | intend sth (as sth) 意指

【例句】What exactly did you intend by that remark? 你那句话到底想说什么？He intended it as a joke. 他只想开个玩笑。

intense /ɪnˈtens/ *adj*. 热情的，强烈的，紧张的；热烈的，认真的；有强烈感情（或意见、想法）的

【例句】①I felt so self-conscious under Luke's mother's intense gaze. 在卢克母亲审视的目光下，我感到极不自在。②That was the cue for several months of intense bargaining. 那意味着几个月的激烈谈判开始了。

【用法】intense concentration 高度集中；intense feelings 强烈的感情；intense relationship 紧张的关系；intense scrutiny 严密仔细的检查

intensity /ɪnˈtensəti/ ***n.*** 强烈；（感情的）强烈程度；强度；烈度

【例句】The most visible sign of the intensity of the crisis is unemployment. 预示危机严重程度的一个最显著的迹象就是失业情况。

intensive /ɪnˈtensɪv/ ***adj.*** 加强的，强烈的；[农] 精耕细作的；[语] 加强语的；（农业方法）集约的

【例句】①She spent the night in intensive care after the operation. 手术后的那个夜晚她在重症监护病房度过。②Boren surprisingly led off the most intensive line of questioning today. 博伦今天出人意料地一上来就开始连珠炮似的盘问起来。③There have been intensive discussions between the two governments in recent days. 近几天，双方政府一直在进行紧张的磋商。

【用法】intensive negotiations 集中谈判；intensive programme 强化项目

intention /ɪnˈtenʃn/ ***n.*** 意图，目的；意向；意义，意旨；[医] 愈合

【例句】The president said he had no intention of deploying ground troops. 总统称并不打算部署地面部队。

【用法】the road to hell is paved with good intentions 黄泉路上徒有好意多；光说不练是不够的

【辨析】intent 指某人做某事的目的，也可作法律术语，指犯罪意图。design 指在头脑中形成的计划，有时含贬义。intention 普通用词，指做某事的打算或计划。

【例句】①The company has declared its intent to get a bank loan. 该公司已宣布打算向银行贷款。②He believed that this had happened by design. 他认为这件事是事先安排的。③I came to London with the intention of studying English literature. 我来伦敦是为了学习英国文学。

intentional /ɪnˈtenʃənl/ ***adj.*** 有意的，故意的；策划的

【例句】①Civil disobedience, violent or non-violent, is intentional law breaking. 公民抗命，不管是暴力还是非暴力的，都是故意犯法。②How can I blame him? It wasn't intentional. 我怎么能怪他呢？那又不是有意的。③Women who are the victims of intentional discrimination will be able to get compensation. 受到故意歧视的女性将会得到赔偿。

interaction /ˌɪntəˈrækʃən/ *n*. 一起活动；合作；互相影响；互动

【例句】①The following excerpt is illustrative of her interaction with students. 接下来的节选部分可以说明她与学生的互动情况。②The interaction of the two groups produced many good ideas. 两个组的相互交流产生了许多好主意。

interest /ˈɪntrəst/ *n*. 兴趣，爱好；利害关系，利益；利息；趣味，感兴趣的事；*vt*. 使产生兴趣；使参与，使加入；引起……的意愿；使产生关系

【例句】①We have to take into consideration the interest of 500,000 customers. 我们得为50万名顾客的利益着想。②Hopes of an early cut in interest rates bolstered confidence. 利率有望早日下调，从而增强了人们的信心。③Interest rates would come down as the recovery gathered pace. 随着复苏的加速，利率会降下来。

【用法】interest（on sth）(finance 财) 利息；have sb's interests at heart 关心……的幸福成功；暗暗地替……着想；to pay interest on a loan 付贷款利息

【例句】When you ask a loan of money from bank, you should pay interest on a loan on time according to the contract. 当你向银行贷款时，应该按照合同按时支付贷款利息。

interfere /ˌɪntərˈfɪr/ *vi*. 干预，干涉；调停，排解；妨碍，打扰

【例句】①He knew when to leave well alone and when to interfere. 他知道什么时候该适可而止，什么时候该插手干预。②Smoking and drinking interfere with your body's ability to process oxygen. 抽烟与酗酒有碍身体处理氧气的能力。

【用法】interfere with sth 妨碍；干扰；ability to interfere 干涉能力；right to interfere 干涉权利

【例句】She never allows her personal feelings to interfere with her work. 她从不让她的个人感情妨碍工作。

interference /ˌɪntərˈfɪrəns/ *n*. 干涉，干扰，冲突；介入；妨碍，打扰，阻碍物；抵触

【例句】①The parliament described the decree as interference in the republic's internal affairs. 议会形容此法令为对共和国内政的干涉。②It is hard to imagine her taking kindly to too much interference. 很难想象她会喜欢被人过多地干涉。

【用法】run interference 掩护阻挡（为己方持球队员让出道路）；（为帮助某人）积极介入

interior /ɪnˈtɪriər/ *n*. 内部；内地；内政；内心；*adj*. 内部的；内地的，国内的；里面的

【例句】①Interior decoration by careful coordination seems to have had its day. 精心搭配的室内装饰似乎已不再受欢迎了。②The interior was shielded from the curious gaze of passersby. 屋子内部被挡住了，以防路人好奇地张望。

【拓展】exterior *adj*. 外面的；外部的；外表的

intermediate /ˌɪntərˈmiːdiət/ *adj*. 中间的，中级的；*n*. 中间物，中间分子，中间人；*vi*. 调解；充当调解人，调解；干涉

【例句】You should consider breaking the journey with intermediate stopovers at airport hotels. 你应该考虑将旅程分为几段，中途在机场旅馆稍作停留。

【用法】an intermediate stage/step in a process 中间阶段/步骤

internal /ɪnˈtɜːrnl/ *adj*. 国内的；内部的；体内的；内心的；*prep*. （机构）内部的；*n*. 内脏，内部器官；本质，本性

【例句】①It took internal whistle-blowing and investigative journalism to uncover the rot. 是内部检举和调查性报道揭露了这一腐败事实。②This cuttlefish has a horny internal shell like a pen. 这只乌贼有一个笔状的角质内壳。

【辨析】inner 指位于某物内部或靠近其中心位置的，也可指想法、情感等藏于内心之中而未表达出来的，只作定语。inside 指在某物内部的，只作定语。internal 指位于身体、公司、组织、国家等内部的，也可指内心的，通常作定语。

【例句】①She lives in inner Paris. 她住在巴黎中心区。②The inside pages of the newspaper have been torn out. 报纸的内页已经被撕了。③Some scientists have been doing research on artificial internal organs. 一些科学家一直在研究人造内脏。

interpret /ɪnˈtɜːrprət/ *vt.* 解释；理解；诠释，体现；口译；*vi.* 做解释；做口译

【例句】①They could interpret it that way if they had a mind to. 如果他们愿意的话，可以那样理解。②The students were asked to interpret the poem. 学生们被要求诠释那首诗的意义。

【用法】interpret sth（as sth）把……理解为；领会；ways to interpret 阐释方式

【例句】I didn't know whether to interpret her silence as acceptance or refusal. 我不知该把她的沉默看作是接受还是拒绝。

interpretation /ɪnˌtɜːrprəˈteɪʃn/ *n.* 解释，说明；翻译；表演，演绎；理解

【例句】①The opposition Conservative Party put a different interpretation on the figures. 反对党保守党对这些数字提出一番不同的解释。②Language interpretation is the whole point of the act of reading. 语言的理解是阅读行为中关键所在。③Their interpretation was faulty—they had misinterpreted things. 他们的理解是错误的——他们将事情曲解了。

【用法】open to interpretation 有待解释；strict interpretation 严谨的解释

interpreter /ɪnˈtɜːrprətər/ *n.* 解释者；口译译员；[军事] 判读员；[自] 翻译器

【例句】①He was an official interpreter to the government of Nepal. 他曾是尼泊尔政府的官方译员。②Speaking through an interpreter, the President said that the talks were going well. 总统通过译员说会谈进展良好。

interrupt /ˌɪntəˈrʌpt/ *vt.* 打断（别人的话等）；阻止；遮挡，截断；*vi.* 暂停；中断；打扰，打搅；*n.* 中断；暂停

【例句】①It's usually thought impolite to interrupt others while they are talking. 打断别人说话通常被认为是不礼貌的。②"If I may interrupt for a moment," Kenneth said. "能打搅一下吗，"肯尼思说。③Taller plants interrupt the views from the house. 稍高些的植物遮挡了房内的视线。

【用法】interrupt（sb/sth）(with sth) 插嘴；打扰；打岔

interruption /ˌɪntəˈrʌpʃn/ *n.* 中断；打断；障碍物；打岔的事

【例句】①There was constant jeering and interruption from the floor. 议员席上不断有人在嘲讽和打岔。② Motherhood did not constitute much of an interruption to her career. 做母亲并没有在很大程度上中断她的事业。③I was able to get on with my work without interruption. 我可以不受打扰继续我的工作了。

interval /ˈɪntəvl/ *n*. 间隔；幕间休息；（数学）区间

【例句】The ferry service has restarted after an interval of 12 years. 时隔12年之后，轮渡服务又重新开通了。

【用法】at（…）intervals 每隔……时间；间或；不时

【例句】Buses to the city leave at regular intervals. 开往城里的公共汽车每隔一定时间发出一班。

【辨析】rest 泛指放松、休息。break 指短暂的中止，如工作或活动之间的休息。interval 指戏剧或音乐会各场次之间的休息。

【例句】①He was so tired that his wife suggested he should get some rest. 他非常累，妻子建议他休息休息。②They worked for 18 hours without a break yesterday. 昨天他们连续工作了18个小时。③There will be a 15-minute interval after the first act. 第一幕结束之后将休息15分钟。

interview /ˈɪntəvjuː/ *n*. 接见，会谈；面试；采访；*vt.&vi*. 面试；*vt*. 访问；会见；采访

【例句】①In the job interview, she performed quite well and aroused the boss's attention. 在面试中，她表现得很好，引起了老板的注意。②As a sports journalist, she often interviews some famous athletes in the world. 作为一名体育记者，她经常采访世界上一些著名的运动员。

【拓展】interviewer *n*. 接见者，会谈者；进行面试者；采访者；interviewee *n*. 被接见者；被采访者；参加面试者

intimate /ˈɪntɪmət；ˈɪntɪmeɪt/*adj*. 亲密的，亲近的；私人的，个人的；内部的；直接的；*n*. 至交；密友；*v*. 暗示，提示；宣布，通知

【例句】①Mr Black went for the jugular, asking intimate sexual questions. 布莱克先生直攻要害，问起了性方面的隐私问题。②France has kept the most intimate links with its former African territories. 法国与其前非洲属地一直保持着最密切的联系。③He surprised me with his intimate knowledge of Kierkegaard and Schopenhauer. 他对克尔凯郭尔与叔本华的深刻了解让我很吃惊。

【用法】 intimate details 不为人知的细节；intimate atmosphere 温馨的气氛

【辨析】 familiar 指关系亲近的，也指某人的言行十分随便，显得过于亲昵的。close 指人与人之间彼此喜爱、关系亲密的。intimate 指关系极其亲密的。

【例句】①She is on familiar terms with all her neighbours. 她和所有邻居的关系都很好。②He felt closer to Susan after the campfire party. 篝火晚会之后，他觉得和苏珊更亲近了。③They have lived here for a year and a half, but are still not on intimate terms with their neighbours. 他们已经在这里住了一年半了，却仍然和邻居不熟。

introduce /ˌɪntrəˈduːs/ *vt.* 提出；介绍；引进；作为……的开头

【例句】 "And now, without further ado, let me introduce our benefactor." "下面，闲话少说，让我来介绍一下我们的赞助人。"

【用法】 introduce sb to sth ｜ introduce sth (to sb) 使初次了解；使尝试；introduce sth (into/to sth) 推行；实施；采用

【例句】①This food was first introduced to China two centuries ago. 这种食物在两个世纪前首次传入中国。②She introduced briefly and clearly and made a very deep impression on us. 她的介绍简单明了，给我们留下了非常深刻的印象。

introduction /ˌɪntrəˈdʌkʃn/ *n.* 介绍；引言，导言；采用，引进；新采用的东西

【例句】①Millions of words have been written about the introduction of the euro. 有关采用欧元的文章已经有很多。②The camera has undergone only two minor tweaks since its introduction. 那款相机自从推出以来仅经过两次小的改进。

invade /ɪnˈveɪd/ *vt. & vi.* 侵犯；侵入，侵略；涌入；干涉，干扰；蜂拥而入，挤满；(疾病，声音等) 袭来，侵袭

【例句】①Some media have been accused of invading public people's privacy unfairly and unjustifiably because of publishing untrue reports. 一些媒体因发布不实报道而被指责不公平地、无理地侵犯公众隐私。②I don't want to invade your private life unnecessarily. 我不想过多地干涉你的私生活。③If the enemy dare to invade us, we'll deal them head-on blows. 敌人胆敢进犯，我们就给以迎头痛击。

invasion /ɪnˈveɪʒn/ *n*. 入侵，侵略；侵害，侵犯；侵袭；[医] 发病

【例句】①When the invasion occurred he ruled as a puppet of the occupiers. 外敌入侵时，他作为占领者的傀儡行使统治。②The secrecy and swiftness of the invasion shocked and amazed army officers. 这次入侵的隐秘和迅速令陆军军官们大为震惊。③There was a peaceful pitch invasion after Milan's eighth goal. 米兰队攻入第八粒进球后，观众有序地涌进球场。

【用法】an invasion force/fleet 侵略军/舰队

invent /ɪnˈvent/ *vt*. 发明，创造；虚构

【例句】①His father had helped invent a whole new way of doing business. 他父亲帮助创造了一套全新的生意经。②We have to invent a new method for sneaking prisoners out without being noticed by the guards. 我们必须想出新的办法使囚犯们偷偷溜出去而不被看守发现。

invention /ɪnˈvenʃn/ *n*. 发明；发明物；捏造；内心捏造的东西，特指谎言；发明才能

【例句】①The new invention ensures the beer keeps a full, frothy head. 这项新发明能保证啤酒始终保持丰富的泡沫。②It's been a tricky business marketing his new invention. 推广他的新发明一直是件棘手的事情。③You can't fault them for lack of invention. 你不能因为他们缺乏创新就指责他们。④Necessity is the mother of invention. 需要是发明之母。

inventor /ɪnˈventər/ *n*. 发明家；创造者；发明者

【例句】①The royalties enabled the inventor to re-establish himself in business. 专利使用费让这位发明家得以再次立足于商界。②He became famous as an inventor of astonishing visual and aural effects. 他因发明了神奇的视听效果而出名。③In my youth my ambition had been to be an inventor. 我年轻时的抱负是成为一个

发明家。

investigate /ɪnˈvestɪgeɪt/ *vt*. 调查；审查；研究；*vi*. 做调查

【例句】①We were asked to investigate the alleged inconsistencies in his evidence. 我们被要求对他证词中的前后矛盾之处进行调查。②The two sides agreed to set up a commission to investigate claims. 双方同意组建一个委员会来调查那些索赔要求。③He felt impelled to investigate further. 他觉得有必要做进一步调查。

【用法】investigate the possibility of something 调查某事的可能性；investigate a crime 调查罪案

【拓展】investigator *n*. 调查者

investigation /ɪnˌvestɪˈgeɪʃn/ *n*. （正式的）调查，研究；审查；科学研究；学术研究

【例句】The allegations are serious enough to warrant an investigation. 这些指控很严重，有必要进行一番调查。

【用法】investigation（into sth）（正式的）调查，侦查

【例句】The police have completed their investigations into the accident. 警察已完成对这次事故的调查。

invest /ɪnˈvest/ *n*. 投资，投资额；封锁；（时间、精力的）投入；值得买的东西

【例句】①Investment could dry up and that could cause the economy to falter. 投资可能会中断，而这会引起经济衰退。②Investment remains tiny primarily because of the exorbitant cost of land. 投资仍然微乎其微，主要原因在于土地成本过高。

【用法】invest in sth 购买昂贵有用的东西；invest sb/sth with sth 使似乎具备某种性质

【例句】①Don't you think it's about time you invested in a new coat? 你不觉得该花点钱买件新外套了吗？②Being a model invests her with a certain glamour. 当模特儿似乎给她增添了一定的魅力。

invisible /ɪnˈvɪzəbl/ *adj*. 看不见的；无形的；隐匿的；*n*. 看不见的人/物

111

【例句】 The invisible press almost overwhelmed every one of us when something unexpected happened. 当一些意想不到的事情发生时，无形的压力几乎压垮了我们每一个人。

invitation /ˌɪnvɪˈteɪʃn/ ***n***. 招待，邀请；请柬，请帖；引诱，吸引，诱惑

【例句】 ①"I can't pass this up." She waved the invitation. "我不能错过这个机会，"她挥舞着请帖说。②Elizabeth had a standing invitation to stay with her. 伊丽莎白受到邀请，可以随时去她家住。

【用法】 accept an invitation 接受邀请；decline an invitation 谢绝邀请；extend an invitation 发出邀请；get/receive an invitation 收到邀请（或请柬）

involve /ɪnˈvɑːlv/ ***vt***. 包含；使参与，牵涉；围绕，缠绕；使专心于

【例句】 ①The 85 million programme will involve an extensive rebranding of the airline. 这个 8,500 万英镑的项目将包括全面重塑该航空公司的形象。②A retrofit may involve putting in new door jambs. 房子翻新可能需要安装新的门框。③A late booking may involve you in extra cost. 预订晚了的话你可能要额外多花钱。

【用法】 involve sb（in sth/in doing sth）（使）参加，加入；involve sb（in sth）表明（某人参与了犯罪等）

【例句】 ①We want to involve as many people as possible in the celebrations. 我们希望参加庆典的人越多越好。②His confession involved a number of other politicians in the affair. 他的自白供出其他一些政治人物也涉及此事。

irregular /ɪˈreɡjələr/ ***adj***. 不规则的，不对称的；无规律的；不合规范的，不合法的；不规则变化的；***n***. 非正规军军人；不规则物；不合规格的产品

【例句】 ①She was taken to hospital suffering from an irregular heartbeat. 她因心律不齐被送往医院。②At least 17 different irregular units are engaged in the war. 至少有 17 个非正规军部队参战。③The paint was drying in irregular patches. 油漆一片片地慢慢变干了。

isolate /ˈaɪsəleɪt/ ***vt***. 使隔离，使孤立；[电] 使绝缘；[化] 使离析；[微] 使细菌分离；***vi***. 隔离，孤立

【例句】 ①Political influence is being used to shape public opinion and isolate critics. 政治影响正被用来左右公众舆论，使批评家们陷于孤立。②A chemist can isolate the oxygen from the hydrogen in water. 一个化学家能把水中的氧和氢分解。③Do not isolate yourself from others. 不要把自己孤立起来。

【用法】isolate sb/yourself/sth (from sb/sth) （使）隔离，孤立，脱离

【例句】Patients with the disease should be isolated. 这种病的患者应予以隔离。

【拓展】isolable *adj.* 可隔离的；isolationist *n.* 孤立主义者；isolationist *adj.* 孤立主义的

issue /ˈɪʃuː/ *n.* 问题；（报刊的）期号；发行物；*vt.* 发行，发布；发给；*vi.* 发行；造成……结果；流出

【例句】The key issue was whether the four defendants acted dishonestly. 关键问题是4名被告是否存在欺诈行为。

【用法】security issue 安保问题；issue an appeal 发出呼吁

4.2 J

journal /ˈdʒɜːrnl/ *n.* （某学科或专业的）报纸，刊物，杂志；（用于报纸名）……报；日志；日记

【例句】①He was a newspaperman for *The New York Times* and some other journals. 他是个记者，为《纽约时报》和其他一些报刊撰稿。②Sara confided to her journal. 萨拉在日记中倾诉心事。

journalist /ˈdʒɜːrnəlɪst/ *n.* 记者，新闻工作者

【例句】①She had taken him for a journalist. 她把他错当成记者了。②A journalist all his life, he's now brought out a book. 他当了一辈子新闻记者，如今已出了一本书。③The last journalist to interview him received a death threat. 上次去采访他的记者受到了死亡恐吓。

journey /ˈdʒɜːrni/ *n.* （尤指长途）旅行，行程；*v.* （尤指长途）旅行

【例句】①We shall start the journey to Europe next week. 下周我们将开始

去欧洲的旅行。②I journeyed to Canada and the United States in December, 2004 for the first time. 2004 年 12 月，我第一次去了加拿大和美国旅行。

【用法】end of a journey 旅程（或历程）结束；first/last leg of a journey 第一段/最后一段旅程（或历程）

joy /dʒɔɪ/ *n.* 高兴；愉快；喜悦；令人高兴的人（或事）；乐事；乐趣；成功；满意；满足

【例句】①Salter shouted with joy. 索尔特欣喜地叫喊着。②One can never learn all there is to know about cooking, and that is one of the joys of being a chef. 钻研烹饪之道是永无止境的，这也是当厨师的乐趣之一。③They expect no joy from the vote itself. 他们对投票本身不抱任何希望。

【用法】cry/weep for joy 喜极而泣；tears of joy 喜悦的泪水

joyful /ˈdʒɔɪfl/ *adj.* 高兴的；快乐的；令人愉快的

【例句】①Giving birth to a child is both painful and joyful. 生小孩是件既痛苦又令人高兴的事。②We're a very joyful people; we're very musical people and we love music. 我们是非常快乐的民族；我们能歌善舞，热爱音乐。③A wedding is a joyful celebration of love. 婚礼就是快乐的爱情庆典。

【辨析】pleasant 多指客观事物令人愉悦的。agreeable 既可指某事物令人开心的，也可指某人很讨人喜欢的。cheerful 形容某事物能令人愉悦或振奋精神的。

【例句】①It had been a pleasant journey. 那是一次令人愉快的旅行。②We spent a most agreeable weekend together. 我们一起度过了一个非常愉快的周末。③This is a cheerful pop song. 这是一首曲调欢快的流行歌曲。

judge /dʒʌdʒ/ *n.* 法官；审判员；裁判员；评判员；鉴定人；鉴赏家；*v.* 判断；断定；认为；估计，猜测（大小、数量等）；裁判；评判；担任裁判

【例句】①A panel of judges is now selecting the finalists. 评判小组现在正选拔参加决赛的选手。②Colin Mitchell will judge the entries each week. 科林·米切尔负责每周对参赛作品进行评判。③It will take a few more years to judge the impact of these ideas. 要再花上几年的时间才能判断出这些想法的影响。

【用法】judge approves something 法官批准某事；judge asks something 法官

询问了某事；decision by/of a judge 法官的判决；don't judge a book by its cover 勿以貌取人；勿只凭外表判断

judgement /ˈdʒʌdʒmənt/ *n*. 意见；判断力；[法] 审判；评价

【例句】①That isn't a value judgement, but it's a fact. 那不是一个价值判断，而是一个事实。②Despite the mixed metaphor, there is some truth in this judgement. 尽管有混用的比喻，这个判断还是有些道理的。③He argues very strongly that none of us has the right to sit in judgement. 他激烈地争论说，我们中任何一个人都无权进行审判。

【用法】sit in judgement (on/over/upon sb) 褒贬（某人）；（对某人）妄加评判

jungle /ˈdʒʌŋɡl/ *n*. （热带）丛林，密林；尔虞我诈的环境；危险地带；丛林音乐

【例句】The hunter seldom goes deeper into the jungle alone incase of wild animals. 由于有野生动物，猎人很少独自深入丛林。

【用法】the law of the jungle 丛林法则；弱肉强食

junior /ˈdʒuːniər/ *adj*. 地位（或职位、级别）低下的；青少年的；（尤用于美国，置于同名父子中儿子的姓名之后）小；*n*. 职位较低者；低层次工作人员；青少年；青少年运动员；小学生

【例句】Junior and middle-ranking civil servants have pledged to join the indefinite strike. 基层和中层公务员已承诺要加入无限期罢工中来。

【用法】junior executive 初级主管；junior whip 初级党鞭

jury /ˈdʒʊri/ *n*. 陪审团；（比赛的）评判委员会，裁判委员会

【例句】①The jury convicted Mr Hampson of all offences. 陪审团裁定汉普森先生全部罪名成立。②I am not surprised that the Booker Prize jury included it on their shortlist. 我毫不惊讶布克奖评委会将其列在入选名单中。③The verdict of the jury was given in his favour. 陪审团做出了对他有利的结论。

【用法】the jury is (still) out on sth （某事）仍无定论，悬而未决；jury duty 陪审团职责；trial by jury 陪审团审判

justice /ˈdʒʌstɪs/ *n*. 公平；公正；公道；合理；公平合理；司法制度；法

律制裁；审判。

【例句】It would have been rough justice had he been deprived of this important third European win. 要是他被剥夺了这一意义重大的第三个欧洲冠军头衔，那对他简直是太不公平了。

【用法】racial justice 种族平等；criminal justice 刑事司法制度；do yourself justice 充分发挥自己的能力

【例句】She didn't do herself justice in the exam. 她在考试中没有充分发挥出自己的水平。

justify /ˈdʒʌstɪfaɪ/ *vt*. 证明……正确（或正当、有理）；对……做出解释；为……辩解（或辩护）；调整使全行排满；使每行排齐；使齐行

【例句】①They justify every villainy in the name of high ideals. 他们打着实现远大理想的幌子为他们的每件恶行开脱。②I give myself treats and justify them to salve my conscience. 我常犒劳自己一番，然后找个说辞让自己良心稍安。③We don't believe that they have the economic reforms in place which would justify putting huge sums of Western money into their pockets. 我们认为他们并没有让经济改革步入正轨，因此不存在把巨额西方资金送进他们口袋的正当理由。

【用法】justify sth/yourself (to sb) 对……做出解释；为……辩解（或辩护）；the end justifies the means 只要目的正当，可以不择手段

【例句】You don't need to justify yourself to me. 你不必向我解释你的理由。

4.3 K

knit /nɪt/ *vt*. 编织；针织；机织；织平针；（使）紧密结合，严密；*n*. 编织的衣服；针织衫

【例句】①The best thing about sport is that it knits the whole family close together. 体育运动最大的益处在于它使整个家庭紧密地团结在一起。②They knitted their brows and started to grumble. 他们皱着眉头抱怨起来。③Ordinary people have some reservations about their president's drive to knit them so closely to their neighbors. 普通百姓对总统号召人们邻里间亲密相处的动机心存疑虑。

【用法】closely/tightly knit 紧密结合；knit together 结合在一起

knob /nɑːb/ *n.* （用以开关电视机等的）旋钮；（门或抽屉的）球形把手

【例句】①He turned the knob and pushed against the door. 他扭动把手推了推门。②The cutters are opened by turning the knob anticlockwise. 逆时针转动旋钮可以开启切割机。③With his left hand he groped for the knob, turned it, and pulled the door open. 他左手摸索着门把手，转动一下，然后推开门。

【用法】with knobs on 有过之而无不及；更是如此；尤其突出

【例句】It isn't art—it's just a horror movie with knobs on! 那不是艺术——只是更为恐怖的恐怖片而已！

knock /nɑːk/ *v.* 敲；击；（常为无意地）碰，撞；把……撞击成（某种状态）；*n.* 敲击声；敲门（或窗等）声；捶击；敲击；撞击

【例句】①She went directly to Simon's apartment and knocked on the door. 她直奔西蒙的房间，敲了敲门。②The stories of his links with the actress had knocked the fun out of him. 有关他与那位女演员有关系的传闻使他很不开。③I'm not knocking them: if they want to do it, it's up to them. 我不是批评他们：想不想做那件事取决于他们。

【用法】knock (sth) (against/on sth) （常为无意地）碰，撞；knock (at/on sth) 敲；击

【例句】①Be careful, you don't knock your head on this low beam. 小心，别把头撞在这矮梁上。②Somebody was knocking on the window. 有人在敲窗户。

knot /nɑːt/ *n.* （用绳索等打的）结；发髻；节子；节疤；*v.* 把……打成结（或扎牢）；缠结；打发髻

【例句】①One lace had broken and been tied in a knot. 一条带子已经断了，打了个结。②They travel at speeds of up to 30 knots. 他们以高达 30 节的速度行进。

knowledge /ˈnɑːlɪdʒ/ *n.* 知识；学问；学识；知晓；知悉

【例句】①She told Parliament she had no knowledge of the affair. 她告诉议

会她对此事并不知情。②Is learning a foreign language a question of learning new skills or a question of acquiring new knowledge? 学习外国语是学习一种新技能，还是获取新知识呢？

【用法】acquire knowledge 获取知识；gain knowledge 获得知识；common knowledge 众所周知的事；general knowledge 常识；prior knowledge 先验知识

【辨析】knowledge、learning 和 scholarship 均有"知识""学识""学问"等之意。knowledge 指对全部已知或可知的知识的理解或了解；learning 指通过研究、总结经验或他人传授而得到的知识，还有"学习"之意；scholarship 尤指经过深入学习、研究而获得的渊博的、严谨的知识，还有"奖学金"之意。

【例句】①A little knowledge is a dangerous thing. 一知半解是很危险的事。②He made a display of his learning. 他夸耀自己有学问。③This is undoubtedly a magnificent work of scholarship. 这无疑是一部学术巨著。

5 L, M, N

5.1 L

liable /ˈlaɪəbl/ *adj.* 有责任的；有义务的；有……倾向的；易……的

【例句】①Offenders will be liable to a seven-year prison term. 违法者可判处7年监禁。②Educational practice is liable to sudden swings and changes. 教学实践中经常会出现突然的变化与改革。③Such a figure is liable to be attacked as a blasphemer. 这样的人物很容易被人抨击为亵渎者。

【辨析】apt 指天生具有做某事的倾向的，其后常接动词不定式。liable 只作表语，指因习惯或倾向性而易做某事或产生某种问题、患上某种疾病等，其后常接动词不定式或介词 to。prone 尤指倾向发生不好的或有害的事情，通常作表语，其后常接介词 to 或动词不定式。

【例句】①This kind of apple is apt to go bad. 这种苹果容易坏。②The dog is liable to bite when angry. 这只狗生气时容易咬人。③You are prone to fall ill if you live in this cold and wet basement for long. 如果你长期住在这又冷又湿的地下室里，很容易生病。

liberal /ˈlɪbərəl/ *n.* 自由主义者；自由党党员；*adj.* 开明的；自由的；慷慨的；不拘泥的

【例句】The attitude of the medical profession is very much more liberal now. 现在，医务人员的态度开明多了。

liberate /ˈlɪbəreɪt/ *vt.* 解放；释放；放出

【例句】①They did their best to liberate slaves. 他们尽最大能力去解放奴隶。②This will liberate him from economic worry. 这将消除他经济上的忧虑。③The government is devising a plan to liberate prisoners held in detention camps. 政府计划释放关押在拘留营内的囚犯。

【用法】liberate sb/sth（from sb/sth）解放

【例句】The city was liberated by the advancing army. 军队向前挺进，解放了那座城市。

liberation /ˌlɪbəˈreɪʃən/ *n.* 解放；释放，逸出

【例句】Women's liberation from the bondage of domestic life. 女性从家庭生活的束缚中解脱出来。

liberty /ˈlɪbərti/ *n.* 自由（自己选择生活方式而不受政府及权威限制）；自由（不受关押或奴役的状态）；自由（做某事的合法权利或行动自由）

【例句】①He firmly believes liberty is inseparable from social justice. 他坚信自由与社会正义是不可分的。②I am afraid we are not at liberty to disclose that information. 恐怕我们无权透露这一信息。③The Puritans became fugitives in quest of liberty. 清教徒变成了追求自由的逃亡者。

【用法】at liberty to do sth 有权做……；有……自由；take liberties with sb/sth（尤指对书）任意窜改

【例句】①You are at liberty to say what you like. 你尽可畅所欲言。②The movie takes considerable liberties with the novel that it is based on. 影片对小说原著做了相当大的改动。

【辨析】freedom 指权利方面的自由，多用于个人言论、信仰、行动等方面；也指不受关押、奴役的自由状态。discretion 指面对某一情况时决定该如何处理的自由或权利。liberty 指生活方式不受政府或权威限制的自由，适用范围比较广泛；也指某方面的合法权利或不受关押、奴役的自由状态。

【例句】①What is your opinion about the rights and freedoms of citizens? 你是怎么看待公民的权利和自由的？②How to deal with these complaints is left to your discretion. 如何处理这些投诉由你斟酌决定。③He believes that everyone should fight for liberty and equality. 他认为每个人都应该为了自由和平等而奋斗。

license /ˈlaɪsns/ *n*. 许可证，执照；特许；*vt*. 同意；发许可证

【例句】The government revoked her husband's license to operate migrant labor crews. 政府撤销了她丈夫管理外来打工人群的许可证。

【用法】a driver's license 驾驶执照；a license holder 许可证持有人

lie /laɪ/ *v*. 躺；平躺；平卧；平放；处于，保留，保持（某种状态）；*n*. 谎言；位置；*v*. 说谎；撒谎；编造谎言

【例句】①Their vessel lay on the shore mirrored in a perfectly unmoving glossy sea. 他们的船停泊在岸边，映衬在一片波澜不惊的湛蓝海水之中。②He lied to his parents that he needed some money to buy some books. 他对父母撒谎说他需要一些钱用来买一些书。

【用法】lie about something 说关于……的谎话；lie to someone 对某人撒谎；tell a lie 撒谎

【辨析】lie 作动词，有"躺""撒谎"等之意。当 lie 有"躺"等之意时，其过去式和过去分词分别为 lay 和 lain；当 lie 有"撒谎"等之意时，其过去式和过去分词分别为 lied 和 lied。

limit /ˈlɪmɪt/ *n*. 限度；限制；极限；限量；限额；（地区或地方的）境界，界限，范围；*v*. 限制；限定；限量；减量

【例句】①In some cases there is a mini-mum age limit. 有些情况下有最低年龄限制。②They struggled to limit the cost by enforcing a low-tech specification. 他们通过实施低技术规格拼命限制成本。

【用法】limit sth to sb/sth 使（某事只在某地或某群体内）存在（或发生）；the sky's the limit 无穷尽；什么都可能；不可限量

【例句】①The teaching of history should not be limited to dates and figures. 教授历史不应该局限于讲年代和人物。②With a talent like his, the sky's the limit. 以他的禀赋，前途不可限量。

limitation /ˌlɪmɪˈteɪʃn/ *n*. 限制；局限；极限；起限制作用的规则（或事实、条件）

【例句】①This drug has one important limitation. Its effects only last six hours. 这种药有一个严重缺陷：它的药力只能持续 6 个小时。②There is to be no limitation on the number of opposition parties. 反对党的数量没有限制。③Parents are too likely to blame schools for the educational limitations of their children. 父母十之八九将子女的教育局限归咎于学校。

line /laɪn/ *n*. 线条；排；行列；界线；*vt*. 排队；用线标出；沿……排列成行；给……安衬里；*vi*. 形成一层；排队；击出平直球

【例句】①Big stores and fast food restaurants line the highway system. 公路系统沿线有大商店和快餐店。②Their first car rolls off the production line on December 16. 他们的第一辆车于 12 月 16 日下线。

【用法】along/down the line 在某一环节；在某一时刻；along/on（the）…lines 按……方式

【例句】①Somewhere along the line a large amount of money went missing. 有一笔巨款在某一环节上不翼而飞。②The new system will operate along the same lines as the old one. 新系统的运作方式将与老系统一样。

【辨析】line 普通用词，指人或物排成的行列；也指人、汽车等在等候时排成的队伍。file 指人站立或行走时排成的列。rank 与 line 基本同义，但多指士兵等排成的队列。

【例句】①There is a line of trees on either side of the road. 道路两旁树木成行。②The soldiers were walking in single file. 士兵们排成一列纵队前进。③On the shelves are rank after rank of liquor bottles. 架子上是一排排的酒瓶。

liner /ˈlaɪnər/ *n*. 邮轮，班轮，班机，衬垫，衬套；衬里；画线者

【例句】①It became impractical to make a business trip by ocean liner. 乘坐远洋班轮进行商务旅行变得不合时宜了。②Jumbo jets somehow lack the glamour of the transatlantic liner. 大型喷气式客机不像横渡大西洋的客轮那么引人注目。

literary /ˈlɪtəreri/ *adj*. 文学的；文学上的；适于文学作品的；有典型文学作品特征的

【例句】①Many literary academics simply parrot a set of impressive-sounding phrases. 许多文人只是机械地模仿一套听上去令人印象深刻的说法。②By the

1920's, he was lionized by literary London. 到了20世纪20年代，他成为伦敦文学界的宠儿。

literature /ˈlɪtrətʃər/ *n*. 文学；文学作品；文献；著作

【例句】Some companies have toned down the claims on their promotional literature. 一些公司已降低了宣传资料中标榜之词的调门。

【拓展】tragedy 悲剧；comedy 喜剧；drama 戏剧；fiction 小说；prose 散文；poetry 诗歌；ode 颂诗；ballad 民谣；epic 史诗

live /lɪv；laɪv/ *v*. 生存；居住；活着；留存；*adj*. 活的；现场直播的；带电的；实（弹）的；*adv*. 在现场直播；在现场表演；在现场录制

【例句】I clearly empathize with the people who live in those neighborhoods. 我非常同情生活在那些地方的人们。

【用法】live and breathe sth 热衷于（某事）；live and let live 自己活也让别人活；宽以待人；互相宽容

【例句】He just lives and breathes football. 他非常热衷于足球。

lively /ˈlaɪvli/ *adj*. 充满活力的；活泼的；充满趣味的；*adv*. 轻快地，富有活力地；轻快地跳起

【例句】①Their 4-1 win in Honduras was a particularly lively affair. 他们在洪都拉斯以4比1获胜的那场比赛尤其激动人心。②The papers also show a lively interest in European developments. 论文对欧洲的动向亦表现出浓厚的兴趣。

【用法】lively atmosphere 热烈的气氛；lively sense of humour 强烈的幽默感

【辨析】vivid 主要指梦境、记忆、描述等生动而逼真的，使人印象深刻或富于想象。lifelike 指图画、模型、刻画的人物等栩栩如生的，如同真实的景物或真人一般。lively 普通用词，指形象、描述等生动而逼真的，可与vivid换用。

【例句】①The book gives a vivid description of the seedy side of city life. 该书生动地描绘了城市生活的阴暗面。②These lifelike statues can only make one marvel. 这些惟妙惟肖的雕像实在令人叹为观止。③A lively/vivid image appeared in his mind. 一个逼真的形象出现在他的脑海里。

load /loʊd/ *n*. 负荷；负担；装载；工作量；*vt*. 使担负；装填；把……装入或装上；装满，堆积；*vi*. 加载；装载；装货

【例句】①His people came up with a load of embarrassing information. 他的部下亮出一大堆令人尴尬的资料来。②An efficient bulb may lighten the load of power stations. 一个节能灯泡也许就能减轻发电站的负荷。

【用法】get a load of sb/sth（用以让人）看，听；load the dice（against sb）使（某人）处于不利地位

【例句】①Get a load of that dress! 你瞧那件衣服！②He has always felt that the dice were loaded against him in life. 他总觉得自己一辈子都背运。

locate /ˈloʊkeɪt/ *vt*. 位于；说出来源；查找……的地点；确定……的位置；*vi*. 定位；定居

【例句】①Try to locate exactly where the smells are entering the room. 找找看气味具体是从什么地方散入房间的。②We've simply been unable to locate him. 我们就是没办法找到他。③Rescue teams are using thermal imaging to locate survivors of the earthquake. 救援队伍正利用热成像确定地震幸存者的位置。

location /loʊˈkeɪʃn/ *n*. 位置，场所；定位；外景（拍摄地）

【例句】①The first duty of a director is to recce his location. 主管的第一项任务是熟悉所在地区的情况。②It has taken until now to pin down its exact location. 直到现在才确定了它的准确位置。

【用法】present location 当前位置；specific location 具体位置

lodge /lɑːdʒ/ *vi*. 存放；暂住；埋入；（权利、权威等）归属；*vt*. 提出（报告、要求、申诉等）；容纳；寄存；把（权利、权威等）授予；*n*. <古>小屋，草屋；（北美印第安人的）锥形棚屋；（森林、猎场等的）看守小屋；（学校、工厂等的）传达室

【例句】①Authorities requisitioned hotel rooms to lodge more than 3,000 stranded Christmas vacationers. 当局征用旅馆房间安顿了 3,000 多名无处落脚的圣诞度假者。②I drove out of the gates, past the keeper's lodge. 我驶出大门，经过守门人的小屋。③My father would occasionally go to his Masonic lodge. 我爸爸

偶尔会到他的共济会分会那里去。

【用法】ski lodge 滑雪度假屋

long /lɔːŋ/ *adj*. 长的；长久的；冗长的；*adv*. 长久地；遥远地；*n*. 长时间，长时期；[语] 长音节；（服装的）长尺寸；长裤；*vi*. 渴望（to, for）

【例句】①I have not read such a good novel for a long time. 我很久没有读过这么好的小说了。②Everyone longs to succeed in life and career. 每个人都渴望在生活和事业上取得成功。

look /luk/ *vt. & vi*. 看，瞧；*vi*. 注意；面向；寻找；看起来好像；*n*. 看；（尤指吸引人的）相貌；眼神；样子；*int*.（插话或唤起注意）喂，听我说

【例句】①It was just then that I chanced to look round. 就在那时，我恰好环顾了下四周。②She had the look of someone deserted and betrayed. 她一副遭人遗弃和背叛的样子。

loose /luːs/ *adj*. 松的；散漫的；*vt*. 释放；松开；射出（子弹、箭等）*vi*. 变得松散；开火；*adv*. 散漫地；*n*. 放任；发射

【例句】Some children played in the seaside and gathered loose sand and let it filter slowly through their fingers. 有些孩子在海边玩耍，捧起疏松的沙子，让其慢慢地从指缝中流过。

【用法】hang/stay loose 保持镇静；不着急；break/cut/tear (sb/sth) loose from sb/sth（使）摆脱，挣脱

【例句】①It's OK—hang loose and stay cool. 没事儿，你要镇定，要冷静。②The organization broke loose from its sponsors. 那家机构摆脱了赞助商。

lose /luːz/ *vt*. 失去；错过；遗失；耽搁；*vi*. 损失；输掉；走慢；降低价值

【例句】①Some battles you win, some battles you lose. 胜败乃兵家常事。②He appealed to his countrymen not to lose heart. 他呼吁自己的同胞不要丧失信心。

loss /lɔːs/ *n*. 损失，减少；丢失，遗失；损耗，亏损；失败

【例句】①Slimming snacks that offer miraculous weight loss are a con. 有神奇减肥效果的瘦身点心是一个骗局。②He always wakes with a sense of deep sorrow

125

and depressing loss. 他醒来时总是满怀哀愁，抑郁惆怅。

【用法】at a loss 不知所措；困惑；cut your losses 不成功就住手（免得情况更糟）；趁早罢手

【例句】His comments left me at a loss for words. 他的评论让我不知说什么才好。

lot /lɑːt/ *n*. 份额；许多；命运；阄；*adv*.（与形容词和副词连用）很，非常；（与动词连用）非常；*pron*. 大量，许多；*vt*. 分组，把……划分（常与 out 连用）；把（土地）划分成块；*vi*. 抽签，拈阄

【例句】①I got quite a lot of ribbing from my teammates. 队友们经常开我的玩笑。②Do you sweat a lot or flush a lot? 你常出汗或是脸上常发烫吗?

loyalty /ˈlɔɪəlti/ *n*. 忠诚，忠实；忠心；忠于……感情

【例句】①There were too many other demands on his loyalty now. 现在有太多其他的事情也要求他忠心。②In his diary of 1944 he proclaims unswerving loyalty to the monarchy. 他在1944年的日记里声称对君主忠贞不贰。

lump /lʌmp/ *n*. 块，团；肿块；许多，大量；笨拙的人；*vi*. 结成块；成团；笨重地行走；*vt*. 使成团，使成块；使团结在一起；把……混在一起；*adj*. 成团的，成块的；*adv*. 很，非常

【例句】We used to buy five kilos of mutton in one lump, but now we seldom do it. 我们过去常买5公斤重的整块羊肉，但现在很少这样做了。

【用法】lump it（因别无选择而）勉强接受，将就，勉为其难

【例句】That's the situation—like it or lump it! 情况就是这样——不管你高兴还是不高兴!

luxury /ˈlʌkʃəri/ *n*. 奢侈，豪华；奢侈品，美食，华服；乐趣，享受；不常有的乐趣（或享受、优势）；*adj*. 奢华的，豪华的

【例句】①We don't live in the lap of luxury, but we're comfortable. 我们的生活虽然并非锦衣玉食，也算是衣食无忧。②He rode on the president's luxury train through his own state. 他乘坐总统的豪华列车经过自己所在的州。

【用法】in the lap of luxury 生活优裕；养尊处优

5.2　M

migrant /ˈmaɪgrənt/ *n*. 移民，移居者；候鸟，迁徙动物；*adj*. 有迁徙习性的，迁移的

【例句】①The migrants from the rural areas make great contributions to the development of the city. 农民工为城市的发展做出了巨大的贡献。②Thousands of migrants looked for shelter in the woods. 大量的动物在森林里寻找避难所。③Thanks to an anonymous donor, the school for children of migrant workers was able to purchase some blackboards, a table-tennis table and a computer. 多亏了一位匿名捐赠者，这个打工子弟学校能够购买一些黑板、一张乒乓球桌和一台电脑。

【拓展】migrate *v*. 迁徙，移居；immigrant *n*. 移民

mingle /ˈmɪŋgl/ *v*. 使混合；应酬，交往

【例句】①The oil will float on water if you mingle the two. 混合以后，油会浮在水面上。②Tom often gets out and mingles with friends. 汤姆经常出去应酬。

【用法】mingle with 使混合

【例句】The princess mingled with the parade and disappeared all of a sudden. 公主混进了游行的队伍中，一转眼就不见了。

miniature /ˈmɪnətʃər/ *adj*. 微型的，小型的；*n*. 微型画，微小模型

【例句】①China Post issued a set of four stamps and a miniature sheet on Saturday to mark the Forbidden City's completion's 600th anniversary. 为纪念紫禁城建成600周年，中国邮政发行特种邮票一套4枚，小型张1枚。②He demonstrated to me the miniature of the new apartment. 他向我展示了新公寓的模型。

【辨析】small、tiny、minute、miniature 都表示"小的"。small 指体积、数量、价值等的小，略低于正常大小；tiny 强调和同类相比，小的超出正常比例，多带有较强烈的感情色彩；minute 指非常细小，仅仅通过显微镜才能看得见；miniature 指正常物体体积缩小的物体。

【例句】①He drank only a small amount of milk. 他仅喝了少量的牛奶。

②Look at the baby! It is so tiny and cute! 看看小宝贝，它是多么娇小可爱啊！
③The water contains the minute amounts of chemicals. 水中含有极少的化学成分。
④The film is a miniature version of the book. 这部电影是书的缩编版。

minimize /ˈmɪnɪmaɪz/ *v*. 使最小化

【例句】Generosity means to maximize others' benefits and minimize the self-interest. 慷慨指对别人的利益最大化，对自己的利益最小化。

【拓展】minimum *adj*. 最小的；*n*. 最小值，最低限度

【反义词】maximize *v*. 最大化，达到最大值

minor /ˈmaɪnər/ *adj*. 较小的，未成年的；*v*. 辅修；*n*. 未成年人

【例句】①He made a minor mistake. 他犯了一个小错误。②Selling wines to minors is illegal in some countries. 在某些国家，给未成年人卖酒是违法的。③I minor in law at college. 在大学我辅修法律。

【辨析】underage 和 minor 都表示"未成年"。underage 是形容词，表示"未到法定年龄的"；而 minor 是名词，与 adult 相对，指未成年人。

【例句】①Underage drinking is illegal in America. 在美国给未成年人喝酒是非法的。②Cigarette sales to minors are not allowed. 禁止向未成年人销售香烟。

【拓展】minority *n*. 少数民族

miracle /ˈmɪrəkl/ *n*. 令人惊奇的人，奇迹

【例句】His survival in the war is a medical miracle. 他能在战争中存活下来是个医学奇迹。

【用法】work/accomplish miracles 产生奇迹；miracle play 奇迹剧；miracle drug 特效药

【例句】①Love could work miracles. 爱能创造奇迹。②After thousands of testing, the miracle drug has come into effect. 经历了上千次的测试，这种特效药终于起作用了。

【拓展】miraculous *adj*. 不可思议的，令人惊奇的

mischief /ˈmɪstʃɪf/ *n*. 恶作剧；麻烦的根源

【例句】①Tom's mischief was troublesome to his mother. 妈妈很头疼汤姆的

恶作剧。②Locusts are a great mischief to the farmer. 对农民而言，蝗虫是大祸。

【拓展】mischievous *adj*. 淘气的；有害的

miserable /ˈmɪzrəbl/ *adj*. 可怜的，悲惨的；令人不快的

【例句】①What a miserable person she was when she paid fifteen years off all the debts for a fake necklace. 她花了15年的时间还清了所欠项链的钱，却得知项链是假的，多么可悲啊！②What a miserable day! 真是令人不快的一天！

【拓展】misery *n*. 痛苦

misfortune /ˌmɪsˈfɔːrtʃuːn/ *n*. 不幸；灾祸

【例句】①I felt more than ordinary human sympathy for him in his misfortune. I was deeply moved as a fellow sufferer. 我对他的遭遇不只是一般的同情，还有一种深切的同病相怜的感触。②Jane faced her misfortune bravely. 简勇敢地面对遭受的灾难。

【拓展】misfortunate *adj*. 不幸的

【辨析】disaster、catastrophe、misfortune 都表示"不幸""灾难"。disaster 指普通用词，指大灾难、痛苦或伤亡。catastrophe 语气最强，指可怕的灾难，强调最终的结局。misfortune 普通用词，多指较为严重的不幸，强调不幸多由外界因素所致。

【例句】①Ten people died in the air disaster. 十人在空难中丧生。②Being unemployed is a catastrophe for her. 失去工作对她来说是场灾难。③Don't gloat over others' misfortune. 不要对别人的不幸幸灾乐祸。

mislead /ˌmɪsˈliːd/ *v*. 误导

【例句】Yet some anti-China elements in the US are abusing the concept of "national security" to mislead the American people in an attempt to cause irreversible damage to China-US relations. 美国一些反华势力滥用"国家安全"概念，刻意误导美国民众，企图给两国关系造成不可逆的破坏。

【拓展】misleading *adj*. 误导的，引入歧途的

mission /ˈmɪʃn/ *n*. 任务；使命；代表团；派遣，向……传教

【例句】①He is proud to accomplish the mission impossible. 他完成了不可能完成的任务，感到很自豪。②We received a trade mission from South America.

我们接待了来自南非的贸易代表团。③Teachers' mission is to impart knowledge to students. 教师的天职是向学生传授知识。

【拓展】missionary *n*. 传教士

mobile /ˈmoʊbl/ *adj*. 可移动的；流动的；腿脚方便的

【例句】①Nowadays nearly every college student is equipped with a mobile phone. 当今大学生几乎人人拥有一部手机。②The door is especially designed for the people who are less mobile. 这扇门是专门为行动不便的人设计的。③The theatre has 300 mobile seats. 剧场拥有300个活动座位。

【拓展】mobilize *v*. 动员；mobility *n*. 流动性，易变性

moderate /ˈmɑːdəreɪt/ *adj*. 适度的，有节制的；温和的，稳健的

【例句】①Prices in the region are fairly moderate. 这个地区的价格很公道。②Qingdao has a moderate climate. 青岛气候温和。

modesty /ˈmɑːdɪstɪ/ *n*. 谦虚

【例句】Modesty pushes one forward whereas conceit makes one lag behind. 谦虚使人进步，骄傲使人落后。

【拓展】modest *adj*. 谦虚；（妇女的）端庄

【反义词】immodest *adj*. 不谦虚的

modify /ˈmɑːdɪfaɪ/ *v*. 修改；减轻，缓和；（语法）修饰

【例句】①Your essay needs to be modified in order to achieve coherence. 你的论文需要在连贯性方面进行修改。②Watch out! You'd better modify your tone of language. 小心！请注意改正你说话的语气。③The word "who" usually modifies a person in the English sentence. 英语句子里"who"一般来修饰人物。

【辨析】modify、alter、transform 都表示"改变"。modify 强调起限定作用的变化或变更，指细小的变化，常含"缓和、降调"的意味。alter 常指轻微的改变，强调基本上保持原物、原状的情况下所进行的部分改变。transform 指人或物在形状、外观、形式、性质等方面发生的彻底变化，失去原状成为全新的东西。

【例句】①The author decided to modify the ending of the play upon the audience's request. 经观众要求，作者打算修改戏剧的结局。②The oversized clothes need to be altered to be put on. 过大的衣服改了才能穿。③A cocoon will finally be transformed to a butterfly. 破茧成蝶。

【拓展】modification *n*. 修改，修正；改变

momentous /moʊˈmentəs/*adj*. 重要的，重大的

【例句】The founding of the People's Republic of China is a momentous event in Chinese history. 中华人民共和国的成立是中国历史上的重大事件。

【近义词】crucial；significant；vital

monopoly /məˈnɑːpəli/*n*. 垄断；专卖；专利品，专卖品

【例句】①The State Administration for Market Regulation recently unveiled proposals that include guidelines on how anti-monopoly measures should be applied to Internet companies. 国家市场监管总局近日发布一份反垄断指南，其中包含了针对互联网企业的反垄断措施。②The company has a monopoly on the mineral resources in the market. 那家公司控制了市场上的矿石专卖权。③Tobacco is a national monopoly in most of the regions. 在很多地区，国家实行烟草专卖。

mortal /ˈmɔːrtl/*adj*. 必死的；致命的

【例句】①Everyone is mortal. It is the natural law. 每个人是必死的，这是大自然的规律。②He died of the mortal wound. 他死于致命伤。

【近义词】lethal

【反义词】immortal

mortgage /ˈmɔːrɡɪdʒ/*n*. 抵押；*v*. 抵押，以某人的前途做代价

【例句】①Paying off the housing mortgage loan disrupted their plan for travelling. 还房贷打乱了他们出去旅游的计划。②He had to mortgage the house in order to open a new company. 为了开公司，他不得不将房子抵押。

motivate /ˈmoʊtɪveɪt/*v*. 激励，激发

【例句】A good teacher should know how to motivate students to work harder. 好老师应该懂得如何激励学生努力学习。

【拓展】motivation *n*. 动机；积极性

multiply /ˈmʌltɪplaɪ/*v*. 乘法；大大增加；繁殖

【例句】①If you multiply two and three, you'll get six. 2 和 3 相乘等于 6。②

Due to the improper measures of protection, the infected patients multiplied during the past few weeks. 由于不恰当的防护措施，感染的病人数量大大增加了。③Rabbits are easy to raise and multiply quickly. 兔子好养，繁殖力强。

【用法】multiply by 乘以

【例句】Two multiplied by three equals to six. 2 乘以 3 等于 6。

multitude /ˈmʌltɪtuːd/ *n*. 大量；群众

【例句】①A multitude of birds flocked southwards to spend the cold winter. 大量的鸟儿南飞过冬。②The singer was surrounded by a noisy multitude. 歌星被喧闹的人群包围了。

【用法】a multitude of 大量，许多

【例句】A multitude of factors can account for the situation. 许多因素可以解释这个情形的出现。

mutual /ˈmjuːtʃuəl/ *adj*. 相互的；共同的，共有的

【例句】①Friendship should be established on the basis of mutual respect and mutual trust. 朋友应该建立在互相尊重、相互信赖的基础上。②The couple set up a harmonious relationship with mutual interests. 因为拥有共同的兴趣，这对夫妻相处融洽。

【近义词】joint; reciprocal; common

【拓展】mutually *adv*. 相互地；mutuality *n*. 相互关系，相关

mysterious /mɪˈstɪriəs/ *adj*. 神秘的；难以理解的

【例句】①The mysterious woman disappeared in the darkness. 那个神秘的女人消失在黑暗中。②His death is still a mysterious puzzle to us. 他的死对我们来说是个谜。

【拓展】mystery *n*. 不可思议的事物，秘密

5.3 N

negative /ˈneɡətɪv/ *adj*. 坏的，有害的；否定的；消极的；负的

【例句】①The pandemic disease had a negative effect on the economy. 流行病对经济发展带来了不利的影响。②He got a negative reply to his proposals. 他的提议被否定了。③The color gray symbolizes negative moods like sadness, fear and disappointment. 灰色象征了消极的情绪, 如悲伤、恐惧和失望。

neglect /nɪˈglekt/ *v.* 忽略, 忽视; 忘记做

【例句】①Don't neglect your studies at college. 大学中千万不要荒废学业。②Mike neglected to write a "thank-you" note to the host. 迈克忘了给主人写便条表示感谢。

【辨析】ignore、neglect、overlook 都表示"忽略"。ignore 指有意识地拒绝, neglect 指无意识地忽视或忘记, overlook 既可以指有意识地遗漏, 也可以指无意识地忽略。

【例句】①She greeted him with a smile but was totally ignored. 她和他打了招呼, 却被忽略了。②I neglected to lock the door. 我忘了锁门。③We should not overlook the warning signals from our brains. 我们不应忽视大脑给我们的警告。

【用法】neglect doing 忘记干某事

【例句】Don't neglect turning off the mobile phone before you go to bed. 睡觉前别忘了关手机。

negotiate /nɪˈgoʊʃieɪt/ *v.* 谈判, 交涉

【例句】The two parties decided to sit down and negotiate about the price. 双方决定坐下来, 就价格进行谈判。

【拓展】negotiate *v.* →negotiator *n.* →negotiation *n.*

nevertheless /ˌnevərðəˈles/ *adv.* 然而, 不过, 尽管如此

【例句】Don't push him so severely. Nevertheless, he is only a small child. 别对他太严厉了, 他还是个孩子。

【近义词】though; whereas; while

nominate /ˈnɑːmɪneɪ/ *v.* 提名; 任命

【例句】①Biden was nominated for the American president. 拜登被提名为美国总统。②The president nominated him to be the US surgeon general. 总统任命他

为美国卫生局局长。

【拓展】nomination *n*. 提名，任命

nonetheless /ˌnʌnðəˈles/ *adv*. 尽管如此，但是

【例句】Deforestation has hit particularly hard sub-Saharan Africa and southeast Asia, where it has accelerated in the last decade, but also Latin and Central America, where it has nonetheless slowed down. 森林砍伐对撒哈拉以南非洲和东南亚的影响尤为严重。在过去十年间，这些地区的森林砍伐速度有所加快，但拉丁美洲和中美洲的森林砍伐速度却有所放缓。

nostalgic /nəˈstældʒɪk/ *adj*. 怀旧的，乡愁的

【例句】The nostalgic photos remind me of my childhood. 怀旧相片让我想起了童年时代。

【近义词】homesick

notable /ˈnoʊtəbl/ *adj*. 显著的，值得注意的；*n*. 名人

【例句】①There has been a notable decline in sales in recent months. 最近几个月销售量出现下滑，值得注意。②The notables attending the conference include three Senators and five State Governors. 参加会议的名人包括三名参议员和五名州长。

【拓展】notable *adj*. →notably *adv*. →notability *n*.

【近义词】personality; celebrity

notion /ˈnoʊʃn/ *n*. 概念，想法；观念

【例句】①The country claims to be established on the notion of freedom and equality. 这个国家声称是建立在自由和平等基础上的。②Some stubborn notions on women should be abandoned. 关于妇女的根深蒂固的旧观念需要被抛弃。

notorious /noʊˈtɔːriəs/ *adj*. 臭名昭著的

【例句】Manhattan used to be regarded as a notorious place for drugs and violence. 曼哈顿过去被认为是以毒品和暴力而声名狼藉的地区。

【近义词】infamous; disreputable

nourish /ˈnɜːrɪʃ/ *v*. 养育；提供养分；怀有情绪

【例句】①She felt a sense of happiness to nourishing two kids. 养育两个孩

子，她感到很幸福。②Reading can nourish our mind. 阅读给心灵提供给养。③They still nourished the hope in face of difficulties. 面对困难，他们仍然满怀希望。

【拓展】nourishment *n.*

novel /ˈnɑːvl/ *n.* 小说；*adj.* 新的

【例句】①My favorite novel is *Jane Eyre*. 我最喜欢的小说是《简·爱》。②The teacher is often inspired by students' novel ideas. 学生的新观点常常让老师深受启发。

【拓展】novelty *n.* 新颖，新奇

【例句】In the contemporary Western world, rapidly changing styles cater to a desire for novelty and individualism. 现代西方社会，不断变化的生活方式满足了人们追求新奇和个性的需要。

nowhere /ˈnoʊwer/ *adv.* 无处；*n.* 无名之地；*adj.* 不存在的，不知名的

【例句】①These non-scientific data will lead you nowhere. 不科学的数据让你得不到想要的结果。② Pursuing unilateralism, protectionism and extreme egoism leads nowhere. 任何单边主义、保护主义、极端利己主义，都是根本行不通的。③The children were nowhere in sight but the parents still watched them off. 孩子们已经走远看不见了，父母却仍然在目送着他们。

numerous /ˈnuːmərəs/ *adj.* 极多的

【例句】Numerous friends came to congratulate her at the wedding. 结婚的时候很多朋友过来祝福她。

6 O, P

6.1 O

order /ˈɔːrdər/ *n.* 次序，顺序；整齐；（社会）治安，秩序；[常 pl.] 命令；订货（单），订购；规则；*v.* 命令，指令；命令去……；订购（制）；安排；整理

【用法】fill an order 供应订货；in order 整整齐齐；情况正常；get out of order 损坏，出故障

【例句】①Please order for me. 请替我点菜。②They ordered everyone out of the house. 他们命令所有人离开房子。③The children lined up in order of height. 孩子们按身高排队。

organization /ˌɔːrɡənəˈzeɪʃn/ *n.* 组织，机构，团体；编制，安排

【用法】World Trade Organization 世贸组织；join the organization 加入该组织

【例句】①The public expect high standards from any large organization. 公众希望任何大型组织都能达到高标准。②Putting on a show of this kind involves considerable organization. 举办这样的演出需要相当多的组织筹备。③The new president plans to make changes to the company's organization. 新总裁计划对公司的组织进行变革。

oriental /ˌɔːriˈentl/ *adj.* 东方的；从东方来的，东方国家的；东方人特有

的；东方式的；*n*. 东亚人，东方人

【例句】①Do you like oriental art? 你喜欢东方艺术吗？②He has a beautiful oriental rug. 他有一块漂亮的来自东方的地毯。

【用法】oriental blood 东方血统；oriental pearl 东方之珠

【拓展】orientalist *n*. 东方通，东方学专家

orientation /ˌɔːriənˈteɪʃn/ *n*. 方向，定位；态度，取向

【例句】①The company has a new eco-friendly orientation. 公司有一个新的环保定位。②We employ people without regard to their political or sexual orientation. 我们雇用的人不考虑他们的政治或性取向。③The building has an east-west orientation. 这座大楼是东西向的。

【用法】the religious orientation 宗教倾向；a two-week orientation course 为期两周的新生训练课程

original /əˈrɪdʒənl/ *adj*. 原来的；独创的；*n*. 原件；原著

【用法】an original version 原来的版本；original design 原创设计；original sin 原罪

【例句】①The land was returned to its original owner. 这片土地已归还原主。②It's a highly original design. 这是一个高度原创的设计。③The original painting is now in the National Gallery in London. 这幅原画现在在伦敦国家美术馆展出。④The colours are much more striking in the original. 原版的颜色更加醒目。

【拓展】original *adj*. →unoriginal（反义词）→originally *adv*.

originate /əˈrɪdʒɪneɪt/ *v*. 起源；首创

【例句】①A lot of our medicines originate from tropical plants. 我们的许多药物来自热带植物。②Many Christmas traditions originated in Germany. 许多圣诞节传统起源于德国。

otherwise /ˈʌðərwaɪz/ *adv*. 不同地；*adj*. 另外的；*conj*. 不然，如果不

【例句】①Finally he chose a path otherwise. 最终他选择了不同的道路。②If this can't work out, take the way otherwise. 这个方法如果行不通，可以试试其他的方法。③Recite the English words frequently, otherwise they will be easily forgotten. 要经常记忆单词，否则单词很容易遗忘。

outcome /ˈaʊtkʌm/ *n.* 结果；后果，结局

【例句】①It was impossible to predict the outcome of the election. 无法预测选举结果。②People who had heard the evidence at the trial were surprised at the outcome. 在审判中听到证据的人对结果感到惊讶。

outlook /ˈaʊtlʊk/ *n.* 观点，看法；前途，前景

【用法】the outlook for...某行业的前景；in outlook 人生观

【例句】①The economic outlook is bleak. 经济前景黯淡。②Tomorrow's outlook is for rain in the morning, clearing up in the afternoon. 明天的天气是早上下雨，下午放晴。③He has a fairly positive outlook on life. 他的人生观相当乐观。

outset /ˈaʊtset/ *n.* 开始，开端

【用法】from/at the outset of...从……开始

【例句】①There have been problems with the project from the outset. 这个项目从一开始就有问题。②I told him at the outset I wasn't interested. 一开始我就告诉他我不感兴趣。③From its very outset, the company has produced the highest quality products. 从一开始，公司就生产出最优质的产品。

overcome /ˌoʊvərˈkʌm/ *v.* 被压倒；克服；打败

【用法】be overcome by 被打败；be overcome with 被压倒

【例句】①Overcome by emotion, she found herself unable to speak for a few minutes. 她激动得说不出话来。②In fact, shyness is difficult to overcome. 事实上，害羞很难克服。③They overcame the enemy. 他们战胜了敌人。

overflow /ˌoʊvərˈfloʊ/ *v.* 溢出，充满着；/ˈoʊvərfloʊ/ *n.* 泛滥，容纳不了的东西

【用法】be overflowed with 充满着；an overflow of...过多的

【例句】①The garden overflows with color. 花园里五彩缤纷。②My heart was overflowing with gratitude. 我的心充满了感激。

overlook /ˌoʊvərˈlʊk/ *v.* 眺望，俯瞰；监督；忽视

【用法】overlook the vital facts 忽略重要事实；overlook from...极目远眺

【例句】①Our room overlooks the ocean. 我们的房间可以俯瞰大海。②She found him entertaining enough to overlook his faults. 她发现他很有趣，可以忽略

他的缺点。

overnight /ˌoʊvərˈnaɪt/ *adv*. 昨晚；通宵，从夜晚到天亮；/ˈoʊvərnaɪt/ *adj*. 昨晚的，昨夜的；通夜的

【用法】overnight stay 留宿一晚；overnight mail 次日送达的邮件

【例句】①Pam's staying overnight at my house. 帕姆在我家过夜。②During the gold rush, many people flocked to San Francisco make a fortune overnight there. 淘金热期间，许多人蜂拥到旧金山，一夜之间就发了财。③Don't forget to pack an overnight bag. 别忘了带个过夜包。④She became a star overnight. 她一夜之间成了明星。

overpass /ˈoʊvərpæs/ *n*. 立交桥，天桥，高架道路

【例句】A train was going by on the overpass. 一列火车正在天桥上经过。

override /ˌoʊvərˈraɪd/ *v*. 否定，推翻，撤销；优先于

【用法】override the objections 不顾反对

【例句】①Parents' concern for their children's future often overrides all their other concerns. 父母对孩子未来的关心往往压倒了他们所有其他的关心。②The needs of the mother should not override the needs of the child. 母亲的需要不应凌驾于孩子的需要之上。③The rights of the individual were being flagrantly overridden. 个人的权利被公然推翻。

overseas /ˌoʊvərˈsiːz/ *adj*. 国外的；*adv*. 在海外

【用法】overseas Chinese 华侨；an overseas training 海外培训

【例句】①We need to open up overseas markets. 我们需要开拓海外市场。②Many more people go overseas these days. 如今，出国的人更多了。

overtake /ˌoʊvərˈteɪk/ *v*. 超过；越过；赶上

【用法】be overtaken by 被超越，被袭击；be overtaken with 被击垮

【例句】①Never try to overtake on a bend. 不要试图在弯道上超车。②Television soon overtook the cinema as the most popular form of entertainment. 电视很快就取代电影成为最受欢迎的娱乐形式。③A terrible sense of panic overtook him. 他突然感到一阵可怕的恐慌。

overthrow /ˌoʊvərˈθroʊ/ *v*. 击倒对手；推翻（政权等）；/ˈoʊvərθroʊ/ *n*. 被

打倒，使屈服等

【例句】①Rebels were already making plans to overthrow the government. 叛军已经计划推翻政府。②A small group of military officers overthrew the President in September. 在9月，一小群军官推翻了总统。

overwhelm /ˌoʊvərˈwelm/ *v*. 压倒；推翻；覆盖，淹没

【用法】be overwhelmed by 极度，使不知所措

【拓展】overwhelming *adj*. 无法抗拒的，压倒一切的；overwhelmed *adv*. 被打败的，不知所措的

【例句】①Harriet was overwhelmed by a feeling of homesickness. 哈里特难以承受思乡之情。②They would be overwhelmed with paperwork. 他们会被文书工作压得喘不过气来。③You are looking a little overwhelmed. 你看起来有点不知所措。

overwhelming /ˌoʊvərˈwelmɪŋ/ *adj*. 极强烈的，势不可挡的；（数量）巨大的，压倒性的

【例句】①She felt an overwhelming desire to hit him. 她强烈地想揍他。②It's an overwhelming task. 这是一项艰巨的任务。

owe /oʊ/ *v*. 欠（钱，账）；应归给，应归功于；欠（情），感激

【例句】①I owe my brother $50. 我欠我哥哥50美元。②I owe my success to my education. 我的成功归功于我的教育。③We owe our great achievements to the wise leadership of the Communist Party. 我们所取得的伟大成就归功于共产党的英明领导。④"I owe my parents a lot," he admitted. "我欠我父母很多，"他承认。

owing /ˈoʊɪŋ/ *adj*. 该付的，欠着的；有负于，受恩于；应归功于

【用法】owing to 由于

【例句】①You need to pay the amount owing, plus the interest. 你需要支付欠款，加上利息。②Most of the money has been repaid but there is still 5 owing. 大部分的钱已经还清了，但是还有5英镑的欠款。

own /oʊn/ *adj*. 自己的，独有的；*v*. 拥有

【用法】on one's own 独自；of one's own 凭借自身的力量

【例句】①Bring your own equipment. 带上你自己的装备。②I'd like to have a place of my own. 我想有一个属于我自己的地方。③You need to get permission from the farmer who owns the land. 你需要得到拥有这片土地的农民的许可。

6.2 P

principal /ˈprɪnsəpl/ *adj.* 主要的，首要的，最重要的；*n.* 负责人，首长，校长；本金，资本

【例句】①His principal reason for making the journey was to visit his family. 他这次旅行的主要原因是去看望他的家人。②Teaching is her principal source of income. 教学是她的主要收入来源。③It's a small school with just three teachers and the principal. 这是一所只有三个老师和校长的小学校。④She lives off the interest and tries to keep the principal intact. 她靠利息过活，尽量保持本金不动。

【拓展】principally *adv.* 主要（地）

principle /ˈprɪnsəpl/ *n.* 法则，原则，原理；道德，准则

【用法】in principle 原则上；on a matter of principle 因原则问题；follow the in principle 遵循原则

【例句】①The general principle is that education should be available to all children up to the age of 16. 一般原则是，所有16岁以下的儿童都应接受教育。②In principle I agree with the idea, but in practice it's not always possible. 原则上我同意这个想法，但实际上并不总是可能的。③On principle, I never eat meat. 原则上，我从不吃肉。

【拓展】principled *adj.* 有原则的，按原则的

prior /ˈpraɪər/ *adj.* 在前的；优先的

【用法】prior to 在……之前

【例句】①His immediate family has a prior claim to the inheritance. 他的直系亲属有优先继承遗产权。②Make sure all revisions are approved by the author prior to publication. 确保所有的修订在出版前都得到作者的批准。

priority /praɪˈɔːrəti/ *n.* 先，前，优先，优先权，优先考虑的事

【用法】give priority to 优先考虑；priority over sb/sth 比……优先；top priority 最先发展的事物

【例句】①The children are our first priority. 孩子们是我们的第一要务。②Banks normally give priority to large businesses when deciding on loans. 银行在决定贷款时通常优先考虑大企业。③Buses should have priority over other road users. 公共汽车应优先于其他道路使用者。

privilege /ˈprɪvəlɪdʒ/ *n.* 特权；荣幸；特别待遇；*vt.* 给予……特权，给予……优待

【例句】①He lives a life of privilege. 他过着特权的生活。②It is a privilege to hear her play. 很荣幸听到她的演奏。③The leaders were often more concerned with status and privilege than with the problems of the people. 领导人往往更关心地位和特权，而不是人民的问题。

professor /prəˈfesər/ *n.*（英国大学的）教授；（美国或加拿大的）大学教师，学院教师

【用法】the professor of …（某领域的）教授

【例句】①She's been named the professor of economics. 她被任命为经济学教授。②She's a professor of nutrition at Columbia University. 她是哥伦比亚大学的营养学教授。③Ted's a college professor. 泰德是大学讲师。

proficiency /prəˈfɪʃnsi/ *n.* 熟练，精通，熟练程度

【例句】①Once children have achieved a certain proficiency as a reader, they prefer to read silently. 一旦孩子们达到一定的阅读能力，他们就更喜欢安静地阅读。②Candidates must be able to demonstrate a high level of proficiency in both languages. 应聘者必须能够表现出对这两种语言的高度熟练程度。③He acquired proficiency at golf through long hours of practice. 他通过长时间的练习熟练地打高尔夫球。

profile /ˈproʊfaɪl/ *n.* 侧面像，轮廓；简介；*vt.* 描述轮廓；写传记

【例句】①Danil has a lovely profile. 达尼的侧面很可爱。②Do you have a job profile? 你有工作简介吗？②The star has a high profile in Britain. 这位明星

在英国有很高的知名度。③Apple kept a low profile for the first few days of the conference, making no major announcements or product introductions. 苹果在会议的头几天保持低调,没有发布重要的公告或产品介绍。④The new Chief Executive was profiled in yesterday's newspaper. 昨天的报纸刊登了新任首席执行官的简介。

profit /ˈprɑːfɪt/ *n*. 利润,好处; *v*. (使) 获益

【用法】gross profits 毛利; net profits 纯利润; make profits 获利; profit from 从中获利

【例句】①The shop's daily profit is usually around ＄600. 这家商店的日利润通常在 600 美元左右。②They were only interested in a quick profit. 他们只对快速获利感兴趣。③There's no profit in letting meetings drag on. 让会议拖下去是没有好处的。④It might profit you to learn about the company before your interview. 在面试前了解公司的情况可能对你有好处。

【拓展】profit *n*. →profitable *adj*. 有用处的,获益的→profitably *adv*. 有利地→profitability *n*. 盈利,收益

progressive /prəˈgresɪv/ *adj*. 进步的;进行中的;进行时态; *n*. 进步分子

【例句】①The left of the party is pressing for a more progressive social policy. 该党的左派正迫切要求一项更进步的社会政策。②We are currently witnessing a progressive decline in the number of students entering higher education. 我们目前正目睹进入高等教育的学生人数逐渐减少。③"I was watching TV when the phone rang" is an example of the past progressive. "电话铃响的时候我正在看电视"就是过去进行时的一个例子。

prolong /prəˈlɔːŋ/ *vt*. 延长,拖延

【例句】①The issue divided the country and prolonged the civil war. 这个问题使这个国家分裂,延长了内战的时间。②I was trying to think of some way to prolong the conversation. 我在想办法延长谈话时间。

prominent /ˈprɑːmɪnənt/ *adj*. 著名的,重要的;显著的,突出的;凸出的

【例句】①The World Cup will have a prominent place on the agenda. 世界杯将在议程上占有重要地位。②The statue was in a prominent position outside the railway station. 这座雕像在火车站外的一个显眼的位置。③He has a prominent nose. 他有一个突出的鼻子。

promise /ˈprɑːmɪs/ *v.* 允诺，答应；大有……的可能，有希望；*n.* 承诺，诺言；希望，出息

【用法】keep the promise 履行诺言；break the promise 未能实现诺言

【例句】①Last night the headmaster promised a full investigation. 昨晚校长承诺要进行全面调查。②Hurry up. And we promised we wouldn't be late. 快点。我们答应过不会迟到的。③It promises to be a really exciting game. 这肯定会是一场非常精彩的比赛。④He would never break his promise to his father. 他永远不会违背对父亲的诺言。⑤He is a young man full of promise. 他是一个充满希望的年轻人。

【拓展】promise *v.* → promising *adj.*

promising /ˈprɑːmɪsɪŋ/ *adj.* 有出息的，有前途的，前景很好的

【例句】①Jonathan is one of our most promising employees. 乔纳森是我们最有前途的雇员之一。②The weather outlook for the weekend isn't very promising. 周末的天气预报不太乐观。

promote /prəˈmoʊt/ *vt.* 推动，促进；营销；提升，发展

【例句】①Fertilizer promotes leaf growth. 肥料促进叶片生长。②Helen was promoted to senior manager. 海伦被提升为高级经理。③The band are currently touring to promote their new album. 乐队目前正在巡回宣传他们的新专辑。

【拓展】promote *v.* →promotion *n.*

prompt /prɑːmpt/ *vt.* 鼓舞，督促；唤起；煽动；*adj.* 敏捷的，迅速的

【例句】①What prompted him to be so generous? 是什么原因促使他如此大方呢？②I just can't understand what prompted him to do something so drastic. 我就是不明白是什么促使他做了这么激烈的事情。③I forgot my line and had to be prompted. 我忘了我的台词，必须找人提词。④She was very prompt in answering my letter. 她很快就给我回信了。⑤Prompt action must be taken. 必须立即采取行动。

【用法】prompt in doing/to do sth 及时做某事，动作迅速去做某事

【例句】They're usually fairly prompt in dealing with enquiries. 他们处理询问通常相当迅速。

【拓展】prompting *n*. 鼓舞，促进，激励

prone /proʊn/ *adj*. 易于……，有做某事倾向的；俯卧的，趴着的

【用法】prone to sth 倾向于某物

【例句】①Some plants are very prone to disease. 有些植物很容易生病。②His eyes shifted to the prone body on the floor. 他的眼睛转向地板上俯卧的身体。③Kids are all prone to eat junk food. 孩子们都喜欢吃垃圾食品。

【拓展】prone *adj*. →proneness *n*.

proof /pruːf/ *n*. 证据，证明；校样，样张；*adj*. 耐……的，能防……的，不能穿透的

【用法】proof against…防止；-proof 防（风，雨，火等）

【例句】①This latest interview was further proof of how good at her job Cara was. 这次最新的面试进一步证明了卡拉在工作上有多出色。②Can you check these proofs? 你能核对一下这些校样吗？

property /ˈprɑːpərti/ *n*. 财产；房产，不动产；性能

【例句】①Property prices have shot up recently. 最近房地产价格猛涨。②We value herbs for their taste, but we forget that they also have medicinal properties. 我们看重草药的味道，但我们忘记了它们也有药用价值。

proportion /prəˈpɔːrʃn/ *n*. 比例，份额；使均衡

【例句】①What is proportion of girls to boys in this university? 这所大学男女生的比例是多少？②The two office buildings are in admirable proportion with each other. 这两座办公楼彼此相当相称。

【用法】in/out of proportion to 和……成/不成比例，a proportion of…一部分……

【例句】①Her feet are small in proportion to her height. 与她的身高相比，她的脚很小。②The porch is out of proportion with the rest of the house. 门廊与房子的其余部分不相称。③You should, however, keep a sense of proportion. 然而，你应该保持一种分寸感。

145

proportional /prəˈpɔːrʃənl/ *adj.* 按比例的；匀称的，平衡的

【用法】be proportional to 与……比例协调的；平衡的，匀称的

【例句】①The punishment should be proportional to the crime. 惩罚应与犯罪相称。②The fee charged by the realtor is directly proportional to the price of the property. 房地产经纪人收取的费用与房地产价格成正比。

proposal /prəˈpoʊzl/ *n.* 提议，求婚

【例句】① He offered a proposal for uniting the two companies. 他提出了合并两家公司的建议。②The committee put forward a proposal to reduce the time limit. 委员会提出了一项缩短时限的建议。③She politely declined his proposal of marriage. 她礼貌地拒绝了他的求婚。

propose /prəˈpoʊz/ *v.* 建议，提议，提出；提名，推荐；打算，计划；求婚；提议祝（酒）

【例句】①In his speech he proposed that the UN should set up an emergency centre for the environment. 在他的演讲中，他建议联合国应该建立一个环境应急中心。②He proposed Mrs Banks for the position of Treasurer. 他提议班克斯夫人担任司库一职。③How does he propose to deal with the situation? 他打算如何处理这种情况？④Shaun proposed to me only six months after we met. 我们见面才六个月，肖恩就向我求婚了。

prosecute /ˈprɑːsɪkjuːt/ *v.* 控告，起诉；（律师在法庭上）指控，公诉

【例句】①Shoplifters will be prosecuted. 入店行窃者将被起诉。②People who give the police false information will be prosecuted. 向警方提供虚假信息的人将受到起诉。③Mrs Lynn Smith, prosecuting, said the offence took place on January 27. 检方的林恩·史密斯夫人说，违法行为发生在1月27日。

prospect /ˈprɑːspekt/ *n.* 前景，前途；展望，设想；景象，景色；可能成为顾客的人，有希望的候选人；*v.* (for) 勘探，勘察

【例句】①I see no prospect of things improving here. 在这里我看不到任何改善的可能性。②I had no job, no education, and no prospects. 我没有工作，没有教育，也没有前途。③The prospect of marriage terrified Alice. 想到结婚把爱丽丝吓坏了。④From the restaurant there was a marvelous prospect of the valley and the mountains beyond. 从餐馆里可以看到山谷和远处的群山的壮丽景色。⑤The company is prospecting for gold in Alaska. 该公司正在阿拉斯中加州勘探金矿。

【拓展】prospector *n*. 勘探者，勘察者

prosperity /prɑːˈsperəti/ *n*. 繁荣，兴旺，昌盛

【例句】①The country hopes to achieve prosperity through increased trade and investment. 该国希望通过增加贸易和投资实现繁荣。②Bush emphasized the linkage between economic prosperity and political freedom. 布什强调经济繁荣与政治自由之间的联系。

prosperous /ˈprɑːspərəs/ *adj*. 繁荣的，兴旺的，昌盛的，富足的

【例句】①It is the middle class that can truly make a nation prosperous and strong. 真正使国家富强的是中产阶级。②He was a prosperous American businessman. 他是一个富裕的美国商人。

protect /prəˈtekt/ *vt*. 保护，保卫

【用法】protect…from 免受侵害；protect against 反对

【例句】①Are we doing enough to protect the environment? 我们在保护环境方面做得够多了吗？②The cover protects the machine from dust. 盖子保护机器不受灰尘的影响。③Waxing your car will help protect against rust. 给你的汽车上蜡有助于防锈。

【拓展】protect *v*. →protective *adj*. 防护的，保护的→protector *n*. 保护者，保护装置→protection *n*. 保护，防卫

protection /prəˈtekʃn/ *n*. 保护，防护；保护费

【例句】①She wore a pair of sunglasses as a protection against the strong sunlight. 她戴了一副太阳镜以保护自己不受强烈的阳光照射。②Zoos fulfil an important function in the protection of rare species. 动物园在保护珍稀物种方面发挥着重要作用。

protective /prəˈtektɪv/ *adj*. 保护的，防护的；呵护的

【例句】①Sunscreen provides a protective layer against the sun's harmful rays. 防晒霜提供了抵抗太阳有害射线的保护层。②He's very protective of his younger

147

brother. 他非常呵护他的弟弟。

【用法】be protective of...保护；protective towards sb 想保护某人的

【拓展】protective *adj*. →protectively *adv*. →protectiveness *n*.

protest /ˈprəʊtest；prəˈtest/*n*.&*v*. 抗议，反对；申辩，申明

【用法】protest against 抗议；under protest 勉强地

【例句】①He protested strongly at being treated unequally. 他强烈抗议受到不平等的对待。②All through the trial she protested her innocence. 在整个审判过程中，她都声称自己是清白的。

【拓展】protester *n*. 抗议者，反对者

proud /praʊd/*adj*. 骄傲的，自豪的，荣誉的（of）；骄傲自大的，自负的，傲慢的（about）；有自尊心的，自尊的，自重的

【用法】be proud of/to do/that...自豪，引以为荣

【例句】①You should be proud of yourself. 你应该为自己感到骄傲。②He is a proud man who would not admit his mistakes. 他是一个不会承认错误的骄傲的人。③Some farmers were too proud to ask for government help. 有些农民自尊心太强，不愿寻求政府的帮助。

prove /pruːv/*v*. 证明，证实；结果是，证明是

【例句】①I really want to prove to you that what I have done is beneficial to you. 我的确想向你证明，我所做的一切都是对你有益的。②Climbing to the top of Mount Tai proved to be more difficult than I had imagined. 事实证明，登上泰山之巅比我想象的要困难得多。

【用法】prove to be...证明了⋯⋯

【拓展】prove *v*. →provable *adj*. →provably *adv*.

provide /prəˈvaɪd/*v*. 供给，提供；（法律或协议）规定

【用法】provide sb with sth = provide sth to/for sb 提供，供给；provided that...假如⋯⋯

【例句】①The project is designed to provide young people with work. 该项目旨在为年轻人提供工作。②The hotel provides a shoe-cleaning service for guests. 这家旅馆为客人提供擦鞋服务。③Health insurance will provide against loss of income if you become ill. 如果你生病了，健康保险将为你的收入损失提供保障。 ④*The Companies Act* provides that the consent of shareholders is required for the sale of assets valued at 100,000 or more to a director of the company. 《公司法》规定，将价值10万英镑或以上的资产出售给公司董事需要股东同意。

【拓展】provide *v*. →provider *n*. 供应者，提供者，维持家庭生计者

provided /prəˈvaɪdɪd/*conj*. 假若，如果；以……为条件

【例句】①He can come with us, provided he pays for his own meals. 只要他自己付餐费，他就可以和我们一起去。②There's no annual fee provided that you use the credit card at least six times a year. 如果您一年至少使用六次信用卡，则不收取年费。

provision /prəˈvɪʒn/*n*. 供应，提供；准备，预备；规定，条款；给养，口粮

【用法】provision of...提供……必需品；provision for/against...防备……

【例句】①He made provisions for his wife and his children in his will. 他在遗嘱中为妻子和孩子做了准备。②The agreement includes a provision for each side to check the other side's weapons. 该协议包括一项条款，规定每一方检查对方的武器。③We had enough provisions for two weeks. 我们有足够两个星期的食物。

【拓展】provision *n*. →provisional *adj*. 临时的，暂时性的→provisionally *adv*.

provoke /prəˈvoʊk/*vt*. 对……挑衅，激怒；激起，引起

【用法】provoke a riot 煽动骚乱；provoke sb to anger 激怒某人；provoke sb to do/into doing sth 刺激某人做某事

【例句】①The proposal provoked widespread criticism. 这项建议招致了广泛的批评。②She hopes her editorial will provoke readers into thinking seriously about the issue. 她希望她的社论能激发读者认真思考这个问题。③The dog would not have attacked if it hadn't been provoked. 如果不是被激怒，那条狗是不会攻击的。

public /ˈpʌblɪk/*adj*. 公众的；公共的，公立的；*n*. 公众，大众

【用法】in public 公开地，公然地；public speech 公众演讲；public

transport 公共交通

【例句】①Public opinion is gradually shifting in favor of the imprisoned men. 公众舆论逐渐倾向于被监禁的人。②It's a public library. 这是一个公共图书馆。③He is adored by his public. 他受到公众的崇拜。

【拓展】public *adj*. →publicly *adv*.

publication /ˌpʌblɪˈkeɪʃn/ *n*. 出版，发行；出版物，发行物；发表，公布

【例句】①She was in England for the publication of her new book. 她在英国出版她的新书。②The local government has taken severe measures to punish those who print and sell illegal publications. 当地政府已采取严厉措施惩罚那些印刷和销售非法出版物的人。

publicity /pʌbˈlɪsəti/ *n*. 宣传，宣扬；公众的关注

【例句】①The movie star always tries to avoid publicity whenever he stays out. 这位电影明星外出时总是尽量避免引起公众的注意。②Who's going to do the show's publicity? 谁来做这个节目的宣传？

publish /ˈpʌblɪʃ/ *v*. 出版，发行，公布，宣传

【例句】①His novel is published by Peking University Press. 他的小说是北京大学出版社出版的。②The firm publishes its accounts in August. 该公司八月份公布账目。

【拓展】publishing *n*. 出版业；publisher *n*. 出版商

punctual /ˈpʌŋktʃuəl/ *adj*. 严守时刻的，准时的

【例句】①She's always very punctual for appointments. 她总是很准时地赴约。②My English teacher is always punctual on every occasion. 我的英语老师在任何场合都很守时。

【用法】be punctual to 准时，按时

【拓展】punctually *adv*. 准时地；punctuality *n*. 准时，守时

punish /ˈpʌnɪʃ/ *vt*. 惩罚，处罚

【例句】①He promised to punish severely any officials found guilty of electoral fraud. 他承诺严厉惩罚任何被判犯有选举舞弊罪的官员。②They deserve to be punished for putting passengers at risk. 他们应该受到惩罚，因为他们把乘客置

于危险之中。③My parents decided to punish me by withdrawing financial support. 我父母决定取消经济资助来惩罚我。

【用法】punish...for 因为……而受到惩罚

【拓展】punish *v.* →punishable *adj.* 可处罚的,该处罚的→punishing *adj.* 十分吃力的,严厉的

punishment /ˈpʌnɪʃmənt/*n.* 处罚,惩罚,惩处;粗暴对待,虐待

【例句】①The punishment for treason is death. 叛国罪的惩罚是死刑。②I was sent to bed as a punishment. 我被罚上床睡觉。③These trucks are designed to take a lot of punishment. 这些卡车设计得很耐用。

purchase /ˈpɜːrtʃəs/*vt.* 买,购买;*n.* 买,购买;购买物;紧握,抓住

【例句】①She paid for her purchases and left. 她付了买东西的钱就走了。②The ice made it impossible to get a purchase on the road. 冰使得车轮很难抓住路面。

【拓展】purchase *vt.* →purchasable *adj.* 可买的→purchaser *n.* 购买人

pure /pjʊr/*adj.* 纯的,纯粹的;纯净的,无垢的;纯洁的;完全的,十足的;纯理论的,抽象的

【例句】①It's a ring made of pure gold. 这是一枚纯金戒指。②My mother's life was pure hell. 我母亲的生活简直就是地狱。③They're too pure and innocent to know what's really going on. 他们太纯洁、太天真了,根本不知道到底发生了什么。④ Critics have argued that an excessive commercial focus will lead researchers to ignore pure science. 批评者认为过度的商业关注会导致研究人员忽视纯科学。

【拓展】pure *adj.* →purely *adv.* →purify*v.* →purity *n.* →purification *n.*

purify /ˈpjʊrɪfaɪ/*v.* 使纯净,净化

【例句】①Chemicals were used to purify the water. 化学物质曾被用来净化水。②It has been found that houseplants help purify the air. 人们发现室内植物有助于净化空气。

purity /ˈpjʊrɪfaɪ/*n.* 纯洁,纯净,纯正,洁净,纯度

【例句】①In literature, the swan has been a symbol of purity and virtue. 在文

学中，天鹅一直是纯洁和美德的象征。②Use of the chemicals could harm the purity of dairy products. 使用这些化学品可能会损害乳制品的纯度。③I was convinced of one thing: of the purity and truth of my love for you. 我深信一件事：我对你的爱是纯洁和真实的。

purpose /ˈpɜːrpəs/ *n.* 目的，意图；计划，目标；决心，意志

【例句】①He came here with the purpose of carrying out the attack. 他来这里是为了发动袭击。②He possessed great strength of purpose. 他有坚强的意志。③You make it sound as if I did it on purpose! 你说得好像我是故意的！

【用法】on purpose 故意地，有意地；one's purpose in doing sth 做某事的目的；to no purpose 无效，毫无结果；to the purpose 中肯的，合适的，得要领的；with/for the purpose of... 为了……

【拓展】purpose *n.* →purposeful *adj.* →purposeless（opposite）*adj.*

pursue /pərˈsuː/ *vt.* 继续；追求，寻求，从事；追赶，追踪，追击；追查，追问

【例句】①Briggs ran across the field with one officer pursuing him. 布里格斯跑过田野，一名军官在追他。②I was pleased, but somewhat embarrassed, when she pursued me. 当她追我的时候，我很高兴，但也有些尴尬。

【拓展】pursuer *n.* 追赶着，追捕着；pursuit *n.* 追求，寻求

pursuit /pərˈsuːt/ *n.* 追求，从事，执行；追踪，追击；消遣，娱乐

【例句】①People are having to move to other areas in pursuit of work. 人们为了工作不得不搬到别的地方去。②There were four police cars in pursuit. 有四辆警车在追捕。③I enjoy outdoor pursuits, like hiking and riding. 我喜欢户外活动，比如徒步旅行和骑马。

【用法】in pursuit of sb/sth 追捕某人（物）；in hot pursuit 穷追不舍

puzzle /ˈpʌzl/ *n.* 智力问题（或游戏，玩具）；难题，谜；*v.*（使）迷惑，（使）为难，迷惑不解

【例句】①Do you like the crossword puzzles? 你喜欢填字游戏吗？②He thought he had solved the puzzle. 他以为他已经解开谜题了。③She had a complex personality that was a real puzzle to me. 她有一个复杂的性格，这对我来

说真是个谜。④What puzzles me is why his books are so popular. 令我不解的是他的书为什么那么受欢迎。

【用法】puzzle over/about sth 为……苦苦思索，因……伤脑筋；puzzle sth out 想出，苦思找出某事的答案或解决办法

【例句】①The class puzzled over a poem by Shakespeare. 全班对莎士比亚的一首诗苦思冥想。②He lay looking at the ceiling, trying to puzzle things out. 他躺在那里看着天花板，想把事情搞清楚。

【拓展】puzzling *adj*. 令人费解的；puzzled *adj*. 无法了解的，困惑的，茫然的；puzzlement *n*. 困惑，大惑不解

7　Q, R, S

7.1　Q

queer /kwɪr/ *adj.* 古怪的，奇怪的

【例句】She seemed very queer since her parents divorced. 自从她父母离婚后，她就很古怪。

quest /kwest/ *v.* 追求，寻求，搜索

【例句】①Nothing can prevent people from questing for happiness. 没有什么能阻止人们追求幸福。②They looked over the pool in quest of the lost ring. 他们仔细搜查这个游泳池寻找到丢失的戒指。

【用法】quest for 寻找；in quest of sth 寻求/寻找某物

queue /kjuː/ *n.* 队列，长队；*vi.* 排队（等候）

【例句】How long have you been in the queue? 你排队多长时间了？

【用法】jump the queue 插队；queue up 排队

【例句】①Those who jump in the queue should be disdained. 插队的人应遭鄙视。②Please queue up to get the ticket. 请排队领票。

quit /kwɪt/ *v.* 停止，放弃；离开，辞职

【例句】①Learning his disease, my father finally quit smoking. 得知病情，我父亲最终把烟戒了。②I will quit if I cannot get the promotion. 如果我升不了职就辞职。

【用法】quit doing sth 停止做某事

quite /kwaɪt/ ***adv***. 完全，十分

【例句】This winter is quite freezing. 今年冬天相当寒冷。

【辨析】fairly、quite、rather、pretty、very 均表示"很""相当"。fairly 语气最轻，常与褒义词连用，常译为"还算""相当"。quite 语气稍重，意为"颇""相当"。rather、pretty 语气更重一些，有"十分""相当"之意。very 语气最重。

quiz /kwɪz/ ***n***. 测验，小型考试

【例句】We have a quiz at the end of each unit. 每个单元结束我们都会有一个测验。

quota /ˈkwoʊtə/ ***n***. （正式限定的）定量，限额；配额

【例句】China has set a strict quota for coal mining. 中国严格设定了石油开采的限额。

quote /kwoʊt/ ***n***. 引文，引语；***v***. 引用；援引

【例句】①This passage is full of quotes. 这篇文章满篇引语。②He quoted the poem of Shakespeare to express his love. 他引用莎士比亚的诗来表达自己的爱意。

7.2　R

represent /ˌreprɪˈzent/ ***v***. 表现，象征；代表，代理；展示，描绘

【例句】①The cooperation is represented by the vice president in the meeting. 这个集团是由副总裁代表出席会议。②His talent agency tends to represent him as a loving father. 他的经纪公司往往把他描述成慈爱的父亲。③This song represents a feeling of departure. 这首歌描绘了离别的感情。

【用法】represent A as B　把 A 描述成 B

【拓展】representative ***adj***. 有代表性的，典型的；***n***. 代表

reproduce /ˌriːprəˈduːs/ ***v***. 复制；重现；繁殖

【例句】①His success cannot be reproduced. 他的成功无法复制。②It is very generous of you to permit us to reproduce these materials. 您能允许我们复制这些资料，真是太慷慨了。③The speed of rat reproduce is amazing. 老鼠繁衍的速度惊人。

republic /rɪˈpʌblɪk/ *n.* 共和国；共和政体；（成员具有平等权利的）团体

【例句】The People's Republic of China was founded in 1949. 中华人民共和国成立于1949年。

【拓展】republican *adj.* 共和国的；共和党的；*n.* 共和主义者

reputation /ˌrepjuˈteɪʃn/ *n.* 名声；名誉

【例句】He rose to his reputation in his thirties. 他30多岁才名声大噪。

request /rɪˈkwest/ *v.* & *n.* 要求，请求

【例句】①The manager refuted their request for raising salary. 经理驳回了他们涨工资的要求。②Her mother cooked beef at her request. 她妈妈应她的要求做了牛肉。③The hostess requested that no one should smoke here. 女主人要求这里任何人不要抽烟。

【用法】request for 要求某事；at sb's request 应某人的要求

require /rɪˈkwaɪər/ *vt.* 需要；要求；想要；命令；*vi.* 要求，规定

【例句】①He requires adequate time to think it over. 他需要充足的时间仔细考虑这些问题。②It is required that each student (should) achieve at least 30 credits. 每个学生应该按要求获得至少30学分。（虚拟语气）

rescue /ˈreskjuː/ *vt.* 营救，救援；*n.* 营救，救援；营救

【例句】①The firefighter rescued a little girl in the fire. 消防员从大火中救出了一个小女孩。②They sent rescue helicopters to disaster-affected area. 他们派出救援直升机前往受灾地区。

【用法】come to the/sb's rescue 援救，营救某人

【例句】There is always a hero comes to the rescue on this occasion. 这种情况下往往会有一个英雄前来营救。

research /ˈriːsɜːrtʃ/ *n.* 调查；探索；研究；探测；/rɪˈsɜːrtʃ/ *v.* 做研究；探究

【例句】①They conducted extensive research before the program. 他们在项目开始前做了广泛的研究。②This team has been researching into the phenomenon for a long time. 这个团队研究这个现象已经很长时间了。

【用法】research into/on sth; research on sb 研究，对……进行调查研究

resemble /rɪˈzembl/ *vt.* 与……像，类似于

【例句】The girl resembles a famous singer. 这个女孩长得像一个著名歌手。

resent /rɪˈzent/ *vt.* 怨恨；愤恨；厌恶

【例句】①I bitterly resent the injustice. 我嫉妒厌恶不公正的情况。②She resents being treated rudely. 她讨厌被粗鲁地对待。

【用法】resent doing sth 厌恶做某事

【拓展】resentful *adj.* 憎恨的；resentment *n.* 愤恨，怨恨

reserve /rɪˈzɜːrv/ *n.* 储备；保留；保护区；替补队员；*v.* 储备；保留；预约

【例句】①Scientists are deeply concerned about our country's oil reserve. 科学家们对我国的石油储备深感忧虑。②There are many natural reserves in the northern part of China. 中国北部有很多自然保护区。③He is a reserve of our school badminton team. 他是我们校羽毛球队的候补队员。

【用法】reserve sth for sb/sth 为……保留某物，为某人保留预定的座位、住处等；in reserve 储存，留以备用

【例句】①You should reserve your energy till the end of the match. 你应该保留体力坚持到最后。②I'd like to reserve a table for two. 我想订一张两人桌。③The money is deposited in reserve. 这笔钱是存以备用的。

【拓展】reservation *n.* 保留的座位、住处等；保留意见；reserved *adj.* 内向的，矜持的

reside /rɪˈzaɪd/ *vi.* 居住，驻在；（权力，权利等）属于，归于

【例句】①Happiness resides in personal feelings rather than money or social status. 幸福存在于个人感觉而非金钱或社会地位。②More and more people prefer to reside in the countryside. 越来越多人更喜欢居住在乡村。③The cause of this accident resides in his bad temper. 这场事故的原因在于他的坏脾气。

【用法】reside in/at...定居于；reside in sb/sth 在于，由……引起；reside in/with sb/sth（权力等）属于

【拓展】residence ***n***. 大宅，官邸；居留期间；resident ***n***. 居民

resign /rɪˈzaɪn/ ***v***. 辞职；放弃；屈从；勉强接受

【例句】①She resigned as president after 30 years. 30 年之后，她辞去了董事长职务。②He had to resign from the board after the merging. 合并之后，他不得不从董事会辞职。③He refused to resign himself to the failure and decided to start over again. 他不甘失败，决定从头开始。

【用法】resign from sth 从某职务辞职；resign as sth 辞去某职务；resign oneself to 听任，只好接受

【拓展】resignation ***n***. 辞职；顺从

resist /rɪˈzɪst/ ***v***. 抵抗，抗拒；忍耐；反对，抵制

【例句】①They resisted the attack with proper tactics. 他们采用了合适的战略抵御袭击。②She is trying to control weight, but she cannot resist delicious food. 她一直努力控制体重，却无法抵抗美食。③This product can resist frost. 这个产品能预防霜冻。

【用法】resist doing sth 忍耐做某事，反抗做某事

【例句】He cannot resist laughing at her hairstyle. 他总忍不住笑话她的发型。

【拓展】resistible ***adj***. 可抵抗的→irresistible ***adj***. 不可抵抗的；resistance (to sth) ***n***. 对抗，阻止；resistant (to sth) ***adj***. 抵抗的；抗/耐……的

【例句】①This attack is resistible/ irresistible. 这次袭击是可抵抗的/不可抵抗的。②A majority of people show resistance to the new policy. 大多数人对这个新政策都表示反对。③This material is resistant to fire. 这种材料可以防火。

resolve /rɪˈzɑːlv/ ***vt. & vi***. 决心；决定；***vt***. 使消释；使分解，使解体；***n***. 决定；决议

【例句】①Nothing can sway her resolve to realize her dream. 没有什么能动摇她实现梦想的决心。②The couple resolved on having a third child. 这对夫妇决定要第三个孩子。③This question can be resolved into several parts. 这个问题

能被分解成几个部分。

【用法】resolve on/upon/against sth/doing sth 决心做某事；resolve sth into 分解成

【拓展】resolved *adj.* （某人）坚定的；resolvable *adj.* 可解决的；resolute *adj.* 坚决的；resolution *n.* 坚定

resort /rɪˈzɔːrt/ *vi.* 求助于，诉诸，采取，对策；*n.* 求助，诉诸；度假胜地

【例句】①Accusing him is a proper resort. 起诉他是恰当的办法。②Huangdao is a beautiful holiday resort. 黄岛是一个美丽的度假胜地。③Violence is never the best resort. 暴力从来不是最佳手段。

【用法】resort to 诉诸，采取

【例句】We may have to resort to starting our back-up plan. 我们可能不得不启动备用计划。

resource /ˈriːsɔːrs/ *n.* 资源；物力，财力；智谋

【例句】①China is a country with vast territory and abundant resources. 中国是一个地大物博的国家。②He is a man of great resource. 他是一个足智多谋的人。③This application can be adopted as a teaching resource in class. 这个应用能作为课堂教学资源使用。

respect /rɪˈspekt/ *vt.* 尊重；尊敬；遵守；*n.* 敬意；尊重；某方面

【例句】①They welcomed the relief heroes with great respect. 他们怀着极大的尊敬欢迎这些救援英雄。②Respect yourself, or no one else will respect you. 尊重你自己，不然没人会尊重你。③A good citizen should respect the law and reject violent. 一个好公民应遵守法律，拒绝暴力。

【用法】in respect of 就某方面而言；with respect to 涉及、提到

【例句】①This proposal is feasible in respect of management. 就管理而言，这个建议是可行的。② With respect to your comments, I made a few improvements. 有关你的评价，我做了一些改进。

【拓展】respecting *prep.* 关于，至于；respectable *adj.* 值得尊敬的；respectful *adj.* 恭敬的；respective *adj.* 各自的，分别的

【例句】①The government issued a law respecting intellectual property. 政府出台了关于知识产权的法律。②He is a decent and respectable scholar. 他是一个体面，值得尊敬的学者。③People should keep a respectful distance on formal occasions. 正式场合人们应该保持表示尊重的距离。④They express their respective opinions during the session. 会议期间，他们都发表了各自的观点。

respond /rɪˈspɑːnd/ *v*. 回答，做出反应；回复

【例句】I sent him a message, but he didn't respond. 我给他发了信息，但他没有回复。

【用法】respond to sb/sth 回答，回应

【例句】Several days later, he responded to my message with an emoji. 几天后，他回复了我一个表情。

【拓展】response *n*. 回复，回应；responsive *adj*. 支持的，赞同的

responsible /rɪˈspɑːnsəbl/ *adj*. 负有责任的；尽责的

【例句】The captain is responsible for the safety of all the passengers. 船长对全部乘客的安全负责。

【用法】be responsible for...对……负责

【拓展】responsibility *n*. 责任

restless /ˈrestləs/ *adj*. 运动不止的；（因烦躁、焦虑等）静不下来的

【例句】The child was restless because of headache. 这个孩子因为头疼而焦虑不安。

restore /rɪˈstɔːr/ *vt*. 归还；使恢复；使复原；使复位；使复职

【例句】①He didn't restore the bike until the police found him. 知道警察找到他，他才归还自行车。②The programmer restored the documents in her computer. 程序员恢复了电脑里的文件。

【拓展】restoration *n*. 物归原主；复原

restrain /rɪˈstreɪn/ *vt*. 制止；抑制，压抑；限定，限制；监禁

【例句】①He tried his best to restrain his anger. 他竭尽全力抑制自己的怒气。②These criminals were restrained in a prison on a remote island. 这些犯人被囚禁在偏远海岛的监狱里。

【拓展】restrained *adj*. 克制的；restraint *n*. 抑制，约束

restrict /rɪˈstrɪkt/ *vt*. 限制，限定；约束，束缚

【例句】①The luggage should be restricted to 5 kg on plane per person. 每个人可带的行李重量应限制在 5 千克以内。②The ability to restrict oneself properly is a symbol of adulthood. 恰当地约束自己的能力是成年的一个标志。

【拓展】restricted *adj*. 有限的，受约束的；restrictive *adj*. 限制性的

【例句】①The access to the building is restricted. 进入大楼受到限制。②We should take restrictive measures to prevent the negative influence. 我们应该采取限制性措施来阻止负面影响。

result /rɪˈzʌlt/ *n*. 结果；*v*. 引发

【例句】The accident was a result of misoperation.（= A misoperation resulted in the accident.）这场事故是由操作失误导致的。

【用法】result of sth 某事的结果；result in 导致

resume /rɪˈzuːm/ *v*. 继续；恢复职位；*n*. 简历；摘要

【例句】①Peace resumed after a few conflicts. 一些冲突过后又恢复了和平。②She resumed her work after the maternity leave. 产假过后她又恢复了她的工作。③The director of human resources only kept these resumes because the applicants are all from famous universities. 人力资源部的部长只保留了这些简历，因为这些应聘者均来自名牌大学。

retail /ˈriːteɪl/ *n*. 零售；*v*. 零售；零卖；/riːˈteɪl/ *adv*. 零售的

【例句】①There are many retail stores in the small town. 这个小镇上有很多零售商店。②The retail price of this toothpaste is ￥16. = The toothpaste retails at ￥16. 这个牙膏的零售价格是 16 元。

retain /rɪˈteɪn/ *v*. 保持；留在心中

【例句】①The customer should retain the receipt at least for 7 days. 顾客应保留发票至少 7 天。②She retains the their first date clearly. 她能清楚地记得他们的第一次约会。

retell /ˌriːˈtel/ *v*.（以不同的方式或语言）复述

【例句】①The story has been retold in many versions. 这个故事已经被复述

为很多版本。②The ability to retell what they've learned in class is vital for English learners. 复述课上所学的知识对英语学习者来说很关键。

retarded /rɪˈtɑːrdɪd/*adj*. 发育迟缓的，智力迟钝的

【例句】He is a little bit retarded because of ill nutrition. 由于营养不良，他发育有些迟缓。

retire /rɪˈtaɪər/*v*. 退休；撤退；退却

【例句】①It is said that women born after 1982 may retire at 65 years old. 据说1982年之后出生的女性可能要65岁退休。②Beepers have retired from history. BP机已经退出了历史。

retort /rɪˈtɔːrt/*v. &n*. 反驳

【例句】He retorted that he should not be punished so severely. 他反驳说他不应受到如此严厉的惩罚。

retreat /rɪˈtriːt/*vi*. 撤退；撤销；*n*. 撤回；静居处；引退期间；静修

【例句】The enemy finally retreated to their own region. 敌人最终撤退到自己区域。

retrospective /ˌretrəˈspektɪv/*adj*. 回顾的；有追溯效力的

【例句】The is an retrospective concert of that musician. 这是那个音乐家的怀旧音乐会。

reunite /ˌriːjuˈnaɪt/*v*. 再次联合；（使）重聚；（使）再结合

【例句】Releasing from prison, he reunited with his children. 从监狱释放出来以后，他和他的孩子们重聚了。

reveal /rɪˈviːl/*vt*. 揭露；泄露；显露

【例句】①He couldn't stop shaking, revealing that he was nervous. 他禁不住抖动不已，透露出他很紧张。②The details of this incident were revealed by reporters. 这个事件的细节由记者揭露出来。

revenge /rɪˈvendʒ/*n. &v*. 复仇

【例句】①She made elaborate plan to revenge her husband. 她制订了详细的计划为她丈夫报仇。②She is willing to sacrifice everything to take revenge on the murderer. 她愿意牺牲所有东西向杀人犯报仇。

【拓展】get/have/take revenge on sb (for sth)（为某事）向某人复仇；out of revenge 为了报复

revenue /ˈrevənuː/ *n*. 收益；财政收入；税收收入

【例句】①The trade war leads to the decrease in annual revenue. 贸易战导致年收益减少。②The tax revenue has reduced by 5%. 税收减少了5%。

reverse /rɪˈvɜrs/ *v*.（使）反转，（使）倒退；（使）颠倒，推翻，撤销；翻转；*adj*. 反面的；颠倒的；倒开的；*n*. 倒转，反向；倒退

【例句】①The decision was reversed by the board. 这个决定被董事会推翻了。②To drive in the reverse direction is dangerous. 反向开车很危险。③The reverse of letters can make a new word. 颠倒字母的顺序能组成新单词。

【用法】in reverse 相反地

review /rɪˈvjuː/ *n*. 回顾；复习；书评、影评等；*v*. 评论；复习；复查

【例句】①The critic made impartial review on this movie. 他对这部电影做出了中肯的评价。②Students should review what they've learned in time. 学生们应当及时复习所学内容。③The newspaper reviewed the big events in this month briefly. 这个报纸大致回顾了本月大事。

revise /rɪˈvaɪz/ *v*. 复习，修正，校订

【例句】①This course revised my value of life. 这个课程修正了我的价值观。②They are revising for the final exam. 他们正在复习准备期末考试。③This book has been revised twice. 这本书已经被修订了两次。

revive /rɪˈvaɪv/ *v*.（使）恢复（健康、力量等），复兴

【例句】①She revived after a cup of coffee. 她喝完一杯咖啡之后恢复了能量。②They make great effort in reviving the old practice. 他们努力恢复旧例。

【拓展】revision *n*. 复查，修订，复习

revoke /rɪˈvoʊk/ *v*. 撤销，废除，吊销

【例句】①His driving license was revoked due to the accident last month. 由于上个月的事故，他的驾驶证被吊销了。②He is a person who cannot be trusted in, because he always revokes his promises. 他是个不值得信赖的人，因为他总是反悔他做过的承诺。

revolt /rɪˈvoʊlt/ *v.* 反叛；反抗

【例句】The peasants revolted against the lords. 农民反抗地主。

【用法】revolt against... 反抗......

revolution /ˌrevəˈluːʃn/ *n.* 革命；重大改变；旋转

【例句】①The widespread of steam engine is the mark of the first industrial revolution. 蒸汽机的广泛应用是第一次工业革命的标志。②The invention of QR code contributes to the revolution of payment. 二维码的发明促进了支付方式的重大改变。③We cannot feel the revolution of earth. 我们感觉不到地球的旋转。

revolve /rɪˈvɑːlv/ *v.* 绕......旋转；以......为中心

【例句】①The earth revolves around the sun. 地球围绕太阳转。②The life of parents revolves around the children. 父母的生活以孩子为中心。

【用法】revolve around sth 绕......旋转；以......为中心

reward /rɪˈwɔːrd/ *n.* 报酬；报答；赏金；酬金；*vt.* 奖赏；报答

【例句】①The manager rewarded the employee for his outstanding performance. 这个经理奖励了这个员工的杰出业绩。②I really don't know how to reward your generosity. 我实在不知道如何报答你的慷慨相助。③Moral encouragement is more inspirational than financial reward. 精神鼓励比经济奖励更鼓舞人。

【用法】reward sb for sth 因某事而奖励某人

rhythm /ˈrɪðəm/ *n.* 节奏；节律，规律；节拍

【例句】①The rhythm of this poem is quite exquisite. 这首诗的韵律十分优美。②He is a so talented that he has a strong sense of rhythm when he was a little boy. 他很有天赋，他还是小男孩的时候就有很强的节奏感。

rib /rɪb/ *n.* 肋骨；*v.* 嘲笑，逗弄，开某人的玩笑

【例句】①He fell of the tree and broke his rib. 他摔下树来，摔坏了肋骨。②They often rib about his baldness. 他们总是嘲笑他的秃顶。

ribbon /ˈrɪbən/ *n.* 带；绶带；带状物；*v.* 把......撕成条带

【例句】The pink ribbon she bought today is fairly fashionable. 她买的这条粉色丝带很时尚。

rid /rɪd/ *vt.* 使摆脱，解除，免除

【例句】There are more villages getting rid of poverty this year. 今年有更多的村庄摆脱了贫困。

【用法】be/get rid of…摆脱……

riddle /ˈrɪdl/ ***n***. 谜语；难解之；***v***. 筛分；解谜

【例句】①That who commit arson remains a riddle. 谁纵的火仍是个谜。②His face is riddled with pimples. 他满脸的粉刺。

【用法】be riddled with…充满……

ridicule /ˈrɪdɪkjuːl/ ***n. &v***. 嘲笑；嘲弄

【例句】①She was often ridiculed by her classmates for her poor grades. 她经常因为成绩差被同学嘲笑。②This short novel is a ridicule of some politicians. 这篇短篇小说是对一些政客的嘲讽。

【拓展】ridiculous ***adj***. 可笑的，荒谬的

rifle /ˈraɪfl/ ***n***. 步枪；来复枪；***v***. 匆忙翻找

【例句】①The thief rifled the drawers for jewels. 小偷搜劫抽屉找珠宝。②The drunkard was killed by a rifle. 这个醉汉是被一把来复枪打死的。

righteous /ˈraɪtʃəs/ ***adj***. 正直的

【例句】He is an honest and righteous person. 他是一个诚实、正值的人。

rightful /ˈraɪtfl/ ***adj***. 正义的，合法的

【例句】She is the rightful owner of the house. 她是这个房子的合法所有人。

rigid /ˈrɪdʒɪd/ ***adj***. 坚硬的；严格的

【例句】①The house needs rigid support. 这个房子需要坚硬的支撑。②This schedule is rather rigid. 这个计划过于死板。③He is a person with rigid aims. 他是个目标笃定的人。

rigorous /ˈrɪɡərəs/ ***adj***. 严厉的；严密的

【例句】①She manages the company with rigorous rules. 她治理公司制度严明。②They conducted a rigorous analysis of this air crash. 他们对这次空难进行了缜密的分析。

riot /ˈraɪət/ ***n***. 骚乱，暴动；欢闹；喧嚣嘈杂；***v***. 暴动，闹事；放荡；挥霍

【例句】The famine is the main reason of this food riot. 饥荒是造成这次争抢食物骚乱的主要原因。

【用法】run riot 肆意妄为；a riot of color 色彩斑斓；ead sb the riot act 严厉警告某人停止闹事

【例句】①Children running riot may end in jail. 肆意妄为的孩子可能最终会进监狱。②There is a riot of color at the flower expo. 花卉展览会上五彩缤纷。③Please stop screaming, or I will read you the riot act. 请不要大喊大叫，否则我就要提出严正警告了。

rip /rɪp/ *n.* 裂口；*v.* 扯破，撕成；锯；裂开

【例句】①His grandma is sewing the rip of his jeans. 他奶奶在缝他牛仔裤上的裂缝。②The postman passed the letter to her, and she ripped it impatiently. 邮递员把信递给她，她着急地撕开了信。

【用法】rip sth up 撕碎某物；rip into/through sb/sth（猛烈快速）穿入，钻透

【例句】①He cannot accept the grievous news in the letter and ripped it up. 他无法接受信中的噩耗，把信撕碎了。②The sword ripped into his arm. 剑刺穿了他的胳膊。

rise /raɪz/ *vi.* 上升；增强；（数量）增加；起身；*n.* 兴起；（数量或水平的）增加；（日、月等的）升起

【例句】①The sun rises in the east. 太阳从东方升起。②The rise of artificial intelligence（AI）will change our lifestyle. 人工智能的兴起会改变我们的生活方式。③She rose to a middle-level cadre in three years. 她花了三年升级至中层领导。

【用法】rise above 战胜困难；超脱；出众；rise to 能够处理；give rise to sth 使发生

【例句】①We have to rise above many difficulties to fulfill our goals. 我们必须克服重重困难来实现目标。②This essay rises above the common ones. 这篇文章很出众。③Only Mary can rise to this situation now. 现在只有玛丽能处理这个情况。④A little mistake may give rise to a big tragedy. 小错误可能引发大悲剧。

risk /rɪsk/ *n.* 危险，风险；危险人物，危险的事；处境危险的人；*v.* 使……遭受危险；冒……风险

【例句】①He risked his life when he entered the wildwood. 他冒着生命危险进入原始森林。②He was a risk. 他是个危险人物。③The president's attitude risked a battle. 那个总统的态度可能会引发战争。

【用法】risk doing 冒……危险；at risk 处境危险；at the risk of 冒着……的危险

【例句】①The disease is spreading, and all children are at risk. 这种疾病正在蔓延，所有的儿童都有被感染上的危险。②At the risk of losing his job, he helped the police investigate the economic problem of his company. 他冒着失去工作的危险，帮助警方调查他所在的公司的经济问题。

【拓展】risky *adj.*

【辨析】risk、danger、hazard 均表示"危险"。risk 指预料不到的危险，特别指在赢利活动中的风险或不幸。danger 为最通俗用语，可以指在任何情况下所面临的不理想的或有害的不测事件或危险。hazard 比较郑重，可以代替 risk，但指更大的危险。

【例句】①To succeed in business, one must be prepared to run risks. 一个人想在商业上成功，必须做好冒险的准备。②His life is in danger. 他的生命处于危险之中。③He will do it at the hazard of his life. 他将冒着生命危险去做这件事。

ritual /ˈrɪtʃuəl/ *n.* （宗教）程序；习惯；*adj.* 仪式上的；惯常的

【例句】①Taking off hat to greet is a ritual. 脱帽致敬是个习惯。②This praise is only ritual. 这只是礼节性的赞美。

rival /ˈraɪvl/ *n.* 对手；竞争；*vt.* 与……竞争；比得上

【例句】①She felt more stressed when she found her rivals were very aggressive. 她发觉她的对手满是挑衅，她更紧张了。②Nobody can rival Yao Ming in basketball all around the country so far. 到目前为止，在篮球方面全国没有人能比得上姚明。

roam /roʊm/ *v. &n.* 漫步；漫无目的地行走

【例句】He used to roam in the village after dinner. 他饭后通常在村里随便

逛逛。

roar /rɔːr/ *v.* 咆哮；吼叫；轰鸣；*n.* 吼叫声，咆哮声，呼啸声；狂笑，大笑

【例句】①The lions in the zoo seldom roar. 动物园里的狮子很少咆哮。②The audience roared with delight learning her triumph. 得知她胜利的消息，观众们高兴地高声呼喊。③The train roared away. 火车呼啸而过。④Her talk show arouses roars of laughter. 她的脱口秀引起了阵阵大笑。

roast /roʊst/ *v.* 烤，烘，焙；*adj.* 烤好的；*n.* 烤肉；户外烧烤

【例句】①The chief is skillful at roasting ducks. 这个主厨非常擅长烤鸭。②We are looking forward to a holiday roast. 我们期待假期烤肉大餐。

rob /rɑːb/ *v.* 抢劫；掠夺；非法剥夺

【例句】They always rob the rich to help the poor. 他们总是劫富济贫。

【用法】rob sb sth/of sth 抢夺/抢劫某人某物

【例句】The gang robbed him of all his money. 这帮家伙抢光了他所有的钱。

【拓展】robbery *n.* 盗窃，偷盗

rocket /ˈrɑːkɪt/ *n.* 火箭；*v.* 飞快地移动

【例句】①The rocket was launched in Jiuquan. 这个火箭于酒泉发射。②The gazelle rocketed away. 这只羚羊火箭般离开了。

rod /rɑːd/ *n.* 杆，拉杆；（打人用）棍棒

【例句】He bought an expensive fishing rod. 他买了一根昂贵的钓鱼竿。

role /roʊl/ *n.* 作用；角色；地位

【例句】They are competing for the role in the play. 他们在竞争剧中的一个角色。

【用法】play a role in… 在某方面起重要作用

【例句】Mobile phones play an indispensable role in people's lives today. 如今移动电话在人们生活中起到了重要作用。

roll /roʊl/ *v.* 滚动；辗；转动眼球；原地转圈；*n.* 名册；滚翻

【例句】①The rocks rolled down the slope. 石头从斜坡上滚下来。②Piggies like to roll in the mud. 小猪们喜欢在泥里打滚。③The teacher reads the roll in class every day. 这个老师每天都点名。④She rolled her eyes at their explanation. 她对他们的解释翻白眼。

romance /ˈroʊmæns/ *n*. 浪漫故事，富于想象力的故事；浪漫气氛，传奇色彩

【例句】This is a romance in Roman. 这是一件发生在罗马的浪漫故事。

【拓展】romantic *adj*. 浪漫的

roof /ruːf/ *n*. 屋顶；顶部；*vt*. 给……盖顶；覆盖；保护，庇护

【例句】①We often climbed on to the roof in childhood. 小时候我们经常爬房顶。②Please roof over the yard in case it rains. 请给院子搭上顶，以防下雨。

root /ruːt/ *n*. 根，根源；本质；祖先；*v*. （使）生根；根源在于；欢呼，喝彩

【例句】①The root of roses were rotten. 这些玫瑰的根腐烂了。②It is said we share the same root. 据说我们有共同的祖先。③This sort of bush can root in desert easily. 这种灌木容易在沙漠中扎根。④I can hear that they are rooting for us. 我能听到他们在为我们欢呼。

rope /roʊp/ *n*. 绳子；*v*. 用绳子绑

【例句】The shepherd tied the sheep to a tree with a rope. 牧羊人用绳子把羊拴在树上。

rotten /ˈrɑːtn/ *adj*. 腐烂的；腐败的；极坏的

【例句】①The vegetables were rotten due to the high temperature. 由于温度高，蔬菜都腐烂了。②The government is rotten. 这个政府腐败不堪。③This is really a rotten day. 今天简直差到极点。

rough /rʌf/ *adj*. 粗糙的，崎岖不平的；粗鲁的；狂暴的；粗略的；*vt*. 粗暴地对待；草拟；*n*. 粗糙的部分；苦难；草图

【例句】①Her hands become rough through years' heavy manual labor. 由于多年繁重的手工劳动，她的手变得很粗糙。②They made a rough calculation of expense this month. 他们对这个月的花费做了大致计算。③This is just a rough of the bridge. 这只是桥的一个草图。④He was roughed up by his classmates. 他受到了同学的粗暴对待。

rouse /raʊz/ *v.* 叫醒；鼓励，鼓舞；使发脾气；使振奋

【例句】①The alarm roused me from a sound sleep. 闹钟把我从酣睡中叫醒。②The faculty were roused by her speech. 所有员工都被他的演讲鼓舞了。③She was roused to interest by the salesman's introduction. 售货员的介绍引起了她的兴趣。

route /ruːt/ *n.* 航线；路；常规路线；途径；*vt.* 按规定路线

【例句】①The find out a best route to travel. 他们发现了一条旅游的最佳路线。②Her route to be a champion is unique. 她成为冠军的道路是独一无二的。

routine /ruːˈtiːn/ *n.* 常规；例行程序；一套动作；*adj.* 常规的；例行的；日常的

【例句】①Wearing make-up before going out has become her routine. 出门前化妆是她必做的事。②The students have to finish the routine of exercises in PE class. 学生们必须在体育课上完成这套体操动作。③There will be a routine inspection this afternoon. 今天下午有一次常规检查。

row /roʊ；raʊ/ *n.* 划船；行，排；吵闹；路；*vt.* 划船；使……成排

【例句】①The students in the first row can concentrate more on the teacher. 坐第一排的学生更能把注意力集中在老师身上。②The team which rowed the fastest won the boat race. 划得最快的队伍赢得了这次船赛。

royal /ˈrɔɪəl/ *adj.* 王国的，王室的；高贵的

【例句】The British royal family has witnessed two spectacular royal weddings. 英国皇室已经历经两场盛大的皇室婚礼了。

rub /rʌb/ *vt.* 擦，摩擦；用……擦；（使）相互摩擦；*n.* 摩擦的动作；表面不平；阻碍，困难

【例句】①My father rubbed the car with an old shirt. 我爸爸用一件旧衬衫擦车。②The puppy rubbed itself against my legs. 这只小狗在我腿上蹭来蹭去。③She is relaxed after the back rub. 做完背部按摩之后她感到很放松。

rubber /ˈrʌbər/ *n.* 橡胶；橡皮；*adj.* 橡胶制成的；*vt.* 涂橡胶于；用橡胶制造

【例句】You need a pair of rubber gloves. 你需要一副橡胶手套。

rubbish /ˈrʌbɪʃ/ *n*. 垃圾；废话；无意义的东西；劣质的东西

【例句】①What he said in the seminar is totally rubbish. 他在研讨会上所说的完全是废话。②Don't litter rubbish on street. 不要在大街上扔垃圾。

rude /ruːd/ *adj*. 粗鲁的；简陋的；狂暴的

【例句】①His manner in the banquet is rather rude. 他在宴会上的举止很粗鲁。②They live in a rude house. 他们住在简陋的屋子里。③They made this table with rude tools. 他们用很简单的工具做了这个桌子。

rug /rʌg/ *n*. 小块地毯；（围盖膝的）围毯，车毯

【例句】This rug is quite exotic. 这个小毯子具有异域风情。

ruin /ˈruːɪn/ *v*. 毁灭；（使）没落，（使）堕落；变成废墟；*n*. 毁灭，灭亡；废墟，遗迹

【例句】①The ugly decoration ruined the party. 丑陋的装饰毁掉了整个派对。②We can find nothing but ruin after the war. 战争后我们只能找到废墟。③His life is in ruins. 他的生活已经毁了。

【用法】in ruins 严重受损

rule /ruːl/ *n*. 规则，规定；统治，支配；章程；*v*. 控制，支配；判定；裁定

【例句】①Everyone should obey traffic rules. 人人都需遵守交通规则。②The country revives under her rule. 在她的统治之下，国家又恢复了繁荣。③The belief that he will succeed ruled him. 他必会成功的信念支撑着他。

【拓展】ruler *n*. 主宰者；尺子

rumble /ˈrʌmbl/ *v*. & *n*. （发出）低沉的声音

【例句】①The thunder was rumbling in the distance. 远处传来轰隆隆的雷声。②My tummy rumbles all day. 我的肚子咕咕叫了一天。

rumor（**rumour** *BrE*）/ˈruːmə(r)/ *n*. & *v*. 谣传；传说

【例句】There is rumor that she is an orphan. 有谣言传她是个孤儿。

rural /ˈrʊərəl/ *adj*. 农村的；田园的；地方的；农业的

【例句】I prefer rural scenery to industrial sights. 相比于工业景点，我更喜欢田园风光。

rush /rʌʃ/ *v.* （使）急速行进，仓促完成；猛攻；急速流动；（使）仓促行事；催促；*n.* 冲；匆忙；繁忙的活动；涌动

【例句】①Take your time. Please don't rush into answers. 慢慢来，不要匆忙回答。②I have to rush this article out before 8：00. 我必须八点前把文章赶出来。③The advertisement fee is rather high during rush hour. 黄金时段的广告费很高。④She was so shy that a rush appeared on her face before her speech. 她太腼腆了，还没开始演讲脸就红了。

【用法】rush into sth/doing sth 仓促（做）某事；rush sth out 将某事匆忙做完；in a rush 匆忙地；rush hour 高峰期，黄金时段

rust /rʌst/ *n.* 铁锈；赤褐色；*v.* （使）生锈

【例句】①His car is full rust spots. 他的车满是锈斑。②This metal doesn't rust in water. 这种金属在水里不生锈。

【拓展】rusty *adj.* 生锈的

rustic /ˈrʌstɪk/ *adj.* 有农村特色的；粗野的

【例句】The design of this hotel is rustic. 这个酒店的设计具有乡村特色。

7.3　S

strain /streɪn/ *n.* 过度的疲劳，紧张，张力，应变；*v.* 扭伤；拉紧，（使）紧张；过滤

【例句】①Do you suffer from the strain of modern life? 你苦于现代生活的紧张吗？②I strained my back when I lifted the box. 我抬箱子的时候扭了背。③He has a strain of melancholy in him. 他有点忧郁。

【用法】strain to do 努力做；a strain of 一种

【例句】I strain to listen but still cannot hear. 我努力听但是仍然听不到。

strand /strænd/ *n.* 绳；串；海滨；*v.* 搁浅；使陷于困境；弄断；搓

【例句】I was stranded in the strange town without money or friends. 我困在那个陌生的城市，既没有钱，又没有朋友。

【用法】a strand of 一缕

【例句】She tried to blow a white strand of hair from her eyes. 她试图吹开眼前的一缕白发。

straw /strɔː/ *n*. 稻草,麦秆;*adj*. 稻草的

【例句】A straw shows which way the wind blows. [谚] 草动知风向,观微知著。

【用法】a straw hat 一顶草帽;man of straw 没有实权的人;catch/grasp at straws 抓住救命稻草;做无成功希望的努力

streak /striːk/ *v*. 飞跑,加上条纹;*n*. 条纹,气质,倾向

【例句】①There was a streak of wildness in him. 他有点儿放荡。②The children streaked off as fast as they could. 孩子们拔脚飞跑。③Bacon has streaks of fat and streaks of lean. 咸肉中有几层肥的和几层瘦的。

stream /striːm/ *n*. 溪流,一股,河流;*v*. 流,涌,流注

【例句】①My eyes were streaming with tears. 我眼里充满了泪水。②Traffic was streaming by. 车辆川流不息。③Streams of people were coming out of the railway station. 成群的人们涌出火车站。④The students streamed into the auditorium. 学生们络绎不绝地进入礼堂。

【用法】stream of consciousness 意识流;go up stream 逆流而上;on stream 进行生产;in streams/a stream 连续,川流不息地

【例句】Part of the new plant is now in operation and the remainder will be on stream later this month. 新工厂现已部分开工,其余部分在本月底前将全力投入生产。

stride /straɪd/ *v*. 大步走(过),跨过;*n*. 步幅,阔步

【例句】①He strode angrily into the classroom. 他气愤地跨进教室。②They are striding forward both in English and in mathematics. 他们的英语和数学都在大踏步地取得进展。

【用法】take in one's stride 轻而易举地解决某事

【例句】He took every obstacle in his stride. 他轻易地度过一切难关。

strive /straɪv/ *v*. 努力;力争;斗争

173

【例句】He strives hard to keep calm. 他努力使自己保持镇静。

【用法】strive against injustice 反抗不公正；strive after/for 为……奋斗；strive toward 为……而努力；strive with 同……作斗争

stumble /ˈstʌmbl/ *v.* 绊倒；使困惑；蹒跚；结结巴巴地说话；*n.* 绊倒；错误

【例句】①I stumbled over a stone and fell. 我在石头上绊了一下跌倒了。②The patient has bones so brittle that a minor stumble could result in a serious break. 这个病人的骨头很脆，轻微的磕绊就会导致严重的骨折。③He always stumbles when he is nervous. 他一紧张就结巴。

【拓展】stumbler 绊跌者；有过失者；结结巴巴说话者

submerge /səbˈmɜːrdʒ/ *v.* 浸没，淹没；潜水

【例句】His talent was submerged by his shyness. 他的才华被其羞怯所遮蔽。

【拓展】submarine 潜水艇

substance /ˈsʌbstəns/ *n.* 物质，实质，主旨；牢固，坚实；财富

【例句】Air has little substance. 空气的密度很小。

【用法】a mineral substance 矿物；a plan without substance 空洞的计划；a person of substance 富有的

substantial /səbˈstænʃl/ *adj.* 大量的；坚固的；实质的，真实的；富有的

【例句】①A substantial number of my colleagues commute to work each day. 我的很多同事每天通勤。②Buildings that were constructed of more substantial materials survived the earthquake. 坚固的建筑材料建造的房屋挺过了地震。

【用法】a substantial breakfast 丰盛早餐；a man of substantial build 体格结实的人

subtle /ˈsʌtl/ *adj.* 微妙的；精细的；敏感的

【例句】①There is a subtle difference in meaning between the two words. 这两个单词之间的区别很细微。②When it comes to giving criticism, sometimes it's best to take a subtle approach. 最好用微妙一点的方法给出批评。

succession /səkˈseʃn/ *n.* 连续，连续性；继承

【例句】①A succession of one-man stalls offered soft drinks. 一连串提供饮料的一人售货亭。②As third in the line of succession, she would only become queen if her brothers both died or became ineligible. 她目前在王位继承顺序的第三位。如果她的两个哥哥都死了，或者没有资格了，她才能成为女王。

【用法】in succession to 继……之后，继位/任；in succession 接连，一个接一个

【例句】Reports of victory came in quick succession. 捷报频传。

suffice /səˈfaɪs/ *v.* 足够，有能力；使满足

【例句】Fifty dollars will suffice for my needs. 50美元足够我的需要。

【用法】suffice it to say that…说……就够了；suffice for 满足，足够

【例句】Suffice it to say that we never talk to each other after that incident. 不必多言，那件事发生以后我们再也没有说过话。

summit /ˈsʌmɪt/ *n.* 顶点，顶峰，最高阶层

【例句】①This appointment had been the summit of Mr. Bertram's ambition. 这曾一直是伯特伦先生的野心的极点。②The leaders of China and the US are expected to meet during the G20 summit this week in Japan, according to earlier reports. 据早先报道，中美两国领导人将共同出席本周在日本召开的G20峰会。

【用法】a mountain summit 山顶；a summit conference 最高级会议

summon /ˈsʌmən/ *v.* 召集，召唤；振作

【例句】①The teacher summoned all the children to the room. 老师把所有的孩子都叫进房间里。②The king summoned him back to the palace. 国王诏他回宫。

【用法】summon (up) one's courage 鼓起勇气

【例句】Since he was painfully shy, it took him a long time to summon up courage to ask her to a game. 由于他太腼腆了，所以花了他好长时间才鼓起勇气请她去看球赛。

【辨析】call、send for、summon 均有"召集""召唤"的意思，call 为非正式，含义广泛，指用说话或呼叫的形式召唤，send for 作"召唤"解时，语气较随便，暗示委派一件工作。summon 正式用词，指官方或正式的召集，召

集者具有权力或权威性。

superior /suːˈpɪriər/ *n*. 长者，上级，超越者；*adj*. 较高的，出众的，高傲的，优越的

【用法】a superior officer 上级官员；a superior court 上级法院

【例句】①He has no superior in this respect. 在这个方面没人能胜过他。②To most major European countries, an outright ban on Huawei does not make any sense, since the US has not produced any evidence of the alleged national security threat. Besides, Huawei's 5G technology is superior and affordable. 对于大部分主要欧洲国家来说，完全禁止华为没有任何意义。因为美国并不能提供它所宣称的华为威胁美国国家安全的证据。另外，华为的5G技术十分领先并且价格合理。

【用法】be superior to 胜过，比……好；不为……所动

【拓展】superiorly *adv*. 超越其他地；卓越地 superiority *n*. 优越，优势；优越性

supervise /ˈsuːpərvaɪz/ *v*. 监督，管理，指导

【例句】①The teacher supervised our drawing class. 老师负责我们的图画课。②In the case of an emergency or a major accident threatening kindergarten safety, supervisors must reach the scene quickly, supervise the emergency response and report the incident to higher authorities. 遇威胁幼儿园安全的紧急情况或重大事故，管理人员应立即到现场，指导应急工作并将事故汇报上级部门。

【拓展】supervisee *n*. 被监督者；supervisor *n*. 管理人

supplementary /ˌsʌplɪˈmentri/ *n*. 增补者，增补物；*adj*. 辅助的；补充的

【例句】①The new students received supplementary instruction. 新生接受补课。②The Ministry of Education said that commercial advertisements must not be included in textbooks for middle and primary school students. The ministry said internet links or QR codes leading to websites containing supplementary learning materials are also prohibited in textbooks. 教育部表示，小学、初中教材不准包含商业广告。包含辅助学习材料的网络连接和二维码也禁止在教材上出现。

【用法】supplementary reading 辅助阅读（材料）；supplementary agreement

补充协议；增补协议；supplementary civil action 附带民事诉讼；supplementary contract 补充契约

suppress /sə'pres/ *v.* 镇压，抑制

【例句】①The troops suppressed the rebellion by firing on the mob. 军队向暴徒开枪镇压叛乱。②The trial's aim is to suppress dependence on methadone. 这项实验的目的是减少对美沙酮的依赖。

【用法】suppress inflation 遏止通货膨胀

supreme /suː'priːm/ *adj.* 至高的，最高的；极其的

【例句】①The board has supreme authority over such issues. 在此类问题上，董事会有最高权威。②He has made supreme effort to construct a modern yard. 为了打造一座现代化庭院，他付出了巨大的努力。

【用法】supreme courage 最大的勇气；the supreme moment 决定性的时刻；在最后关头；supreme court 最高法院；supreme commander 最高指挥官；最高统帅；supreme being 上帝；至高无上的力量

【例句】The most important law court is called the Supreme Court. 最重要的法院叫作最高法院。

surge /sɜːrdʒ/ *n.* 巨涌，澎湃；*v.* 汹涌；上涨

【例句】①The fans surged forward to see the movie star. 影迷们汹涌地奔去看那个影星。②Some first-tier cities saw a surge in housing prices because of China's rapid urbanization process several years ago. 几年前，由于中国快速的城市化进程，一些一线城市的房价出现了飙升。

surplus /'sɜːrplʌs/ *n.* 剩余，过剩，盈余；*adj.* 剩余的；*v.* 卖掉

【例句】①Brazil has a big surplus of coffee. 巴西有很多剩余的咖啡。②These are countries where there is a surplus of labour. 这些是劳动力过剩的国家。③Rich people tend to have large sums of surplus cash. 富人往往有大笔的闲钱。

【用法】surplus funds 剩余基金；surplus population 过剩人口；surplus value 剩余价值

surrender /sə'rendər/ *v.* 交出，投降，听任；*n.* 交出，放弃，投降

【例句】No terms except unconditional and immediate surrender can be accept-

177

ed. 除去无条件立即投降，其他条件一概无法接受。

【用法】surrender oneself to... 向……投降；surrender to... 屈服于……；(an) unconditional surrender 无条件投降

【例句】He surrendered himself to despair. 他绝望至极。

survival /sərˈvaɪvl/ *n*. 生存；幸存，残存；残存物

【例句】All animals need food and water for survival. 所有的动物都需要食物和水来生存。

【用法】survival rate 存活率；survival equipment 救生设备；the survival of the fittest 适者生存；a survival from ancient times 古代遗物

【拓展】survive *v*. 幸存，残存；比……活得长；survivor *n*. 幸存者，残存者，生还者

susceptible /səˈseptəbl/ *adj*. 易受影响的；易感动的；容许……的；*n*. 易得病的人

【例句】①Teachers should help students to objectively and sensibly evaluate the proposed amendments so that young people could acquire critical thinking and become less susceptible to incitement and blind faith. 教师应该帮助学生客观、理性地评价拟议的修正案，这样年轻人才能具备批判思维能力，不轻易受到煽动和盲目迷信的影响。②Walking with weights makes the shoulders very susceptible to injury. 负重行走易使肩膀受伤。

【用法】susceptible heart 敏感的心；a susceptible young man 一个易动情的青年；be susceptible to 对……敏感；容易受到……影响

【例句】She is always susceptible to other's remarks on her. 她总是容易受到别人对她的评价的影响。

suspicion /səˈspɪʃn/ *n*. 猜疑，怀疑

【例句】①Suspicion crept into his mind. 不由得他不怀疑。②I have a suspicion that she is not telling the truth. 我有点疑心她讲的不是真话。③His strange behaviour aroused the police's suspicion. 他奇怪的行为引起了警察的怀疑。

【用法】on suspicion of 因……受到嫌疑，作为……的犯罪嫌疑人

【拓展】suspicious *adj*. 可疑的；怀疑的；多疑的；suspect *v*. 怀疑

swamp /swɑːmp/ *n*. 沼泽，湿地；*v*. 陷入沼泽，淹没

【例句】①The horse was swamped in the mud. 马陷入泥潭。②In summer night I like to sit by the swamp behind the road listening to frogs. 夏天的晚上我喜欢在这条路后面的一个沼泽地旁听蛙鸣。③I am swamped with work. 我工作忙得不可开交。

sway /sweɪ/ *v*. 摇摆，摇动

【例句】① The trees swayed in the wind. 树在风中左右摇动。② His splendid speech swayed thousands of votes. 他美妙的演说影响了成千上万的选票。

【用法】be swayed by 受到……的影响；under the sway of 在……支配、影响下；hold sway 支配；统治

【例句】Don't be swayed by his words. Stick to your own opinion. 别受他的话影响。坚持自己的观点。

symptom /ˈsɪmptəm/ *n*. 症状，征兆

【例句】①Fever is a symptom of many illnesses. 发烧是许多疾病的症状。②Inflation is a symptom of weak economy. 通货膨胀是经济不景气的征兆。

【用法】symptom complex 症候群

synthetic /sɪnˈθetɪk/ *adj*. 合成的，人造的；综合的；虚伪的；*n*. 合成物，合成纤维

【例句】This synthetic dress material does not crush. 这种合成纤维衣料不会皱。

【用法】synthetic fabrics 人造纤维织物；synthetic method 综合法；synthetic sympathy 虚假同情

8 T, U, V, W, X, Y, Z

8.1 T

token /ˈtoukən/ *n*. 标志，象征；证明；纪念品；礼券；*adj*. 象征性的

【例句】Please accept this small present as a token of our gratitude. 我们谨以这件小礼品表示我们的感激之情，请笑纳。

tolerance /ˈtɑːlərəns/ *n*. 容忍，宽容；公差；忍受能力

【例句】①It is a country with a reputation for tolerance towards religious minorities. 这个国家以对占少数的宗教人士持宽容态度而出名。②Many old people have very limited tolerance to cold. 许多老年人对寒冷的忍受力极其差。

torch /tɔːrtʃ/ *n*. 火炬；手电筒

【例句】①They lit a torch and set fire to the cabin's thatch. 他们点着一支火把，放火烧了小木屋的茅草屋顶。②A boy followed the shepherd, carrying a torch to light his way. 一个男孩跟在牧羊人后面，举着火把照路。

torment /tɔːrˈment/ *n*. 痛苦，苦恼，使人痛苦或苦恼的人或物；*vt*. 使痛苦，使苦恼，戏弄，折磨

【例句】①Years of turmoil and torment make her hard to be at peace. 多年的动荡与痛苦使她很难安心下来了。②A cat usually torments the mouse before really eating it. 猫总是会在吃老鼠前先折磨这只老鼠一会儿。

torture /ˈtɔːrtʃər/ *n*. 折磨；拷问；拷打；苦难；*vt*. 折磨；拷问；使遭受

苦难

【例句】①It was sheer torture to hear him play the piano so badly. 听他那样糟糕的拉小提琴真是一种受罪。②She was tortured with guilt. 她因内疚而倍感痛苦。

tournament /ˈtʊrnəmənt/ ***n***. 比赛，锦标赛，联赛

【例句】A golf tournament is going to be held in Qingdao. 青岛将举行一场高尔夫锦标赛。

【拓展】invitational tournament 邀请赛；tournament committee 竞赛委员会；open tournament 公开赛

toxic /toxic/ ***adj***. 有毒的，中毒的

【例句】①It costs millions of RMB to clean up toxic waste. 清除有毒废弃物的成本高达数百万。②The factory was required to protect workers from being poisoned by toxic gas. 这家工厂被要求保护工人不受有毒气体的危害。

tragedy /ˈtrædʒədi/ ***n***. 悲剧；不幸事件，惨事

【例句】The family suffered an enormous personal tragedy: The youngest child died in a car accident. 他们遭受了一场巨大的个人灾难：他们最小的孩子在车祸中不幸遇难。

trait /treɪt/ ***n***. 品质，特性，特点

【例句】Being keen is an attractive trait for volunteers. 对志愿者来说，热心是一个迷人的品质。

tranquil /ˈtræŋkwɪl/ ***adj***. 宁静的，安宁的

【例句】The hotel is located in a tranquil lake area. 这个宾馆坐落在安静的湖区。

【拓展】tranquilly ***adv***. 平静地，安静地；tranquility ***n***. 宁静；tranquilizer ***n***. 镇静剂；tranquilize ***v***. 使安静

transaction /trænˈzækʃn/ ***n***. 交易

【例句】The bank charges a fixed rate for each transaction. 银行对办理的每一项业务都收取一定的费用。

transcend /trænˈsend/ ***vt***. 超出，超越，胜过

181

【例句】①The size of the universe transcends human understanding. 宇宙之大超越了人类的理解范围。②Short video apps, for instance, have to innovate to meet the growing demand for fresh forms of entertainment in those countries. Also, they need to transcend cultural barriers. 例如，短视频应用需要创新以满足那些国家的新形势的娱乐。另外，它们也需要超越文化障碍。

transient /ˈtrænʃnt/*adj*. 短暂的，易逝的；*n*. 流动人口

【例句】① Climate change accelerated by anthropogenic factors is not a transient or a regional problem. 由人为因素所加剧的气候变化问题不是一个暂时的，也不是区域性的问题。②The couple suspected in the disappearance of a 9-year-old girl were longtime swindlers and transients who had run out of money and decided they no longer wanted to live. 涉嫌九岁女孩失踪案的夫妇一直是骗子，流动人员，他们花光了身上的钱，并打算轻生。

transition /trænˈzɪʃn/*n*. 转变，过渡

【例句】It takes time to help developing countries in their transition from high carbon to low carbon to zero carbon economies. 帮助发展中国家从高碳过渡到低碳，再由低碳过渡到零碳，需要一定的时间。

transmit /trænzˈmɪt/*v*. 传输；传播；发射；传达；遗传

【例句】①The basketball game was transmitted live. 这场篮球比赛被现场直播。②Mosquitoes transmit diseases to humans. 蚊子向人类传播疾病。

transparent /trænsˈpærənt/*adj*. 透明的；显然的；坦率的；易懂的

【例句】①All of this information is transparent to the user. 所有这些信息对用户而言都是透明的。②Shoe of Cinderella is totally transparent. Nobody knows when you wear them. 灰姑娘的水晶鞋是完全透明的，没有人知道你穿它。

transplant /ˈtrænsplænt/*v*. 移植，移种；迁移；*n*. 组织或器官的移植

【例句】He was recovering from a liver transplant operation. 他正从肝脏移植手术中康复。

treasure /ˈtreʒər/*n*. 财富，财宝；*v*. 珍爱，珍藏

【例句】①Chinese should first try their best to dig out and digest their own culture, and then extend the wisdom of Chinese traditional culture as a treasure to the world. 中国人首先应当尽最大努力去挖掘并消化自己的文化,然后再将中国文化的智慧作为财富传递给世界。②She treasures the days that they spent together when they were at universities. 她十分珍惜他们一起在大学里度过的时光。

tremendous /trəˈmendəs/ ***adj***. 极大的,巨大的;极好的,非凡的

【例句】We had a tremendous amount of rain recently. 我们这里最近雨量大。

trend /trend/ ***n***. 趋势;时尚

【例句】With the increase of per-capita income and the ongoing consumption upgrade trend, Chinese consumers are eating more and more snacks. 随着人均收入的增加以及消费的上涨趋势,中国消费者对零食的消费越来越高。

trial /ˈtraɪəl/ ***n***. 试验;审讯; ***adj***. 试验的

【例句】①New evidence showed the accused lied at the trial. 新的证据表明被告在审判时撒了谎。②The trial program is expected to establish specific waste management regulations. 这个试验性计划旨在制定一个废物管理规定。

triangle /ˈtraɪæŋgl/ ***n***. 三角形;三角形物;三角关系

【例句】China seized 29.6 metric tons of drugs smuggled from the Golden Triangle, one of the largest overseas drug sources. 中国警方从最大的海外毒品来源地之一的金三角截获29.6公吨的毒品。

tribute /ˈtrɪbjuːt/ ***n***. 贡品,贡金;颂词,称颂

【例句】The book is a tribute to my parents. 这本书是敬献给我父母的。

【用法】pay tribute 致敬;朝贡;…is a tribute to……有成效的结果

【例句】His success is a tribute to hard work, to professionalism. 他的成功是辛勤工作和兢兢业业的结果。

trifle /ˈtraɪfl/ ***n***. 琐事;少量的钱;无多大价值的东西

【例句】I don't know why you waste your time on such trifles. 我不明白你为什么在这种鸡毛蒜皮额小事上浪费时间。

【用法】a trifle 有一点

【例句】As a traveller, he'd found both locations just a trifle disappointing. 作为一名旅行者,他发现这两个地方都有点儿令人失望。

trigger /ˈtrɪgər/ *n.* 枪等的扳机引爆器；扳柄；*vt.* 扣扳机开枪；引发

【例句】①A gangster pointed a gun at them and pulled the trigger. 一个匪徒用枪指着他们，扣动了扳机。②The incident triggered the outbreak of the First World War. 这件事引起了第一次世界大战的爆发。

trim /trɪm/ *adj.* 整齐整洁的；苗条的；优美的；*vt.* 修剪；删掉，消减

【例句】You must trim your costs if you want to increase your profits. 如果你想增加利润，你就必须削减开支。

triumph /ˈtraɪʌmf/ *n.* 凯旋，胜利；伟大成就；喜悦；*vi.* 取胜，成功

【例句】The victorious army returned in triumph. 得胜的部队凯旋而归。

trivial /ˈtrɪviəl/ *adj.* 琐细的，无足轻重的

【例句】Why do you get so angry over such trivial matters? 你为什么为这些琐事生气？

troop /truːp/ *n.* 一群，军队，童子军中队，骑兵或炮兵、装甲兵连队；*vi.* 成群结队地走，列队行进

【例句】They gave her information about Japanese checkpoints and troop movements in the area. 他们给了她该地区日军检查站和军队调动的情报。

trophy /ˈtroʊfi/ *n.* 奖品，战利品，胜利纪念品

【例句】The special trophy for the best speaker went to Wendy. 最佳演讲者的特别奖给了 Wendy。

tropical /ˈtrɑːpɪkl/ *adj.* 热带的；炎热的

【例句】Tropical storm Barry made landfall near Intracoastal City, US state of Louisiana, and weakened to a storm again from a hurricane on Saturday afternoon. 热带风暴巴瑞在美国路易斯安那州的因特拉科斯特尔城登陆，并在周六下午由飓风再次减为风暴。

【用法】tropical cyclone 热带旋风；tropical storm 热带风暴；tropical depression 热带低压；tropical fruit 热带水果

trumpet /ˈtrʌmpɪt/ *n.* 喇叭，号；*v.* 宣扬，鼓吹；大象吼叫

【例句】①I played the trumpet in the university orchestra. 我在学校管弦乐队吹小号。②They trumpet "free, fair and reciprocal trade", but in fact do whatever they can to bypass multilateral mechanisms and exert unilateral pressure on other countries. 他们鼓吹"自由""平等""互惠"，但实际上却肆意妄为，置多边体制于不顾，向其他国家施加单边压力。

trunk /trʌŋk/ *n*. 树干；躯干；大衣箱；象鼻子；游泳裤，运动裤；汽车

【例句】①The road network is made up of three expressways, three fast lanes, and eight trunk roads within the logistics hub. 道路网由物流枢纽内的三条高速公路、三条快车道和八条主干道组成。②Mary unlocked her trunk and took out a red dress. 玛丽把她的大箱子的锁打开了，拿出了一件红色的裙子。

tuition /tuˈɪʃn/ *n*. 尤指对个人或小组的教学，讲授；学费

【例句】Mary's 5,000 RMB tuition at university this year will be paid for with scholarships. 玛丽今年五千元的大学学费将用奖学金来支付。

tunnel /ˈtʌnl/ *n*. 地下通道，隧道，地洞；*v*. 挖掘地道或隧道

【例句】Qingdao is famous for its underwater tunnel. 青岛因海底隧道而闻名。

8.2 U

uniform /ˈjuːnɪfɔːrm/ *n*. 制服，校服；*adj*. 一致的，统一的

【例句】①The hat is part of the school uniform. 帽子是校服的一部分。②Growth has not been uniform across the country. 全国各地的发展程度不一致。

【拓展】uniform *adj.* →uniformly *adv.* →uniformity *n.*

unify /ˈjuːnɪfaɪ/ *v*. 统一，使一元化

【例句】The new leader hopes to unify the country. 新领导人希望统一国家。

unique /juˈniːk/ *adj*. 独一无二的；独特的

【例句】①Each person's fingerprints are unique. 每个人的指纹都是不同的。②The town is fairly unique in the wide range of leisure facilities it offers. 该城市在提供广泛的闲暇活动设施方面是独特的。

universal /ˌjuːnɪˈvɜːrsl/ *adj*. 全体的，影响全体的；普遍的，一般的

【例句】①There was universal agreement as to who should become chairman. 谁该当主席大家意见一致。②This is a subject of universal interest. 这是一个普遍关心的题目。

unleash /ʌnˈliːʃ/ *v*. 引发

【例句】The announcement unleashed a storm of protest from local people. 公告引发了一场当地人的抗议风暴。

unload /ˌʌnˈloʊd/ *v*. 从……卸下货物，卸；退出（枪的）子弹，倒出（相机）的胶卷

【例句】①Have you unloaded the parcel from the car? 你把包裹从车上卸下来了吗？②The ship is unloading its cargo in the harbor. 这艘船在港口卸货。

upright /ˈʌpraɪt/ *adj*. 垂直的；诚实的，正直的；*adv*. 垂直地

【例句】①Make sure you stand that bag upright so it doesn't fall over. 确保把那个包放正了，以免倒了。②He is an upright citizen. 他是一个正直的市民。

upset /ˈʌpset/ *v*. 打翻，使倾覆；打乱，搅乱；使不安，使心情不好；*n*. 搅乱，倾覆；不适；出乎意料的结果

【例句】①If they develop these new weapons, it will upset the balance of the power. 如果他们研制这种新武器，那么力量平衡将会被打破。②He upset the cup and the coffee went all over the floor. 他把杯子打翻了，咖啡流了一地。③It was a major upset when our local team beat the big league. 我们地方队打败了大联队，这课真是个意想不到的结果。

urban /ˈɜːrbən/ *adj*. 城镇的

【例句】The minimal basic pension standard for rural and urban residents will be increased to 103 yuan from 98 yuan. 城乡居民的最低养老金标准将从98元提高到103元。

urge /ɜːrdʒ/ *v*. 敦促；大力推荐；驱赶；*n*. 冲动，强烈的欲望

【例句】The report urged that all children be taught to swim. 报告敦促所有的孩子学习游泳。

urgent /ˈɜːrdʒənt/ *adj*. 紧急的；迫切的

【例句】①Take this to the minister now because it is very urgent. 把它交给部

长，现在，很紧急！②The law is in urgent need of reform. 这项法律亟待修订。

usher /ˈʌʃər/ *n*. 引坐员；*v*. 引导，引领

【例句】①The secretary ushered me into his office. 秘书把我领进他的办公室。②The usher will show you to your seat now. 引座员会指示你的座位在那里。

utensil /juːˈtensl/ *n*. 家具，器皿

【例句】Cooking utensils include bowls, steamers and frying pans. 厨房器皿包括碗、蒸锅、煎锅等。

utilize /ˈjuːtəlaɪz/ *v*. 使用，利用

【例句】①The resources at our disposal could have been better utilized. 我们所掌握的资源本来可以利用的更好。②I would like to see more people utilize public transport. 我愿意看到更多的人使用公共交通。

utmost /ˈʌtməʊst/ *adj*. 极端的，最大的

【例句】①Health is a matter of the uttermost concern for us. 健康是我们最为关心的问题。②I did my utmost to prevent it. 我尽了最大努力去阻止它。

utter /ˈʌtər/ *adj*. （尤指不好的事情）完全的，全然的，十足的；*v*. 发出

【例句】①It was an utter waste of time. 这完全是浪费时间。②The wounded man uttered a groan. 那个受伤的人发出痛苦的呻吟。

8.3　V

vicinity /vəˈsɪnəti/ *n*. 附近

【例句】A school library is under construction in the vicinity. 学校附近在建一所图书馆。

【用法】in the vicinity of …在……附近

【例句】There are a few hotels and restaurants in the vicinity of the university. 大学附近有几家饭店和旅馆。

vicious /ˈvɪʃəs/ *adj*. 邪恶的；恶性的，不正确的

【例句】①The vicious wizard got punished and the prince and princess lived happily after. 邪恶的巫师受到了惩罚，从此王子和公主过上了幸福的生活。② We need to break the vicious circle of newspaper. 我们需要打破报纸业的恶性循环。

victim /ˈvɪktɪm/ *n.* 受害者

【例句】More donations have arrived to help the victims. 更多的捐赠涌入，来帮助受害者。

【用法】fall victim to 成为受害者

【例句】The young man fell victim to the struggle for power. 年轻人成为权力斗争的牺牲品。

vigorous /ˈvɪɡərəs/ *adj.* 精力充沛的

【例句】China will be more vigorous in integrating with the global market and will take greater initiative in deepening international cooperation. 中国将更加积极地融入全球市场，更加主动地深化对外合作，为世界经济复苏发展创造更多机遇和空间。

【近义词】passionate; energetic; vibrant

violate /ˈvaɪəleɪt/ *v.* 违反

【例句】Under no circumstances could we violate the law. 在任何情况下我们都不能违反法律。

【拓展】violation *n.* 违反，违背

violence /ˈvaɪələns/ *n.* 暴力

【例句】New measures should be taken to fight against campus violence. 制定政策制止校园暴力。

【用法】the outbreak of violence 爆发暴力事件

【例句】The outbreak of violence can be attributed to the unfair treatment. 不公正的对待导致了暴力事件的爆发。

【拓展】violence *n.* →violent *adj.* →violently *adv.*

virtual /ˈvɜːrtʃuəl/ *adj.* 虚拟的；实际的，事实上的

【例句】①We lived in a virtual world created by the internet. 我们生活在计算机带来的虚拟世界中。②He is the virtual owner of the company. 他实际上是

公司的主人。

【拓展】virtually *adv*. 实际上

【辨析】actually，virtually，practically 都表示"实际上"。actually 表示"事实上""实际上"，用来说明事情的真实情况。virtually 和 practically 的意思都是"几乎"，practically 强调现实情况中想法或理论的可行性。

【例句】①Actually he is the boss of the company. 他才是公司的老板。②The plan is practically feasible. 这项计划切实可行。③The twins are virtually identical. 这对双胞胎长得一样。

visible /ˈvɪzəbl/*adj*. 看得到的，可视的

【例句】There was visible light in the far distance of the village. 远处的村庄依稀可见灯光。

【拓展】visible *adj*. →visibly *adv*. →visibility *n*.

vision /ˈvɪʒn/*n*. 远见，愿景；视力，想象力

【例句】①We will strive for a vision of a community of shared future for mankind. 我们要努力建立人类命运共同体。②The boy was born with poor vision. 男孩天生视力欠佳。

vital /ˈvaɪtl/*adj*. 非常重要的，至关重要的

【例句】Nowadays computers play a vital role in human communication. 如今计算机在人类交往中起着重要的作用。

【拓展】vitality *n*. 活力，生命

【近义词】pivotal；crucial；critical

vocational /voʊˈkeɪʃənl/*adj*. 职业的，行业的

【例句】The government has laid down the vocational standards to restrain the behaviors. 政府制定了行业规范标准来约束人们的行为。

【拓展】vocation *n*. 职业，使命，天职

volume /ˈvɑːljuːm/*n*. 音量；体积，容量；一册书

【例句】①Could you turn down the volume of the radio a little bit? 能把收音机音量调小一些吗？②Don't underestimate the volume of the schoolbag. You can still put two books in it. 别小看了书包的容量，你还能往里放两本书。③The recent volume of the magazine will be published in two weeks. 最近一期杂志将在两周后出版。

volunteer /ˌvɑːlənˈtɪr/ *n*. 志愿者

【例句】Working as a volunteer makes his life fulfilling. 志愿者活动让他的生活充实。

【用法】volunteer to do sth/for sth 自愿提供，自愿效劳

【例句】He volunteered to introduce the Chinese culture for the foreigners. 他自愿为外国人讲解中国文化。

【拓展】voluntary *adj*. 自愿的

voyage /ˈvɔɪɪdʒ/ *n*. 航行，旅行；*v*. 航行，航海

【例句】①He met with an old friend on his voyage home. 在回家的路上他遇见了老朋友。②He set on voyage to the deep blue sea. 他打算进行深海航行。

【近义词】trip, excursion

【辨析】trip, journey, excursion, voyage 都表示"航行"。trip 为一般用语，指"任何方式的，从事业务或游览的旅行"，往往着重于"短途旅行"；journey 指"有预定地点的陆上、水上或空中的单程长、短途旅行"，一般来说，它着重指"长距离的陆上的旅行"；excursion 指"娱乐性的短途旅行"；voyage 主要指"乘船作水上旅行"，也可指"空中旅行"。

【例句】①They are planning a trip to Qingdao this summer. 他们计划今年夏天去青岛旅行。②The airhostess wished us to have a good journey. 空姐祝我们旅途愉快。③At weekends we made an excursion to the village nearby and tasted the local food. 周末我们旅行参观了小村庄，品尝了当地的美食。④We were thrilled to go on a voyage through the sea. 我们非常激动地进行了航海之旅。

vulnerable /ˈvʌlnərəbl/ *adj*. 易受伤害的，易受攻击的

【例句】Children and the elderly are the vulnerable group of people. 孩子和老人是弱势群体。

【用法】be vulnerable to...易受……伤害的，易受……攻击的

【例句】His works are vulnerable to criticism. 他的作品容易受到攻击。

8.4　W

whatever /wɒtˈevər/ ***pron***. 无论什么；诸如此类；***adj***. 都，任何；***adv***. 一点儿都不，丝毫；（非正式）不管怎样

【例句】①Wherever you go, whatever you do, I will be right here waiting for you. 不论你去哪里，干些什么事，我都在这里等着你。②Whatever difficulties we may meet with, we should never give up. 不管遇到什么困难，我们都不应该放弃。

whatsoever /wɒtsoʊˈevər/ ***adv***. （用于名词词组后，加强否定陈述）丝毫，任何，无论什么

【例句】There is no evidence whatsoever to back up his argument. 没有证据支持他。

whereas /ˌwerˈæz/ ***conj***. 然而

【例句】He is talkative in the public, whereas quiet in private. 他公共场合很健谈，但是私下很安静。

【近义词】while; by contrast; although; however

whereby /werˈbaɪ/ ***conj***. 凭借，通过；借以……；***adv***. 凭此，借此

【例句】①Psychologists say the result could be down to the "lipstick effect", whereby using make-up boosts self-esteem and has a knock-on effect on memory, confidence and mental ability. 心理学家称，该结果可归因于"口红效应"，即通过化妆提升自尊心，对记忆力、自信心和心智能力产生连锁反应。②Alipay is often used in China instead of cash whereby similar to WeChat Pay, you scan a QR code provided by the seller using the App to make payment. 在中国，支付宝这种支付方式与微信支付类似，通常是通过扫描卖家提供的二维码来支付。

withdraw /wɪðˈdrɔː/ ***v***. 撤退；取钱

【例句】①The American army finally withdrew the troops from the Iraq. 美军最终从伊拉克撤军。②Mother withdrew some money from the bank to pay for the kid's tuition. 母亲从银行取了钱，给孩子付学费。

【拓展】withdrawal *n*. 撤走，退出；提款

wither /ˈwɪðər/*v*. 凋谢，枯萎；变虚弱

【例句】①The flowers wither instantly without good irrigation. 花没有好好浇水，很快就枯萎了。②He withered after a big operation. 一场手术过后，他变得虚弱起来。

【用法】wither away 枯萎，幻灭

【例句】Her hope withered away finally. 她的理想最终幻灭了。

withstand /wɪðˈstænd/*v*. 抵挡，经得起

【例句】Unlike traditional glass, the transparent wood can withstand much stronger impacts. 和传统玻璃不同，这种透明木材可以承受更强烈的冲击。

【近义词】bear; tolerate; stand

witness /ˈwɪtnəs/*v*. 目睹；*n*. 证人

【例句】①He witnessed an accident on the way home. 回家的路上他目睹了一场车祸。②The past decades witnessed the tremendous changes in China. 近十年来，中国发生了巨大的变化。③He appeared in court as the only witness to the accident. 他作为这场事故的唯一目击证人出庭作证了。

worthwhile /ˌwɜːrθˈwaɪl/*adj*. 值得做的，有价值的

【例句】It is worthwhile to take part in such a meaningful activity. 很值得参加这样有意义的活动。

【辨析】worthwhile, worthy, worth 都表示"值得做某事"的意思。worthwhile 用在句型"It is worthwhile to do sth"中，表示做某件事是值得的；worthy 用在句型"Sth be worthy of being done"中，表示值得做某事；worth 用在句型的"It is worth doing sth"中，表示值得做某事。

【例句】①It is worthwhile to teach the kids in the mountains. 给大山中的孩子们教书是值得的。②The man is worthy of being trusted. 他值得信赖。③The book is worth reading. 这本书值得一读。

8.5　X

xylograph /ˈzaɪləʊɡrɑːf/ *n.* 木板印刷，木版画；*vt.* 木板雕刻印刷

【例句】Different styles of xylograph are on display in the museum. 博物馆展出了不同风格的木版画。

【拓展】xylograph *n.* →xylography *n.* 木板术→xylographic *adj.* 用木头雕刻的，木板印刷的

xylophone /ˈzaɪləfəʊn/ *n.* 木琴

【例句】It is said that the xylophone originated from 14th century in Africa. 据说木琴起源于14世纪的非洲。

xyster /ˈzɪstə(r)/ *n.* （医用）刮骨刀

【例句】His finger was bleeding by the sharp xyster. 他的手被锋利的刮骨刀刮出了血。

8.6　Y

yield /jiːld/ *v.* 出产，产量；屈服，放弃；*n.* 产量

【例句】①The research yielded new findings in teaching. 这项研究对教学产生了新的发现。②Under no circumstance will he yield to the enemies. 在任何条件下，他都不会向敌人屈服。③Thanks to the modern technology, the yield has increased by 10%. 由于新技术的使用，产量增加了10%。

【用法】yield to 屈服于

【例句】He would rather die than yield to the enemies. 他宁死不屈。

8.7　Z

zoom /zuːm/ *v.* （尤指汽车、飞机等）疾行，升起；（价格、费用等）猛涨；镜头放大或缩小；*n.* 急速上升；视频软件

【例句】①The plane zoomed shortly after it took off. 飞机起飞后开始直线上升。②The prices zoomed as a result of recession. 经济衰退，物价上涨。

后　记

  自从 2016 年我们的"英语教育研究科研团队"成立以来，在学院各位领导和老师的大力支持和帮助下，经过团队成员的不懈努力，陆续出版了相关研究成果。《英语词汇习得研究》作为《英语词汇记忆研究》的姊妹篇，力求将团队成员的研究成果提供给英语学习者和研究者，一方面帮助学习者提高英语词汇学习效率和词汇能力，达到提高英语语言综合英语能力的目的，有助于学好本专业知识，进行国际化交流，能够用英语讲好中国故事，向世界传播中国声音；另一方面希望得到广大英语教师和研究者的指导和帮助，我们将继续努力，在英语词汇方面做更多的研究。

编著者
2022 年 7 月于青岛